Passion & Principle

Also by Jane Aiken Hodge:

Passion & Principle

THE LOVES AND LIVES OF REGENCY WOMEN

Jane Aiken Hodge

JOHN MURRAY
Albemarle Street, London

For my daughters

First published in 1996
by John Murray (Publishers) Ltd.,
50 Albemarle Street, London WIX 4BD

A catalogue record for this book is available
from the British Library

ISBN 0-7195-5551-5

Typeset in Monotype Fournier
by Servis Filmsetting, Manchester

Printed and bound in Great Britain by
The University Press, Cambridge

Contents

Contents

Illustrations

(between pages 118 and 119)

Author's Note

This book is intended as a pleasure cruise, not a learned work. I have admired and loved the women of the Regency ever since I started using them as background for historical novels, and the chance to write about them was irresistible. But to understand their lives, one needs to know something about their world and my first chapter gives an amateur's eye-view of the eventful forty years during which they flourished.

I owe an immense debt to the people who have worked on these women before me. I would particularly like to thank I. N. Davis for *The Harlot and the Statesman*, Edna Healey for *Lady Unknown*, Lucille Iremonger for *Love and the Princess*, Molly Lefebure for *The Bondage of Love*, Elizabeth Mavor for *The Ladies of Llangollen* and Claire Tomalin for her books on Mrs Jordan, Shelley and Mary Wollstonecraft.

I am most grateful to Caroline Knox and John Murray for asking me to write this book. I would also like to thank Austen Gee for historical advice, Jessica Hodge for getting the pictures, Douglas Matthews for the index and Christine Padmore for the patient typing.

A crowd is not company, and
faces are but a gallery of pictures,
and talk but a tinkling cymbal,
where there is no love
Francis Bacon

I

Setting the Scene

THE WORD REGENCY is often misused, and I have misused it. This is a book about women and love during the forty odd years of the Prince Regent's active life, between 1780, when he was eighteen, and 1820, when he became king. This was a time of quite as much international tension and domestic change as we have seen in the last forty years, but the position of women, central to the stories I am going to tell, was both more hazardous and more restricted than it is today. In the upper classes, boredom threatened, in the lower ones, starvation and death. A woman could be deported or even hanged for stealing a pocket handkerchief, and burned at the stake (until 1790) for what was called petty treason, coining or husband murder, offences against property and the patriarchy. Until she married, she was her father's chattel; afterwards, she was her husband's. Widowhood might just give her a chance of freedom, if she was strong enough to survive to it and rich enough to enjoy it. Marriage meant a child a year, since birth control was almost unknown and a husband had as unquestioned rights to his wife's person as to her property. An active male would run through three or four wives in the course of his lifetime; a clever one would improve his finances by a series of well-dowered matches.

The matrimonial negotiation took place amid the constraints of an apparently rigid class structure, lubricated and modified by money. A woman took her class from her husband, never vice versa. A banker's daughter might become a countess by marriage, if she was rich enough, and an actress could do it if she was sufficiently beautiful and played her cards right, but a woman who married below her, sank.

A woman who did not marry at all might almost as well not have existed. She could make herself useful in the family as daughter, sister and aunt. With money, she might become an eccentric. Without it, she might be reduced to teaching in one of the amateur schools that were long matriarchy which may have come a little hard on her children. At last, at sixty-two, she suffered the classic fate of dowagers when her oldest surviving son married and she had to take second place to the new mistress of Charlecote. In fact, she made a good job of that too, but her story does sum up the female predicament at the time. The rules of the marriage game were loaded against the woman. Marriage was about property and the succession. Estates passed to the eldest son: there must be no doubt about his legitimacy. Husbands could do as they pleased, and did. Wives must be above suspicion.

The matrimonial rules had changed a little in the course of the eighteenth century. Marriage was made more difficult in 1753 when Parliament acted to end the abuse by which eloping couples could be married within the Rules of the Fleet prison as well as being immune from arrest for debt while living there. The immunity from arrest continued, but from then on runaway couples had to go as far as Scotland, where marriage law was still lax. And if marriage had become more difficult, divorce was still to all intents and purposes impossible. A few aristocrats, with the succession at stake, managed the lengthy and expensive business of suits both in the law courts, where they claimed damages against the man involved for what was called criminal conversation, or 'crim con' for short, and the ecclesiastical court, followed by an Act of Parliament. It was not for the man in the street, who was compelled to resort to bigamy, violence, or in extreme cases wife sale, which had a kind of dubious legality. A legal separation was another possibility and if things were bad enough a woman could actually initiate this, but to do so meant to risk losing her children, her reputation and her fortune.

Unless the wife's family protected her property with a special trust, it became her husband's when they married, and even if there was a trust, he might compel her to break it by brutal treatment. He was her absolute master, with total rights in the children. If they separated, however much it might be his fault, she was dependent on his good will for access to her children. That was the legal background, but in the late eighteenth century society was working out its own rules for the mating game. Nobody suggested, or expected, that husbands would be faithful. It was assumed that a well-bred wife would ignore her husband's extra-marital affairs, both before and after marriage. In return, a social convention was growing up among the younger members of society, that gave just a suggestion of similar licence to the wife. Once she had borne her husband the essential heir, she might, if she was very careful, take a lover of her own. It must be done with the utmost discretion. Society would forgive almost anything except an open scandal. It did not much matter that everybody knew, so long as it remained possible to pretend not to. Lady Oxford's brood might be known as the Harleian Miscellany after her husband's famous manuscript collection, because their origin was just as varied, but everybody received Lady Oxford. When Lady Melbourne's eldest son Peniston Lamb died and his younger brother William became next in line to the title, society knew that he was probably Lord Egremont's son, but the dissolute, feckless Lord Melbourne said nothing and society followed his lead. It gave William Lamb the dubious advantage of suddenly being eligible for the hand of the Countess of Bessborough's daughter, Caroline Ponsonby. But that is another story.

What it was really all about, was property. The Duke of Devonshire might eventually forgive his wife a son by Charles Grey, born after she had produced the essential heir to the title. It was her gambling debts that were her undoing. Like the lottery today, gambling was endemic in eighteenth-century society. There was nothing dishonourable about winning (or, aside from the inconvenience) losing a fortune at cards. Betting was also a universal pastime. Parson Woodforde betted on a change in the weather; James Boswell wagered that he would not catch a venereal disease for three years. He lost. The government itself cashed in on this mania by running lotteries, which were finally prohibited by Act of Parliament in 1826.

The upper classes had so much time on their hands. Armies of servants did everything for them. A man's estates were run for him by his agent, who probably cheated him and then lent him (at interest) the money to pay the expenses he had run up for him. George III was known as Farmer George because he actually took a personal interest in the running of his farms in Windsor Great Park. The appellation was probably as affectionate from the lower classes of society as it was scornful among the aristocracy. It was not 'done' to work. Men could fill in a great deal of time hunting and shooting in the country, while in London there were politics, the clubs, the gaming houses, the brothels and the theatre.

After a lady had told her maid what she wanted to wear, and given her orders for the day to the tyrant who ran her house, she was left with an immense amount of time on her hands. Another tyrant ran the nursery, from which the children were produced, elegantly turned out, for a formal evening appearance. Pious Lady Spencer, anxious about her daughter's early marriage to the Duke of Devonshire, and more anxious still as it developed, did a great deal for her grandchildren when she provided them with learned Miss Selina Trimmer as an unusual governess. Babies were normally farmed out to some hearty country woman who was expected to neglect her own infant in their favour, if it had not been so obliging as to die already. This habit simplified the problem of illegitimate children. They, too, could be farmed out and, if required, neglected to death.

Husbands and wives did not necessarily appear in public together. He had his interests, she was expected to have hers, but they must be suitable. When the newly married Duchess of Devonshire planned her own laboratory, in emulation of her husband's cousin, the scientist Henry Cavendish, the Duke told her to give it up and cut the connection. 'He is not a gentleman,' he explained. 'He works.' It really served him right when the Duchess took to gambling instead. Another respectable woman's pursuit was the writing of immensely long letters, of which they kept copies. They also kept diaries; they read; they practised new dances, the harp and singing, all useful social accomplishments. In the country they drove or rode, or even walked with a footman in attendance. The more enterprising ladies might hunt; the Royal Princesses went out with their father at Windsor. In town there were exhibitions and lending libraries to be visited and calls to be paid. They stayed up very late at balls and the theatre, and got up equally late, but even that left a great deal of the day to fill. A lover, with all the anxiety and contriving, often helped to fill the void in their lives, but it was a dangerous business, particularly when love entered into it. Here again the double standard obtained. The Marlborough heir got his cousin Harriet Spencer with child. It changed her life, not his. In an illicit affair, the woman was always at greater risk, both of heartbreak and of social disaster.

The mechanics of an affair remain something of a mystery. The upper and middle classes lived their lives entirely surrounded by servants, taken entirely for granted. Even the smallest and most frugal household had several. The comfortable country houses in Jane Austen's novels must have been full of servants, but, significantly, they are hardly ever mentioned. A place like Goodwood or Chatsworth would have had well over a hundred, indoors and out. They opened doors, stood behind chairs, emptied slops, carried coal, put warming-pans into beds, brought up water in the morning and lit the bedroom fire. They were everywhere, scuttling about the big houses in tunnels and separate passages made specially for them, bouncing out of doors hidden in the panelling. A servant met in a corridor by a guest was liable to be dismissed, or raped. They must have seen and known everything: the four chairs put together, the screen disturbed, the marks in the bed. In the main, they were amazingly discreet, but the opportunities for blackmail were immense. In her novel *Belinda*, Maria Edgeworth paints a chilling picture of a society lady dominated by a maid who knows too much. But it was very much in the servants' interest that the great houses should keep going. A separated couple might mean a closed house and all the staff out of work, in a cold world of unemployment and no welfare state. There was an elaborate system of bribes. Ladies passed on their little-used clothes to their maids, for use or sale; guests must give a finely graded set of tips, or vails as they were called, to their hosts' servants. A round of country house visits was a serious drain on a gentleman's purse. But if he wished to carry on an affair with a lady in the house, he was wise to be generous.

Affection entered into it too. With the significant exception of her husband's agent, all the Devonshire servants loved their lady. When she came back from her years of exile abroad there was rejoicing all through Devonshire House in Piccadilly. Servants had their own class structures, and there must have been an elaborate underground network, connecting with the baby farms to which a woman inconveniently pregnant could apply. Emma Hamilton contrived to give birth to twins in London in 1801 without anyone being the wiser. She had, of course, the advantage of being enormously fat to start off with. When Lady Elizabeth Foster found herself pregnant by the Duke of Devonshire she went abroad and gave birth in dramatic circumstances near Naples. It was risky for any society lady to disappear from her usual haunts for too long. Talk was bound to start about a secret pregnancy. The princesses suffered from this a great deal. It was not an easy world for a woman, but it must have been an interesting one. They were still part of the world, not marginalised, as they were to become in the nineteenth century. It might not be with their husbands that they appeared in public, but they did appear, and at home they could make their houses into political or social centres. The Duchess of Devonshire's house became the Whigs' meeting ground, and the 'bluestocking' ladies ran well attended literary salons.

The English scene was changing dramatically in those turn of the century years between 1780 and 1820. The war that lost England her American colonies ended with defeat at Yorktown in 1781 but peace was not signed with America, France and Spain until 1783. The loss of the American colonies might be a shock to public pride, but it was outweighed by immense financial gains in the West Indies and India. Huge fortunes were being made there. Nabobs and their heiress daughters figure largely in the novels and plays of the time, and as always in good times, bankers and industry throve too. There was new money about for the marrying. Thomas Coutts the banker married his brother's nursemaid, but their daughters all married titles, and were all received at court.

The court of George III and his wife Charlotte formed the apex of this structured society, and it is impossible to understand how it functioned without some idea of what went before. The rest of this chapter will be devoted to a brief outline of the events that made George III's court what it was, as well as a quick sketch of the years when his son was first Prince of Wales and then Regent.

The older George was the third Hanoverian king of England. His great-grandfather had been summoned to London in 1714 after the childless death of Queen Anne, much to the disappointment of Jacobite Tories who had hoped for the return of her Catholic half-brother James Stuart, the Old Pretender. But a country that had been riven by civil war in the previous century was content to settle for Anne's German cousin, though he proved far from glamorous and spoke no English. Coming rather reluctantly to England, he left his divorced wife behind, shut up in a castle. She had got tired of his infidelities twenty years before and taken a lover of her own. The lover disappeared, the Queen never emerged from the castle. In her place, George brought two large, middle-aged Hanoverian mistresses with him, and soon acquired some local ones. He spent a good deal of time back in Hanover and never became central to British society, and his son, another George, was soon running a parallel court of his own, establishing what was to be a family tradition of dislike and distrust between monarch and heir.

The second George and his wife Caroline were devoted, if not faithful to each other, and he respected her political judgement. They were united in detesting their eldest son, Frederick, Prince of Wales, and he returned the feeling. Hating his clever, political mother, he kept his wife Augusta rigorously out of politics. Their eldest son was a disappointment to them. Born two months early, the future George III was a sickly, backward child and his parents made no secret of their preference for his next brother, Edward, later Duke of York. Luckily George liked Edward too, and the two boys shared a house next door to their parents', where they grew up isolated from other children, George shy, Edward outgoing.

Everything changed when their father died suddenly in 1751 and thirteen-year-old George found himself Prince of Wales. He had been brought up to hate and fear his grandfather the King and undoubtedly knew about the mistresses with whom George II consoled himself both before and after the death of his wife. He must have heard the talk about his politically interfering grandmother and seen his father exclude his mother from his councils. And there was vicious talk about his mother and her friend and adviser Lord Bute. There is no touching scene recorded in which George recognized his fate and said, 'I will be good' like his grand-daughter Victoria but he clearly made himself some such promise. He would be King and his own man. The shy, backward (some said retarded) boy put himself into training for the royal job. And he found a father figure in Lord Bute himself, his mother's friend and adviser, though probably not her lover as the gossips said. But while it did not affect his passionate devotion to Bute, the gossip about them may have hardened George's determination that his would be a moral court and that he would be its absolute master, and his family's.

He was a moral, but he was also a susceptible young man. There were stories about a secret marriage to a young Quaker, Hannah Lightfoot, and then, at eighteen, he fell in love with the Duke of Marlborough's handsome daughter, Lady Elizabeth Spencer, only to see her swiftly married off to the Earl of Pembroke, who left her six years later. George next fell seriously in love when he was twenty-one, again with an English girl. He had seen the Duke of Richmond's youngest sister, Lady Sarah Lennox, snubbed by his grandfather at court, which may have added to her attractions in his eyes, but she was on her way to being one of those women who, though not strictly beauties, are always surrounded by men. And she had intelligence, maybe inherited from her astute great-grandfather Charles II and his French mistress, Louise de Keroualle. Sarah's own parents had been forced into a juvenile marriage to settle a gambling debt. Her father, then Lord March, had gone straight from the unwelcome wedding and his plain little bride to Europe for the Grand Tour. Returning, he went to the theatre, saw a stunner surrounded by men in her box, asked who she was and was told, the reigning beauty, Lady March. They fell in love and had twelve children, of whom seven survived, but they both died when Sarah, the youngest, was six. Brought up by her older sisters, she came to court at fifteen and caught the Prince of Wales's eye. She was staying with her older sister, Lady Caroline, who had made a runaway marriage with Henry Fox, the Whig politician.

Lovelorn George put his case in a letter to Lord Bute. Highly sexed like all his family, but puritan with it, he spoke of his 'boiling youth' and went on:

> 'She is everything that I can form to myself lovely . . . I am daily grown unhappy, sleep has left me which never was before interrupted by reverse of fortune. I protest before God that I never had any improper thought with regard to her. I don't deny with [*sic*] often having flattered myself with hopes that one day or other you would consent to my raising her to a throne . . . I submit my happiness to you . . . whose friendship I value if possible above my love for the most charming of her sex; if you can give me no hopes how to be happy I surrender my fortune into your hands, and will keep my thoughts even from the dear object of my love, grieve in silence, and never trouble you more with this unhappy tale; for if I must either lose my friend or my love, I will give up the latter, for I esteem your friendship above every earthly joy.'

Lady Sarah might have had her doubts about the balance between love and friendship in this letter, and Lord Bute said no. He was not a large-minded or imaginative man, and as a minor player in the complex political arena must have felt the threat of Lady Sarah's powerful Whig connection. It is interesting, but idle, to speculate how different the reign of George III would have been if he had been allowed to court and marry this lively young English aristocrat, whose startling career was to run curiously parallel to his.

At the time, he bit the bullet and suggested a quiet investigation of 'Various princesses in Germany. That binds me to nothing.' He did not mean to marry during his grandfather's lifetime, telling Bute that he 'would undergo anything ever so disagreeable than [*sic*] put my trust in him for a single moment in an affair of such delicacy.' When the old king died in 1760, the scene changed. In those days, a new king meant new ministers and there was a good deal of confusion at first, but in the end Bute emerged as a rather unsatisfactory First Minister.

In the spring of 1761 Lady Sarah came to court again. What happened next is open to different interpretations. It is a sad little story whichever way you look at it. Of course, everyone was watching. The King's mother and his older sister, Princess Augusta, kept as close to him as they could at court; Henry Fox was all agog and wrote about the courtship to his wife; Lady Sarah herself described it in letters to her cousin and close friend Lady Susan Fox-Strangways. Lady Susan, who was soon to make a runaway marriage of her own, played a part in the affair. She interpreted a conversation she had with the young King as a kind of roundabout proposal to her cousin, and passed it on as such. But was it really a proposal or a suggestion that Sarah would make an ideal bridesmaid at a royal wedding? At this point, in the spring of 1761, nobody knew that George was in fact busy investigating German princesses. So when he talked about a coronation, and how much better it would be with a queen, and how fit her friend would be, what else was Susan to think?

Not unnaturally, the roundabout way it was done irked Sarah, a spirited girl, and besides she had just been affronted by another young man. When George asked her if her cousin had told her what he had said, and what she thought of it, she would not answer, and looked furious. She was sorry afterwards, but quite convinced that she had been proposed to, however awkwardly. Urged by her family to accept him next time, she meant to, but while on a country visit she fell off her horse, broke her leg and was away from court for a few vital weeks. Henry Fox was sure that the King meant to speak when she came back, and she went to the Sunday court expecting a proposal. 'I am allowed to mutter a little,' she wrote to her friend Lady Susan before she went, 'provided the words *astonished, surprised, understand,* and *meaning* are heard.' But in the event Princess Augusta 'watched as a cat does a mouse.' She went hopefully to court again the following Sunday, 'But nothing was said; I won't go jiggitting for ever if I hear nothing I can tell him.'

That was written on June 10th. On July 7th she heard something indeed. There was to be a council the next day and the King was to announce his engagement to a Princess of Mecklenburg Strelitz. Sarah wrote her outraged astonishment to Susan:

'He must have sent to this woman before you went out of town; then what business had he to begin again? . . . I have almost forgiven him; luckily for me I did not love him, and only liked him, nor did the title weigh anything with me . . . I did not cry I assure you . . . The thing I am most angry at, is looking so like a fool.'

It was all over. Her brother the Duke of Richmond had a ferocious private quarrel with the King soon afterwards, about which neither of them would say a word. And Sarah wrote to Susan many years later, in 1789, when the King had just recovered from his first serious bout of madness:

> 'I am one who will keep the King's marriage day with unfeigned joy and gratitude to Heaven that I am not in Her Majesty's place . . . I like my sons better than I like royal sons, thinking them better animals, and more likely to give me comfort in my old age . . . I am delighted to hear the King is so well . . . I always consider him as an old friend, who has been in the wrong.'

And when she fell on hard times, her old friend the King gave her a pension.

In fairness to George III one has to remember that what seemed all important to Lady Sarah and her confidante would have been just one small item in the social and political vortex into which the twenty-two year old King had plunged. And George was no fool. He must have known that the Whig Henry Fox was right behind Lady Sarah, maybe even hoping that, if not Queen, his sister-in-law might become the King's influential mistress. If George had not seen this for himself, there were his mother and sister to tell him, not to mention his adored Lord Bute. It may well have helped to contribute to his strong views about the kind of wife he wanted. During that first winter of his reign, his emissaries had worked their way round to Charlotte of Mecklenburg Strelitz by a process of elimination. She was not on the original shortlist, but while he was flirting with Sarah, the King had been taking some firm decisions. He did not want a member of the House of Brunswick, perhaps because George II had suggested one. And he did not want a woman who would play politics or answer back. It was to be husband, church and children for his wife. Two princesses were rejected because they were reported to be stubborn and ill-tempered and, besides, there was a threat of illness in one family which gave him, he wrote to Bute 'melancholy thoughts about what may perhaps be in the blood.' He was selecting a royal brood mare and being careful about it.

There may have been more to it than that. Did he perhaps know that he had inherited a family problem of his own? Was he afraid then of developing the symptoms of what recent research has revealed as the inherited nervous condition, porphyria? In their book, *George III and the Mad Business*, Ida Macalpine and Richard Hunter argue that this affliction can be traced back to Mary Queen of Scots and her son James I of England. A family tradition of a sinister health threat would explain both George's careful choice of bride and also the austere lifestyle to which he confined himself. If he was aware of the threat of an illness, part nervous part physical, he must have watched both himself and his children for signs of it, and been appalled at what he saw. Whatever else he may have been, he was a brave man.

Having selected his wife, he hurried on the arrangements. Naturally Charlotte's family were delighted when the proposal reached them, and agreed to everything. She was a Lutheran but would be glad to conform to the rites of the Church of England, and the Church of England agreed that this was no problem. No one pretended that Charlotte was anything but plain, but George made the most of a lock of soft brown hair. Her mother died; the arrangements went on just the same. She was measured for the wedding dress that was to be made for her in England and told to bring as few servants as possible. A practical girl, she spent the ten-day voyage cheering up her seasick retinue and learning her first English, and *God Save the King* on the harpsichord. She landed at Harwich on September 7th, 1761, reached London next afternoon, met the King, dined with the royal family, and was married at about nine o'clock that evening, with Lady Sarah Lennox as a dignified chief bridesmaid. She and her new husband did not get to bed till three. They had one significant thing in common, they were both strong as horses. They were to have fifteen children, only two of whom failed to grow up, something of a record in those days of high infant mortality. George must have been pleased with his brood mare.

But if she had expected a glamorous life as centre of one of the great courts of Europe, Charlotte was to be disappointed. George had planned her life as carefully as he had selected her. Besides, Parliament held the purse strings, and money was tight. His court was to be a frugal as well as a moral one. He had already issued a proclamation against sin, and in favour of Sunday observance, and had cancelled those dangerous Sunday courts as part of his moral drive. Anxious not to put on weight, a family tendency, he cut down drastically on royal entertaining, and kept his Queen in a kind of purdah. His domineering mother made rules for her; his unmarried sisters mocked her German ways; she was not even allowed to play cards with her waiting women. She was to learn English, read Shakespeare with her husband, appear at court and the theatre with him and bear his children. And she did it all. They were an apparently devoted couple, but isolated behind a rigid screen of etiquette. Even their children, and pregnant women, must stand in the royal presence. It hardly made for close friendships, still less for family love.

Charlotte was to say later that she was 'Truly sensible of the dear King's great strictness, at my arrival in England, to prevent my making acquaintances, for he was always used to say that . . . there never could be kept up a society without party, which was always dangerous for any woman . . . Particularly so for the royal family . . . I feel thankful for it from the bottom of my heart.' But it dried up the springs of love in her.

George might tame his wife, his children were another matter. His sons were brought up as he had been, isolated from other children, in their own rooms in the palace, their own houses on Kew Green. Letters of heavy parental advice sped from wing to wing of the palace; boyish wrongdoing was punished by savage beatings. With the most high-minded of intentions, he was bringing up an inevitable pack of rebels. As soon as they could, the boys kicked over the traces, went out into the world and enjoyed themselves. Their father must often have congratulated himself that early in his reign he had pushed through a Royal Marriage Act, intended to prevent the kind of mis-alliances that had been made by two of his brothers. Under its provisions no descendant of George II could marry without the consent of the Crown. If they did, the marriage was null and void and anyone who helped in it was liable to penalties. Children of princesses who married abroad were exempt, and family members over twenty-five could marry without consent on giving twelve months' notice and getting the tacit approval of both Houses of Parliament. Not a popular measure, it was ferociously opposed by Sarah Lennox's nephew, the young Charles James Fox, and the King never forgave him for this. It is still in force today.

The six daughters were more amenable but not necessarily happier than their brothers. Their mother could not love them. George was a devoted father who did not want his children to grow up. He kept the Prince of Wales in baby clothes long after he should have been breeched, and wanted his handsome, spirited, highly-sexed daughters to stay at home and be a comfort to their parents. He had in fact grounds for caution about dynastic marriages. His divorced great-grandmother had died in captivity only twelve years before he was born. And he himself had consented to his youngest sister's marriage to the imbecile King of Denmark in 1766. Finding life with her husband intolerable, Caroline Matilda conspired with her lover against him, but their plot failed and it took her brother's intervention and a British fleet to ensure at least her safety in a fortress in Hanover, where she died, at twenty-four, in 1775. Later, the court of Denmark suggested a marriage between her son and his cousin, the Princess Royal, but George would have none of it. His sister's sad story must have confirmed him in his views of the unsuitability of women's mixing in politics.

His eldest son, inevitably another George, was brought up starved of love, and was a bad son and a worse husband and father. Yet he was fond of and good to his sisters, who loved him and were grateful, and he almost managed to love Maria Fitzherbert, but self-love and vanity were too strong in him. His achievements were all ostentatious. He patronized the arts and architecture, employing both James Wyatt and John Nash, but his Pavilion at Brighton is a fantasy palace without a heart. He also remodelled Windsor and Buckingham Palace, gave his name to a street, and spent the public's money wisely, for once, when he bought the pictures that were to form the basis of the National Gallery, but he left no creation of his own behind him, except the daughter he neglected. Thackeray, writing a mere thirty years after his death, called him an 'empty scapegrace' who 'never could have real friends.' In the end, he convinced himself that he had fought at Waterloo. 'So you have often told me, sire,' said the Duke of Wellington, tactful for once.

When young, the Prince of Wales was handsome and had immense charm. The public loved him at first, calling him Prince Florizel after the hero of *The Winter's Tale*. He was having an affair with the actress who played the heroine, but the affair, and the public enthusiasm, soon cooled. He and his equally spendthrift brothers were swimming against the tide of public opinion. Their father might be a domestic tyrant and threatened with madness, but he was much more in touch with the mood of the general public than they were. Surrounded by sycophants, it was easy for them to ignore the rise of an increasingly prosperous and vocal middle class. Below the surface froth, the balls and masquerades, there was a strong evangelical tide running, and the Quakers were active too. It has been argued that it was this strain of moral seriousness in the nation that made it proof against the revolutionary frenzy that engulfed France at the end of the century.

There were serious minds among the aristocracy too. The Countess of Huntingdon, the 'Queen of the Methodists', had perhaps as many as sixty-four active chapels in the Calvinist Methodist Connection named after her. Her friend the Countess Spencer was another strongly religious lady, but she was a society one too. She brought up her children to observe the laws both of God and man. Her two entrancing daughters both made brilliant, arranged marriages, but found love elsewhere.

The aristocracy was a small, close-knit world, with its own tribal rules, dangerous to break. Below it, the members of the burgeoning middle class were working out their own rules, creating their own snobberies and aping the manners of their assumed betters. Jane Austen, a member of the rising middle class, was infinitely aware of fine social shades, from overbearing Lady Catherine de Bourgh to illegitimate Harriet Smith, and middle-class Emma's fantasies about her birth. Jane Austen's novels and letters show her equally aware of the importance of money in the social structure. Emma was rich and could afford her fantasies; and Harriet Smith was lucky to have been sent to school by her anonymous father. Otherwise, she would have been voiceless, like the great mass of the lower classes.

Politics also played its part in the social scene, since Whig and Tory did not mix or marry much, keeping apart, with their own clubs and great houses as social centres, both in London and in the country. When the young Tory Lord Granville Leveson Gower became devoted to the older Whig Countess of Bessborough it was surprising politically as well as socially, though in fact there was a certain amount of blurring both within and between Whig and Tory, with smaller cliques forming around outstanding individuals.

The difference between Whigs and Tories is about as hard to pin down and describe as that between Democrats and Republicans in the United States. To over-simplify, the Whigs, like the Democrats, were the more radical party, dominated by great country landowners like the Dukes of Devonshire and Bedford, but open to the progressive young. The Tories, more conservative, many of them small country squires, were still recovering from the disaster of backing the Stuart claimant at the beginning of the century. The King was theoretically above politics, but he was dependent on Parliament for his (and his family's) income and became an active and ruthless player of the political game. He was the fount of honour and patronage, immensely important in those days, as always. The promise of a title or a pension then was as influential as that of a title or a highly paid directorship is now, but then it was in the absolute gift of the monarch.

George III was not a well man. Despite his stringent regime, he had been ill in 1762 and 1765. His first serious bout of madness occurred in the winter of 1788 to 1789. By then, he had become identified with the Tory party, who were then in power, and his son with the opposition Whigs, who hoped passionately that the King's madness would prove so incapacitating that his son had to take over as Prince Regent. There were bitter battles in Parliament that winter about the terms of the Regency Bill, with the Whigs wanting unlimited powers for their friend the Prince of Wales and the Tories entrenched against this. In the end, the Whigs were disappointed when the King recovered just when a modified Regency Bill had been passed, in the spring of 1789. Revolution broke out in France that autumn, and France declared war on England in 1793. The expense of the war, the industrial revolution to which it contributed and the revolutionary influence of France all combined to make the seventeen nineties years of extreme social unrest, with consequent government oppression, treason trials and deportations. The rising cost of living also contributed to the unpopularity of the flagrantly extravagant royal princes.

Pitt and the Tories had been in office since 1783, but trouble over Ireland caused Pitt's resignation in 1801 and the stress of it all contributed to George III's new bout of insanity. A brief peace with France did not last beyond 1803 and after that the war continued with fluctuating alliances and varying fortunes until campaigns both in Spain and Central Europe forced Napoleon back on Paris in 1814. By then, the Prince of Wales had been Regent for three years. He hosted triumphant celebrations in London, but the international peace conference that followed at Vienna was interrupted by the news that Napoleon had escaped from imprisonment on Elba. He was to be defeated at last at Waterloo in 1815. The blind, mad old King lived on at Windsor until 1820, but by then the Prince Regent was too worn out by self-indulgence really to enjoy the position he had longed for, still less to remarry on the death of his detested wife the following year. He died in 1830, mourned by his first wife, Mrs Fitzherbert, and by four of the sisters who had been the first and perhaps the best loves of his life.

In the following chapters, I propose to talk about the lives and loves of a very varied group of women who were the Prince of Wales' contemporaries. Some of them were born before him, some lived long after, but they all shared in some way the experience of those eventful years when the eighteenth century gave way to the nineteenth.

2
Six Frustrated Princesses

T HE NINE SONS and six daughters of George III and Queen
Charlotte were all born between 1762 and 1783, so they were
all growing up, looking for life and love, during the years I
am considering. Boys and girls do tend to be brought up differently,
but they were brought up very differently indeed. The boys may
have been beaten, but they had independence and establishments of
their own from as early as eleven, while the girls were kept at home
under the parental eye. The boys had money, the girls did not, but the
girls, brought up as a group, had each other in a sense that the boys
never did. They grew up capable of love and knowing they needed
it.

The princes, surviving their loveless childhoods, plunged swiftly
into the pleasures of life. Of course one reacts against one's parents,
and the sight of George and Charlotte playing Darby and Joan at
Windsor might have turned any lively young man to dissipation, even
without the beatings, but the Royal Marriage Act also had its impact
on their emotional lives. Their father had the whip hand in every
sense. Given a chance, most of his sons might well have been happy
to settle for domesticity and a comfortable wife to whom to be
unfaithful. Everyone said that the future George IV was at his most
agreeable when he was living with Mrs Fitzherbert, and William IV
had many contented years with Mrs Jordan and then a surprisingly
happy marriage with his dynastic Princess Adelaide of Saxe-Coburg-
Meiningen. Augustus Duke of Sussex might have been happy with his
older wife Lady Augusta Murray and their two children had their
marriage not been annulled under the Act, and the Duke of
Cambridge, marrying in his fifties after the death of Princess
Charlotte, apparently lived happily ever afterwards with Princess
Augusta of Hesse-Cassell. Even the Duke of York's marriage to
Frederica of Prussia seems to have gone well enough so long as she

stayed in the country with her dogs and he in London with his mistresses. He was the only one of the nine brothers who made what their father considered a suitable marriage at a reasonable age. It was, unfortunately, childless.

Their sisters, the six unlucky princesses, were equally cut out for domesticity, and they longed for homes of their own. 'Never in tale or fable,' wrote the diarist Fanny Burney, who worked for the Queen, 'were there six sister Princesses more lovely.' Even allowing for the author's prejudice, they were indeed good-looking, well mannered, highly marriageable girls, but doomed to late marriage, spinsterhood, or worse. Their father had ring-fenced them. There were sightings of course. They appeared at their mother's side at court, they joined the ceremonial family parade on the terrace at Windsor, they went to the theatre, to concerts and, sometimes, to balls. Lord Elgin danced with Princess Augusta Sophia at a ball on board ship at Weymouth in 1798, and this is probably significant; they were freer away from London. You do not hear of them dancing the night away at Devonshire House. Of course not. The Devonshires were Whigs, anathema to their parents. So was Lady Melbourne, the other great society hostess. The Princess Royal actually and boldly once took exception to the fact that their mother only invited the daughters of loyal Tories to Windsor. It did no good. Queen Charlotte was a tyrant in her quiet, dutiful way. When he was mad, George III said her daughters hated and feared her and he may well have been right. Her daughter Mary wrote, after a painful scene in 1812, that, 'It was the object of the dear King's life to keep from the world *all* he *suffered* and *went through* with her *temper.*'

Her daughters could not get away from her. They loved their father, and he loved them dearly. Fanny Burney reports that when they met their parents in the morning their father kissed them and they kissed their mother's hand. But though he loved them, he did not want them to marry. Before he went mad in 1788 he actually apologized to his older daughters for his failure to provide them with husbands, and said something about taking them to Hanover to find them some suitable young princes. But what with his madness, and the French Revolution, nothing came of this. And there was no hope of support from their mother. He had tamed her too successfully, and, besides, his early illnesses of 1762 and 1765 had been alarming enough. According to Mrs Papendiek, wife of one of the royal pages, the Queen knew of her husband's inherited health problem, described as 'scrofula', and watched her children anxiously for signs of it. But she was one of the wives for whom the husband always comes first. Her prime concern was to keep his life as free from stress as possible. Everything else must give way to that. It was a sound instinct but it was hard on the children.

Various hopeful young princes had been turned away, and Charlotte Augusta Matilda, the Princess Royal, was still unmarried at the ripe age, for those days, of twenty-two, when her father's illness developed into madness in 1788. It was a moment when Queen Charlotte might have asserted herself. There is a healthy English tradition of functioning queens, whether regnant or regent. Her son the Prince of Wales might be twenty-six, but his life was a public scandal and he was deeply involved with the party in opposition. If she had been firm, she might have managed to take over the royal reins. Instead, she collapsed into nonentity, a pitiful helpless figure wailing, 'What will become of me?' On one occasion the King actually attacked the Prince of Wales at the family dinner table, banging his head against the wall so violently that he burst into tears and his sisters had to revive him with smelling salts. The King could be so violent that they had the mahogany doors of his rooms at Windsor reinforced. No one knew whom he might attack next. The Queen took no chances. She kept a lady in waiting or a daughter always with her and huddled in her rooms, while the Prince of Wales took charge of everything.

Of course there could be no talk of marriage for his daughters while the King's illness lasted. When he confounded Prince and politicians by recovering in 1789, the Princess Royal (she was known in the family as such since she shared her mother's first name) was a year older and her position much worse. Her mother had proved herself a broken reed, and the danger of crossing her father was common knowledge. If his ministers had to tailor their policies to his whim, what chance had his daughters of defying him? And, besides, they loved him, and had seen him mad and tormented by his doctors with their barbarous remedies. How could they risk that again? Approaches were made from Denmark, from Orange, from Brunswick, from Württemberg, and the King turned them all down. Between public appearances, the Princess Royal acted as a kind of superior governess to her younger sisters. Aside from that, what else was there for her to do? Brought up for the role of wife, and probably consort, she was condemned to play second fiddle to a mother who brought out the worst in her. Was Charlotte jealous of her husband's devotion to their eldest daughter? Gossipy Mrs Papendiek said the Princess Royal was, 'Always shy with the Queen . . . out of the Queen's presence she was a different being.' Dress bored her and her appearance showed it. She was tone deaf, so her father's weekly concerts must have been a misery to her. And she had been with her father in the carriage when he first went out of his mind. No wonder that by the time she was twenty-eight her doctor Sir Lucas Pepys was reported as saying that he thought her 'quiet, desperate state' a threat to both her life and her understanding, so dangerous that only marriage would save her.

The Prince of Wales tried to arrange a match for her with the heir to the Duke of Oldenburg, but nothing came of it. And then, at last, in 1795, when she was twenty-nine, a suitor appeared in the robust form of the Hereditary Prince of Württemberg. He was an immensely fat man with children by a first wife who had died under sinister circumstances after bearing an illegitimate child in Russia. To make matters worse, she had been the King's own niece, daughter of his sister Augusta, the Duchess of Brunswick. He quite reasonably insisted on an investigation into the circumstances of her death, which delayed matters, but he continued his delaying tactics when the Prince was finally cleared and landed in England early in 1797. The bride was thirty by now, large and plain, the groom was forty and so huge he had to have special holes cut in his tables. She was so nervous when they first met that she could not speak and her mother spoke for her. The cartoonists were savage, but the marriage went ahead, with the Princess looking unusually well, having been firmly dressed by her mother. There was a tear-drenched parting with her father, whom she never saw again.

The new bride put her heart into her marriage, and managed to be happy in Württemberg. Her only child was stillborn, but she became a loving step-mother to her husband's children and stood by him through the hazards of life in Europe with Napoleon on the rampage. They had had to flee from French troops a couple of times before Napoleon swept into Württemberg unopposed in 1805. Accepting the inevitable, she advised her husband to hide his treasures from the predatory conqueror and she herself received him with dignity. He was impressed, behaved politely to her, and said later that he had stopped her husband ill-treating her. He made them King and Queen of Württemberg the following year as a reward for good behaviour, and she was able to write to her mother as '*chère mère et soeur*,' which must, one feels, have been satisfying, but which infuriated Queen Charlotte, who refused to reciprocate.

The new Queen helped arrange a match between her step-daughter Catherine and Napoleon's brother Jerome, which made Catherine Queen of the new Kingdom of Westphalia. Her own husband changed sides again when Napoleon began to be defeated late in 1813 and after nine isolated years she was back in touch with her family. But when her brother, now Prince Regent, wrote to her personally to invite her to the 1814 victory celebrations in England her husband was affronted and would not let her go. She had to pretend illness so as to save everyone embarrassment. She always maintained that she was happy with her man and when he died in 1816 she wore black for the rest of her life, finally returning to England for a visit in 1827, the year before she died. Before that, she had been visited by her sister, another Augusta, who found her very much altered: 'Very large and bulky . . . not wearing the least bit of a corset.' Opinions differed about the success of the marriage, but Charlotte was in no doubt. She had found someone to love, and loved him. When her sister Mary married in 1816 she wrote that she was convinced that her sisters, 'Would all have been happier had they been properly established.'

But the Princess Royal's marriage probably made things harder for her sisters. Her father, anxiously watching the tide of war wash to and fro over Württemberg must have been strengthened in his resolve not to let his other darlings go into such danger. And it never for a moment occurred to him that they might make English marriages, as he himself had once wished to do. One of the disconcerting features of his madness was his preoccupation with Lady Elizabeth Spencer, the Duke of Marlborough's daughter, whom he had loved at eighteen. Unfortunately the Countess of Pembroke, as she now was, had become lady in waiting to Queen Charlotte after being abandoned by her husband. She had always been tall and handsome and did not lose her looks. Queen Charlotte had always been plain, and constant childbearing had not improved her, though someone did remark that the bloom of her ugliness was going off. The contrast between the two women must have been striking. It has been suggested that this is what drove George mad, and it does seem that the emotional conflict may have finally upset the balance of a brain tormented both by savagely painful illness and the ruthless ministrations of the doctors. Fifteen children prove him an uxorious man, but now when the doctors did let him see his wife she always kept someone with her until he had retired to his rooms. It casts a glum light on the royal bedchamber, but she was only forty-four in 1788 and may well have thought that fifteen children were enough. But it is not altogether surprising that her passionate, frustrated husband fantasized marriage with a complaisant Lady Pembroke. Recovering, he remembered his ravings about her and apologized. It must have been hideously embarrassing for everyone. And when he went mad again, the pattern repeated itself. He seems not to have raved about Lady Sarah Lennox.

The second daughter, Princess Augusta Sophia, was forty-three when the King was finally declared insane in 1811 and immured at Windsor. Next year, she wrote a passionate appeal to her brother, now Prince Regent, begging him to connive at a secret marriage with the English officer she had loved for years. She, too, had been the subject of abortive proposals. Fanny Burney gives an interesting and significant description of the gossip about one of these in her *Journal* for 1787. She describes a scene in which the Queen's lively French reader, a married clergyman, teased the Princess unmercifully about her love for all things Danish and actually got between her and the door when she blushed and tried to escape, appealing to Fanny for help. All Fanny did was write it up as comedy afterwards. These days I think it would be considered sexual harassment. Naturally nothing came of the Danish proposal since the young man in question was son of the King's unlucky sister Caroline Matilda and her mad husband and had already been rejected as a candidate for the Princess Royal's hand.

Fanny Burney said Augusta had 'a great deal of sport in her disposition.' She got on well with her brothers and seems to have been a comfort to her mother during her father's first outbreak of madness, since it was for her that a tent bed was put up in the Queen's room at Kew when the King was brought there from Windsor in 1788. In the early years of the next century, she gave up thoughts of a foreign marriage when she fell in love with an Englishman. She never named him, but all the evidence points to a successful Irish career officer called Brent Spencer. The handsome son of a country squire, he had joined the army at seventeen and was well advanced in a dashing career when they first met, probably early in 1800 after he had served in Holland with her brother, the Duke of York, in 1799. The Duke spoke highly of him in despatches and might well have introduced him to his sisters. He then served with distinction in Egypt, returning to

England in 1805, when he was promoted to major-general, appointed equerry to the King and placed on the staff. After that they were bound to meet. He was abroad again in 1807, commanding a brigade in the surprise attack on Copenhagen, and next year he served in the Peninsular War as second in command to Sir Arthur Wellesley. He fought courageously, but the future Duke of Wellington found him unreliable, describing him years later as 'exceedingly puzzle-headed, but very formal.' He sounds a perfect son-in-law for George III. The Peninsular years were the high point and end of his career. He resigned on being superseded by Sir Thomas Graham in 1811 and returned to England. Made a general on retirement, he bought a small estate at Lea, within easy distance of Windsor, and settled there.

Next year, Princess Augusta wrote her appeal to her brother, describing the twelve years she had known her beloved, and the anxiety she had suffered when he was in action. She referred to a previous conversation with the Prince in 1808 when she had told him about her lover's handsome offer to give up his position as equerry so as to spare her the constant frustrating meetings. She had urged him not to do so, obviously hanging on to her crumb of happiness. Now she wanted more. Her brother was Regent, could he not sanction a waiver, or a dodging of the Royal Marriage Act for her and her man? If he could not actually attend the wedding, would her dear brother allow the Duke of York to represent him? And perhaps most important of all, would he speak to the Queen on her behalf?

> 'I am certain the Queen cannot approve if she merely thinks of my birth and station . . . But when she considers the character of the man, the faithfulness and length of our attachment, the struggles that I have been compelled to make, never retracting from any of my duties . . . I am sure that she will say that long and great has been my trial, and correct has been my conduct . . . I am proud of possessing the affection and good opinion of an honest man and highly distinguished character, and I am sure that what you can do to make us happy, you will not leave undone.'

We do not know what, if anything, the Prince Regent did, but he was always loving and good to his sisters and when his daughter died in childbirth in 1817 he chose Brent Spencer to break the terrible news at Windsor. Spencer was installed as a Knight of the Bath the same year and Princess Augusta was present at the ceremony. They may have had private happiness, but anything public was impossible. She achieved a small measure of freedom when Queen Charlotte died in 1818 and, perhaps significantly, left her a house and farm at Frogmore.

She lived there after her father's death and we are free to imagine that Spencer came over from Lee to visit her there until his death in 1828. She lived on until 1840, great friends with Queen Adelaide and with her niece Victoria and her husband, and called 'a capital aunt' by another niece, the Duke of Cambridge's daughter.

The next sister, Elizabeth, liked to refer to herself as 'Sally Blunt'. She was a plump, lively girl with artistic leanings, but often ill. Like several of her sisters she suffered from 'spasms' and was bled and blistered for 'a scrofulous abscess on her left side,' according to Mrs Papendiek. She was ill so much as a young woman that there were persistent rumours of a secret marriage and concealed pregnancies, but she was in fact presumably suffering from a mild case of porphyria which a resilient constitution helped her to live with. She liked her food (her sisters called her Fatima) and she made no bones about wanting to be married. 'I trust that the P R's being determined upon may open the way for others,' she wrote hopefully when the Princess Royal married in 1797, but it did not work out like that. She got into debt that year and appealed to her brother George for help. She needed £600 urgently for some unnamed reason and he sent it to her at once, like the good brother he was. The sisters had only £1,000 a year each from their mother, who was known for her meanness, and one of the things George did on becoming Prince Regent was to arrange adequate allowances for them. This made the Queen furious. She was even angrier when the four sisters still at home agreed to join George's daughter Charlotte in the House of Lords for his first state opening of parliament in the autumn of 1812, while she remained at Windsor with her mad husband. George needed his sisters there partly to keep his lively daughter in order and partly as moral support against the propaganda campaign being waged against him by his estranged wife. In the end, Princess Elizabeth and Princess Mary went, and when they got back to Windsor it was to face an appalling scene with their mother. The Prince Regent had to intervene to calm her down, which he could usually manage.

But before this, in 1808, a chance of marriage for Elizabeth had come and gone. When her brother the Duke of Kent had been in Canada with the army back in 1794 he had met three impecunious young French exiles, the sons of Philippe Égalité, the Duke of Orleans, who had signed the death warrant of his brother the King of France and then in the end followed him to the guillotine. The eldest son, Louis Philippe, was trying to support himself by teaching and the

Duke of Kent lent him a much needed £200. Now Louis Philippe was back in Europe, looking for a wife. He renewed his friendship with the Duke of Kent and his mistress Madame St Laurent and dined with them on Christmas Day 1807. By next autumn things were so well advanced that Elizabeth was writing hopefully to the Prince Regent about the legitimisation of any children of the match. The question of religion seems to have been overcome, but the Queen was the obstacle. She refused to discuss the proposal at all, still less put it to the King. Elizabeth wrote that she 'Would *never give it up* – for it was hinted many, many things had been brought forward and rejected without a word from us, and therefore we all felt the Sun of our Days was set.' Their only hope was in their brother.

But the Prince was not Regent yet; his father was still technically sane, a powerful weapon in the Queen's hands. Louis Philippe eventually gave up and went to the Kingdom of Naples and Sicily where, despite some opposition from her powerful mother, he managed to marry a grand-daughter of the Empress Maria Theresa who became his Queen when he succeeded to the throne of France in 1830. Elizabeth was thirty-eight when he failed to marry her in 1808, so he would probably not have had eight children by her, as he did by his Marie-Amélie, but what an interesting set of possibilities it raises. Years later, when he was King of France, Elizabeth, sitting by her own widowed hearth, said that Marie-Amélie was an angel and that his 'conduct has been perfect since he has been where he is.'

She resigned herself to spinsterhood in the cottage on Kew Green that had been assigned to her when she was ill. All she wanted now, she wrote to her brother, was 'kind and good friends, A Great chair, a pinch of Snuff, a Book, and a good Fireside.' Her health was still not sound; in the great row between the sisters and their mother over the opening of parliament in 1812 she had a fit of hysterics so serious that she found herself thinking of 'what I had always thought with horror of, a sudden death.' She and her mother seem to have made it up, for they were in Bath together for the Queen's health in 1817, when the death of Princess Charlotte in childbirth suddenly raised the whole question of the succession and the royal dukes began to think about dynastic marriages.

And then, suddenly, in 1818, Elizabeth received a proposal of her own. The Hereditary Prince of Hesse-Homburg had been one of Augusta's unsuccessful suitors back in 1804. But he had come to England for the great celebrations of 1814 and had a chance to meet the sisters and perhaps to hear the rumours about Augusta's secret marriage. Now he was proposing in form for Elizabeth, and she meant to have him. She was forty-eight. 'In our situation,' she realistically wrote to her brother, 'there is nothing but character to look to . . . I wish to accept this offer. I am no longer young, and fairly feel that having my own home will be a comfort in time.' The Queen's health was visibly deteriorating and she cried a great deal, but the sisters were supportive and the Prince Regent finally talked their mother round. The gossips were scathing. The Hereditary Prince was a poor man, and plain, and stank of tobacco and garlic. They had to clean him up for the wedding, and he was horribly sick on the bridal journey to Windsor, but his bride was happy: 'I am so contented with my lot that I can never be too thankful . . . Single I should have been wretched.'

Her new home was a shock, deficient in many of the basic comforts she was used to, but she set to work to clean it up and perhaps her husband too, and apparently succeeded. The diarist Cornelia Knight, visiting them, reported that 'Bluff', as Elizabeth called her Fritz, 'Was remarkably neat in his person and never came into company without changing his dress if he had been smoking.' Tobacco was a more serious matter than drink in those days. When her father-in-law the old Landgrave died and Fritz succeeded, Elizabeth shocked her family by allowing her mother-in-law to go on taking precedence of her. Her husband had been left a burden of debt along with the title and she was soon hard at work trying to raise the money to pay it off without hurting his feelings. She outlived both her husband and her eldest brother, and compared George IV with their father in a letter to a friend: 'My Father was a man after God's own heart . . . the other God made perfect but the world spoiled him.' And each year on February 14th she would look back to meeting her Fritz for the first time, and, 'The sun beginning to shine upon me, as it did when he arrived, and I am sure it never set afterwards.'

The next sister, Mary, was the acknowledged beauty of the handsome sextet. She had beautiful manners, too, and no talents at all, except, perhaps, for people. She was a great talker, but not always discreet; her sisters learned not to tell her anything that they did not want their mother to hear. But they loved their 'dearest Minny' just the same and she was the family nurse. When their youngest sister Amelia was dying in 1809 Mary was chosen to go with her to Weymouth, a place she disliked. And when the Regency was established and the

Queen was given custody of the old, mad King at Windsor, Mary was the one who wrote daily bulletins to the Prince Regent about their father's condition. According to her, seeing the Queen made him worse because of her lack of 'warmth, tenderness, affection.' She suggested that it would be a good thing if she and her sisters were to visit the poor King, two at a time, so as to ease things between the unhappy couple, who would never again be 'a real comfort' to each other.

The Queen thought her daughters should share her cloistered existence at Windsor, and there were fierce battles every time they tried to escape. After getting away for a few days to the Queen's House, now rebuilt as Buckingham Palace, they 'lived upon very cross words and sour looks.' They did not dare go and stay with their brother in the luxury he had achieved at Carlton House. But they did manage to get to town for the victory celebrations in 1814, when Princess Mary opened the Grand Ball at Carlton House with the Duke of Cumberland. Augusta, older than her, must have been known to be out of the running and Mary functioned as the oldest unmarried Princess. When the Prince Regent gave a fête for the Duke of Wellington even the Queen went, and Princess Mary opened the ball with the young Duke of Devonshire and said afterwards that she, 'Never saw the Queen more pleased.'

But each escape from the stifling unhappiness of Windsor must have made the return worse. So when Mary's cousin William Frederick, Duke of Gloucester, came forward as a possible suitor in 1815 she was all eagerness, ignoring the fact that he had recently been an unsuccessful candidate for the hand of her niece Princess Charlotte. She ignored a good deal else. William Frederick was the son of one of the unsuitable marriages that had driven George III to the Royal Marriage Act. His father was George III's brother, but his mother was one of the three beautiful Waldegrave sisters, the illegitimate daughters of Sir Edward Walpole and his gutter-bred mistress. Unfortunately the son did not inherit his mother's charm and intelligence. A tall, thin, stupid young man, he was known as 'Slice' or 'Silly Billy', but stood touchily on his rights as a member of the royal family. At thirty-eight, he was a year younger than his bride. She had some doubts about the match, but he promised that she would be allowed to visit her family whenever they needed her, and also agreed to some other unnamed provision of hers. Reporting this to her brother, she wrote: 'We compleatly [*sic*] understand each other.' And then went on: 'I don't know what other people feel when going to be married, but as yet I have done nothing but cry.' Oddly enough, the Queen chose to approve of this marriage of cousins, which would have appalled her husband, had he been sane to witness it. The wedding was celebrated at the Queen's House in July 1816 and every-body cried.

They probably showed good sense. Gloucester, who had shocked his royal relations and embarrassed the Whigs themselves by coming out as a Whig, was not an easy husband. But he kept his word about letting his wife go to help in family crises. When her mother was dying in 1818 he tactfully went abroad to leave his wife free to go and support her sisters through the illness at Kew, and then for the painful first journey back to Windsor where their sister Sophia had stayed to keep the rule that a member of the family must always be in atten-dance on the mad King. Mary found it less easy to get leave to visit the family on pleasant occasions. Her husband was an Evangelical as well as a Whig and knew the Quaker Gurney family. Like them he dis-approved of Sunday travel and the Prince Regent, and tended to limit the length of the visits to the Brighton Pavilion that she enjoyed so much. 'Man is man,' she wrote to her brother on one occasion, 'and does not like to be put out of his way, and still less by a Wife than anybody else.' In fact, she had married a petty tyrant who locked up the downstairs reception rooms because, he said, they were not kept tidy enough, so that she had to entertain her friends in her rooms at the very top of the house. Childless, she loved children. In 1847, her niece Queen Victoria wrote to thank her for her presents to the royal children: 'Alice was quite *beside herself* at her first earrings and is in all anxiety to have her ears bored.'

The Duke of Gloucester died, probably of the family complaint, in 1834. His wife nursed him devotedly and Princess Lieven, the Russian Ambassador's wife who had become such a figure in English society, wrote, 'You will see that the Duchess of Gloucester will now get perfectly well.' The Duchess indeed lived to be eighty, always available for family crises, witnessing the Great Exhibition and the birth of all her niece Victoria's children. The future King Edward VII sent her gifts of game and she described him as charming but lazy. She had always been sound about people, if not necessarily discreet. She was the last of George III's children to die, and Harriet Martineau, the Victorian author, used the occasion for a powerful plea for the repeal of the Royal Marriage Act, the 'narrow and artificial law ordained by a wilful King of England.' 'Marriage is too solemn and sacred a matter to be so treated as a piece of state politics,' she wrote, but nothing was done.

Princess Sophia was almost as beautiful as her sister Mary and a great deal more intelligent. She tended to be people's favourite among the sisters. Her niece Charlotte, the Prince Regent's daughter, described her as a true friend: 'She is a very sweet dear, being so true to me, so sencible [*sic*], so right on all subjects.' But Sophia had inherited the family malady and suffered like her father from 'spasms', together with bouts of depression and a throat problem that sometimes made it hard for her to swallow. The doctors feared for her life and her reason, but she had her father's strong constitution too, and lived to be seventy-one.

Hers is an extraordinary story and much of it inevitably remains conjecture. But all the evidence – and all the gossip – point to her having borne an illegitimate son in the summer of 1800. Gossipy Lord Glenbervie, whose wife knew the Princesses, reported the rumours in his *Journal* as early as 1801, his informant being the irresponsible Princess of Wales, who loathed the Royal Family by then. By 1804 he was writing that, 'The foundling which was left at the Taylors . . . is now in a manner admitted by the Court to be Princess Sophia's, and, as the story generally goes, by General Garth.'

Charles Greville, writing much later in his *Memoirs*, said: 'The Princesses lived at the Lower Lodge. Pss. Sophia, however, was unwell, and was removed to the Upper Lodge, and a few days after the K. and Queen went to town, leaving the Pss. there. Garth, who was one of the King's equerries, remained also, and his bedroom at the Lodge was just over hers. Nine months from that time she was brought to bed.' Greville had the story from Lady Caroline Thynne, whose mother, the Marchioness of Bath, was Mistress of the Robes to Queen Charlotte. He added: 'The old King never knew it. The Court was at Weymouth when she was big with child. She was said to be dropsical, and then suddenly recovered. They told the old King that she had been cured by *roast beef*, and this he swallowed, and used to tell it to people.'

The *Morning Chronicle* of March 15th, 1829, when the scandal finally broke, had another version of the story in which the birth took place in the course of the royal family's annual move from Windsor to Weymouth for their summer holiday. Princess Sophia was taken so ill on the journey that she and her party had to stop for a night at

Andover, and when she reached Weymouth the next day she had to be carried upstairs to her lodgings. Soon afterwards, she suddenly recovered. And at the same time a baby appeared mysteriously at the house of a Weymouth tailor, or a man called Taylor, whose wife had just had a son of her own. The child was brought up as theirs until he was four or five when they started asking awkward questions, and he was swiftly removed and brought up as his own child by General Garth, the King's equerry, who was known as 'the King's Garth' because he was such a favourite with him.

Back in 1798, Princess Mary had written to her brother the Prince of Wales, 'As for General Garth, the Purple Light of Love, *toujours le même*!' Garth had a hideous port-wine coloured birthmark on his face; the Princess's remark could have meant anything. On the other hand Greville reported Lady Caroline Thynne as saying that the Princess was so violently in love with Garth that everyone could see it. But then he also reported a rumour that the child was the son of the King's page, Papendiek, who was married, unlike Garth.

Princess Sophia wrote a curious letter to the family's good friend and confidante Lady Harcourt in December of 1800. Thanking her for her kindness during some 'distressed and unhappy days and hours,' she goes on: 'I have no doubt that I was originally to blame, therefore I must bear patiently the *reports*, however unjust they are . . . It is grievous to think what a little trifle will slur a young woman's character for ever.'

It seems an odd way to refer to the birth of an illegitimate son. Dorothy Margaret Stuart, in her book *The Daughters of George III*, assumes that there must have been a secret marriage, invalid of course, because of the Royal Marriage Act. This would go far to explain Sophia's feeling of innocence and also the strong support she received from her brothers and sisters, though her mother does seem to have liked her even less than the others.

General Garth was thirty-three years older than Sophia, a rich, ugly man with a respectable army career behind him and a house called Ilsington conveniently placed for a stopover between London and Weymouth. Princess Mary and her sick sister Amelia spent the night there on their way to Weymouth in 1809 and Mary described it as a comfortable bachelor residence. Fanny Burney described him as 'A man of real worth, religious principles, and unaffected honour, with a strong share of wit and a great deal of literature.' He was also devoted to George III. It all makes him seem a most improbable partner in an illicit royal romance. The one solid fact is his behaviour to young Tom Garth. He told him he was his son and brought him up as such, doting on him and spoiling him badly in the process. In 1814, when the Prince Regent was having trouble with his tempestuous daughter Charlotte, he put General Garth in charge of her, and she wrote cross letters to her friend Margaret Mercer Elphinstone from Ilsington about how Garth spoiled the boy (now at Harrow) and threw him embarrassingly in her way. She implied that something very odd was going on, and as her indiscreet mother was the source for the stories about the child she must have been aware of them.

Glenbervie said the boy looked every inch a member of the royal family, and he certainly behaved like one of the princes. Brought up too much with servants, according to Princess Charlotte, he had an unsuccessful army career, got into debt and, in 1829, precipitated the scandalous revelations in the press by a complicated attempt at blackmail. By now the stories had grown more sinister. General Garth was said to have simply acted as a loyal cover for something much worse. A faithful servant, he had agreed to bring up the child of a liaison between Sophia and her brother, the detested Duke of Cumberland. The papers fell on it, hoping to drive the Duke out of England, but instead of giving in, he brought his wife and son over from Hanover and sat it out, his friends maintaining that the allegations could be proved to be physically impossible. The royal family said nothing. Sophia was her own mistress by now. When the Prince Regent had arranged allowances for her and her sisters in 1812 she had written him a grateful letter. Dated 'from the Nunnery', it thanked him for his kindness, 'To *four old cats* . . . I wonder you do not vote for putting us in a sack and drowning us in the Thames.' She was very ill for a year and a half after that, and when her father died she moved to quiet quarters in Kensington Palace. There is a tradition that from time to time all the servants were sent away for the day. Perhaps she was receiving her unregenerate son. He certainly got money from somewhere after his attempts at blackmail failed. And who was his father? Why did they all, except for Queen Charlotte, close ranks so firmly around Sophia? There is one explanation much sadder than the story about Cumberland. When she was living in the Upper Lodge nine months before her son's birth, Sophia's frustrated father the King was living there too. He had been mad before. He was to go mad again the following year; did a moment of madness strike him then? It would explain everything.

Born in 1783, Princess Amelia was the last of the family and every-one loved her, especially her father. Two little brothers, Octavius and Alfred, had died before she was born and she was never strong. Queen Charlotte was probably right to think it was time she stopped bearing children. Amelia spent a good deal of her childhood at Worthing because of a tubercular knee and when she was coming up for eighteen in 1801 she was left behind at Weymouth for some more healthy sea air after the rest of the family went back to Windsor. In attendance were Miss Jane Gomm, her governess, and the King's equerry, Colonel the Honourable Sir Charles FitzRoy, a handsome descendant of Charles II. The family should have had more sense. Hanover was always falling in love with Stuart, as witness the King himself and Lady Sarah Lennox. Charles FitzRoy was unmarried, a sedate, successful soldier of thirty-nine who had won the good opinion of such diverse characters as Frederick the Great and the King's sister, the Duchess of Brunswick. Amelia was the romantic novel reader of the sisterhood; of course she fell in love with him. She seems to have made the running and Miss Gomm soon noticed her tendency to hang back in order to ride with him, and gave her a friendly warning. She took it in ill part, there was a row, her sister Mary was involved and the Queen soon heard about it. Her first thought was that it must be kept from the King, whose favourite Amelia was. The couple were corresponding by now, FitzRoy even lent Amelia £5,000 at some point. Her letters survive, his do not, but hers suggest that the impetus was on her side. He presumably enjoyed the situation but valued his job.

Rumour was soon rife about a possible marriage and probable babies; it does seem remarkable if they did contrive to keep it from the King. FitzRoy was probably too cautious a man for a secret marriage, still less a secret affair, but she began to sign her letters Amelia F.R. and had her silver engraved with his initials.

There was a great family row in 1807 when anonymous letters accused the two governesses, Miss Gomm and Miss Goldsworthy, of winking at the affair because they knew the Queen had agreed that the two could marry 'the moment the King was dead.' The Queen was outraged; the castle seethed; Amelia and Mary quarrelled and may not have made it up until towards the end of Amelia's short life. By 1808 she was getting a friend to find out the terms of the Royal Marriage Act for her, and building her hopes on that, though it would mean waiting until she was twenty-five. Of course there was also always the painful hope and fear that if her father, who adored her, were to die, or go permanently mad, her brother would almost certainly let her marry her beloved. On learning the terms of the Royal Marriage Act she drafted letters to the Privy Council and to her brother. To the former she wrote: 'I would never marry where I could not give my affections, and General FitzRoy possesses all my affection.' To her brother: 'Deceive you I never will, and I think it best to tell you I have delayed taking any step with him from his peculiar position about my father, and not to hurt my father. That being removed, I feel it owing to myself to act decidedly.' But the moment to send the letters never came.

For a while, during the hopeful beginning of the affair, her health improved. Her tubercular knee got better, and she could ride and dance with her beloved, but in the end the strain told on her health as it very likely did on the King's, who must have known that something was going on. The family atmosphere must have been appalling. She wanted to tell her father about her lover, but the Queen fiercely forbade it, and she convinced herself that her mother wanted her to die. By 1809 she was so ill with pain in her side that the doctors advised a trip to Weymouth. Their treatments were exquisitely painful and Mary, now in attendance, wrote that her physicians said she, 'Must be *worried* about nothing, which, *Entre Nous*, in our House is very difficult.' When she was at Windsor the King visited her constantly, trying to raise her spirits and his own. She did not want to leave for Weymouth, because it meant leaving FitzRoy, but in some ways it may have been a relief to get away. Her father ordered elaborate arrangements for her comfort, and Princess Mary wrote to him after a few days that her sister had actually slept all night 'without moaning in her sleep.' She tended to dream that she was in prison.

Mary would not let her talk about FitzRoy, writing after her death that, 'On the subject that I look upon as having *killed her* . . . I was never in her confidence . . . I don't believe I named the subject *three times*.' It makes one's heart bleed for Amelia. Her mother was impatient with her too, writing loving letters to Mary, but speaking briskly of Amelia. When it was decided that Amelia should go home to Windsor, in effect to die there near her family and, of course, FitzRoy, Mary wrote a note to her father warning him that her sister was in too low a state to stand sharp words. It was arranged that they should come back not to the castle itself but to a house in Windsor. The invalid was so weak that they had to take the journey very slowly, spending a night at Ilsington where faithful General Garth gave them 'a famous dinner and very good beds'.

Settled with Mary at Augusta Lodge in Windsor, Amelia was prescribed Madeira wine (as well as calomel) by an intelligent doctor, but her mother was still brisk, and financial problems plagued her. She had only managed to pay back one thousand of the five General FitzRoy had lent her and wanted to make him her heir. She wrote a sad little note to her brother George in the summer of 1810, asking him to act as her executor and going on to ask him to speak to her doctor, the fashionable Sir Henry Halford: 'He is now become so good a courtier that he does not venture to oppose anything that the King and Queen like, tho' it may be very contrary to my wishes. For instance they want me to see all the Ladies and others who are in the Castle, whether I like them or not.' Amelia was dying in some discomfort. But her sisters stood by her. Princess Augusta contrived a meeting for her with General FitzRoy, but her pulse was lower after it.

Everyone but her father knew she was dying, but he would not admit it. She had a keepsake made, with a lock of her hair in it, and 'Amelia' and 'Remember Me' inscribed on it. Although the family urged her not to, she gave it to her father: 'Remember me, but do not grieve for me,' she told him. He was so blind she must have had to read the inscriptions for him. They had loved each other dearly, he had ruined her life, she probably helped contribute to his final madness.

Amelia died late in 1810, only twenty-seven, and the Prince of Wales as her executor had a problem with her will. She had left her jewels to FitzRoy and made him her residuary legatee, presumably hoping in this way both to declare their relationship and to pay off her debt to him. She left more muddle than money. The Prince of Wales persuaded FitzRoy to renounce the jewels, which went to Princess Mary, and probably never repaid the balance of the £5,000. FitzRoy wrote about her as 'the adored and departed angel', and married a few years later.

3
Married to Order

YOUNG MEMBERS of the aristocracy had no Act of Parliament to bind them, but the pressures were there just the same, with not much room for love in their matrimonial arrangements. Marriage was about blood, property and money, not necessarily in that order.

Lady Georgiana Spencer made a marriage very much by the rules. Her mother, a 'mere Miss Poyntz' when she married John, first Earl Spencer, had a strong connection with the powerful Cavendish family. She had watched William Cavendish, Fifth Duke of Devonshire, grow up and known him for the steady young man he was, as well as being head of one of the great Whig families. She presumably thought the two young people an admirable pair of opposites. Where Georgiana was lively and outgoing, the young Duke was quiet, reserved and almost pathologically lazy. He found dogs easier to get on with than people. But he was the great matrimonial catch of the day. When he was six his only brother had been born and his mother had died, and he became Duke at sixteen, on his father's death. One way and another, he had experienced even less of family life than most of his contemporaries. When he proposed for Georgiana's hand he was twenty-four and she only sixteen, but she had already refused several eligible connections, according to her mother, who thought her too young to marry. She was delightful but 'giddy, idle and fond of dissipation.' The Duke was a young man used to getting his own way. They were married on June 7th, 1774, Georgiana's seventeenth birthday.

The new Duchess was by no means a complete *ingénue*. She had travelled abroad with her parents and brother and sister, meeting Marie Antoinette in Paris, and the young Duke of Devonshire at Spa. Now she was married to him, the first Duchess of Devonshire for eighteen years, and her world was agog to meet her. She had red gold curls and a golden nature, and London society welcomed her with open arms. She was soon its leading lady, a lively rival to dull Queen Charlotte, down at Windsor half-way through her succession of babies. A potential rival in town, Lady Melbourne, already established as a great Whig hostess, very sensibly decided to be friends instead, and they were soon exchanging letters of passionate friendship, full of the endearments and nicknames in which fashionable ladies indulged. Devonshire House in Piccadilly became the centre of Whig society.

It may all have been a bit of a shock to the introvert Duke. He fathered an illegitimate daughter at about the time of his marriage, so he was not entirely without experience, but nothing can have quite prepared him for this whirl of tempestuous petticoats into his life. And his mother-in-law kept sending them letters of the best possible advice. It was hard on a young man used to having his way in everything. How did they get on? Georgiana's great-great-granddaughter, Iris Leveson Gower, who wrote her life based on family papers, gives a vital clue as to what went on behind the scenes of their drama of social success. In the early, glowing days of the marriage, Georgiana once ebulliently plumped herself down on her new husband's lap in the presence of her mother and younger sister. He pushed her roughly off his knee and rushed from the room. There may of course have been a simple physical explanation for this rudeness, but it cast a chill on the relationship which cannot have been helped by an early miscarriage. The facts of women's lives come hard on young husbands. Love does not necessarily flourish in a sickroom.

And then there were no children for nine years. Georgiana danced till dawn; her husband came home from his club, Almack's (later to become Brooks') at about the same time. This was the Whig club, but he was too idle to become their political leader. It was thanks to her that their house became the Whig stronghold. She was friend and hostess to promising young Whigs like Charles James Fox and Richard Brinsley Sheridan. When the Prince of Wales bounced on to the social scene, having escaped at last from Windsor and, after a ferocious row about money with the King, set up his own establishment at Carlton House, he naturally followed the family pattern of taking the opposite political side from his father. He threw in his lot with the opposition Whigs and became an habitué of Devonshire House. A delightful, totally selfish young man, he was already well advanced in debt and mistresses. Society was soon laying bets as to whether he was the Duchess's lover or her friend Lady Melbourne's, or even the lover of both. It must have been Lady Melbourne. The Duchess of Devonshire had not yet borne her husband the essential heir. And she was beginning to worry about it. She distracted herself with the gambling habit she had inherited from her mother, and soon had debt to add to her worries. It is revealing of her relationship with her immensely rich husband that she did not dare tell him about her debts, resorting instead to money lenders for expensive loans that plunged her deeper and deeper into trouble.

A marginally less hazardous occupation of Georgiana's during these first years of marriage was the writing of a novel. Published anonymously in 1779, *The Sylph* was an instant success, and was at first attributed to Fanny Burney. Her father, Dr Burney, indignantly denied this, and suspicion then centred on Georgiana, who said nothing. One does wonder if her husband read it. He may have been too lazy, but he must have heard it being talked about. Like Fanny Burney's *Evelina*, it is a novel in letters and describes the adventures of a country girl who marries a London rake and plunges as suddenly into society as Georgiana had herself. The lap-sitting scene is described, and the heroine learns not to expect tenderness from her husband in public: 'Marriage is now a necessary kind of barter . . . an alliance of families but little else.' In the end the neglectful husband obligingly commits suicide, leaving the heroine free to remarry. I find it baffling that this book did not cause as much furore as Lady Caroline Lamb's *Glenarvon*, a savage attack on Lord Byron, published in 1816.

The letters in *The Sylph* are written to a younger sister, perhaps because Georgiana was now acting as chaperone to her own beloved younger sister Henrietta. Their brother Lord Althorp was busy wooing stiff Lady Lavinia Bingham, but Henrietta, four years younger than her sister, had grown up with a mind of her own. She was less of a beauty and more of a charmer than her sister, and more intelligent. And she must have seen enough of Georgiana's marriage to be cautious about her own. She had already rejected at least two suitable young men when her parents decided to send her to London to try her fortunes there. It consolidated the already strong bond between the two sisters, but Henrietta, too, gave in to family pressure in the end and married young Lord Frederick Duncannon, a connection of the Devonshires. He was another quiet young man, but not so rich, and Henrietta wrote to a friend, 'I wish I could have known him a little better first . . . He is so grave and I am so giddy.' They were married in 1780, when she was nineteen, and at least the physical side worked. She had her first child, a boy, nine months later. It must have been hard on her still childless sister, but nothing was ever to shadow the deep affection between these two.

In 1782 Georgiana and her husband made a new friend who was to change their lives. Lady Elizabeth Foster was the daughter of the erratic Earl-Bishop of Bristol and Derry. He had stopped speaking to his wife, and would not help his daughter when her marriage broke down and she lost her two sons to their impossible father. Now she and her equally unlucky sister Lady Erne were living forlornly together, the impecunious half-life of separated wives. Lady Spencer knew the Earl and his wife, and, good interfering woman that she was, suggested that her daughter and son-in-law be kind to the two poor waifs. She must have regretted it. Lady Elizabeth was soon their 'dearest Bess', best friend of both of them. In an age given to nicknames, the Duke was Canis, the dog, the Duchess was Mrs Rat and Bess was Racky, short for raccoon, or perhaps because of her cough. In Bess's lively company, the Duke livened up too, and Georgiana was soon pregnant at last, devotedly nursed through some early ailing months by her 'dearest Bess'. There was talk, of course. Lady Spencer wrote volumes of warning about the odd relationship and in the end Bess went abroad for her health, taking the Duke's illegitimate daughter, eight-year-old Charlotte Williams, with her. Learning about Charlotte two years before, Georgiana had reacted with characteristic generosity, despite the fact that the child had been born at the time of her own marriage. She described her to Lady Spencer as, 'The best humoured little thing you ever saw . . .' [but] 'the most nervous little thing in the world, the agitation of coming made her hands shake so.' Charlotte was also the image of the Duke which endeared her to kind Georgiana.

Bess found Charlotte a bore, but at least she was a source of income. And life abroad was far from dull for a beautiful young grass widow. She was publicly crowned with flowers at Nice and was soon answering anxious letters from Georgiana about suitors, referred to cautiously as, 'Monsieur P and Mr G'. Her 'idolizing G' wrote urging her to live with women as much as she could, 'let them be ever so disagreeable.' But Georgiana had problems of her own, writing to Bess that the Prince of Wales had kissed her in public: 'You cannot think how uneasy it made me. And what do you think I did – I told Canis who, Dear Dog, instead of being angry said it was not my fault.' Despite all this excitement she gave birth to her first child, Georgiana Dorothy, on June 6th, 1783. The celebrations were almost as great as if it had been a boy and Georgiana's letters to Bess were a mixture of anxious advice about 'Mr G and the Chevalier,' and talk of the baby, whom she was suckling herself as she did all her children. She had just dismissed the baby's attendant, known as the Rocker: 'She was only rather dirty till last night, when she was so drunk as to fall down and vomit.' It is a useful reminder of the filthy, dangerous, starving mob that always seethed behind the scenes of polite society. It had broken loose with the savage anti-Catholic Gordon riots three years before, and the Duchess had behaved with admirable common sense, as had the King. As for the Duke, it would take more than a riot to shake him out of his habitual calm. On one occasion when waked to be told that Chatsworth was on fire, he just told them to put it out and went back to sleep.

Georgiana was soon back in the thick of things. The birth of little Georgiana had closed Devonshire House to society for a few weeks, causing some inconvenience to the French Ambassador, who had got into the habit of meeting Charles James Fox casually there. Next year, when Fox found his parliamentary seat at Westminster under threat in a general election, Georgiana threw convention to the winds, and led a group of her friends in canvassing for him. It was an unusually ribald and riotous campaign even for those violent days, but Georgiana and her friends, bribing shopkeepers and kissing butchers for their votes, managed to sway the balance so far as Fox himself was concerned. Unfortunately it was a disaster for the Whig party in general and Fox was to be out of office for years. But at the time they celebrated as if they had won a tremendous victory and did their best to ignore the libellous comments of the press. Inevitably, Georgiana was hinted to be Fox's mistress, though everyone knew he was really devoted to Mrs Armistead, whom he had acquired from the Prince of Wales.

What did the Duke do? Nothing, presumably. He had something to look forward to. Bess was coming home. She joined them at Chatsworth that summer, tried and failed to ingratiate herself with Lady Spencer, and became the Duke's mistress. Convinced of her own good intentions she kept an agitated diary: 'Depositary of both their thoughts, I have sought when her imprudences have alienated him, to restore him to her, and when my full heart has mourned over her avowal of his returning caresses, I have checked and corrected the sensation.' By December, both women were pregnant. Bess went abroad, flirted with the charming Duke of Dorset in Paris, and then travelled south, telling nobody her secret, hoping for a miracle, thinking of an abortion, desperately frightened, desperately sorry for herself. In the end, she told her brother, who stood by her and arranged a sinister backstreet birth near Naples. Her daughter Caroline was born on August 16th. Georgiana's Harriet (always known as Harryo) was born two weeks later, in some comfort, at Devonshire House, just when Bess was parting with her baby and putting flannels on her breasts in order to appear as usual in Neapolitan society, where she was snubbed by Georgiana's sister-in-law, the starchy young Lady Spencer. But she had avoided a scandal, and so long as Georgiana and the Duke stood by her, nothing else mattered. And Georgiana and the Duke did.

What was it like for Georgiana? When did she learn about Caroline's birth? Her letters to her mother were heavily edited after her death and her letters to her sister destroyed. All we have are some facts. Bess returned to England in the summer of 1786, leaving the baby behind in France, and was actually met at Southampton by the Duke. With the outstanding exception of Lady Spencer, society welcomed her back and she was now firmly settled as part of the Devonshire household. The *ménage à trois* was established. Bess throve on it, Georgiana's health began to show the effects of stress. She had terrible headaches and frequent colds and suffered increasingly from inflammation and pain in her eyes. But she still sat up to all hours playing faro and running up more debts, and though she was beginning to put on weight she was still surrounded by an adoring public. Among them was a rising Whig politician, Charles Grey, a handsome young northerner, who had scored an instant success with his maiden speech in parliament in 1780. It was pleasant to be told that she and Grey were the best-looking couple in England but for the moment that was all there was to it. Two daughters meant nothing. She had not yet borne her husband an heir and must content herself with platonic enjoyment of this adoration by a younger man. Her place at the heart of Whig politics must have added to her attractiveness in Charles Grey's eyes. When the King went mad in 1788 and the Prince of Wales and his Whig friends thought their moment of power had come, the Duchess was in the thick of the excitement. While the doctors tortured the King with their treatments at Windsor, the

Prince and the Duchess exchanged breathless, shamelessly hopeful reports of his worsening condition. But the King was too tough for them and recovered suddenly, just when the Prince thought a regency within his grasp.

Meanwhile Bess had gone quietly off to France in the spring of 1788 to bear the Duke a son, Augustus Clifford, in a good deal more comfort this time, and also to make some arrangements for her daughter. Caroline had a name now, she was Mademoiselle St Jules, and Bess found her a home in Paris. Back in England, she planned for her two children, while Georgiana drifted further and further into debt. In 1789 the Devonshire House party left *en masse* for the continent, ignoring danger signs in France, where the National Assembly was in session. Georgiana's two little girls were left behind in the nursery ruled by formidable Selina Trimmer, daughter of a minor bluestocking and protégée of Georgiana's mother. Fifteen-year-old Charlotte Williams went with them to be left in Paris with little Caroline. They got there in June and were actually at Versailles, calling on Marie Antoinette, when the revolutionary mob broke in on the royal family. Unalarmed, they were still in Paris two weeks later when the Bastille fell. As good Whigs, they were delighted about this, never dreaming that there might be any threat to themselves or to their friend the Queen. Besides, the Duke had met his two-year-old daughter Caroline for the first time and taken a fancy to her. But they left her and Charlotte Williams behind in Paris when they moved on to Spa, hoping that the waters would be good for the Duke's gout and help achieve the longed-for heir. The news from Paris got worse and worse; the mob was loose in the streets; the two little girls were there. The Duke cried for the first time in his life. It was for Caroline, not Charlotte.

The waters of Spa worked. The Duchess was pregnant at last. Every one was sure it was the heir. Obviously he should be born at Devonshire House, but the Duke said he was afraid the journey would bring on a miscarriage. The whole party stayed abroad, and in the spring of 1790 Georgiana's two daughters, Georgiana and Harryo, came out to join them in Brussels, as did the Duncannons and Lady Spencer herself. There was a complicated negotiation going on about Georgiana's debts at this time, with no one telling anyone the whole truth and the creditors suffering. Georgiana took two of the successful banker Thomas Coutts' three daughters under her wing while they were in Paris as some kind of recompense for his infinite patience with her.

The revolutionary tide spread to Brussels, but still the Duke did not take his wife home to England. Instead they all went back to Paris later that spring, so that Bess could quietly add little Caroline to the party. Georgiana went into labour as they were moving from cramped quarters at an hotel to a borrowed house in Passy and her son Hartington was born that night. It was all a tremendous muddle. Bess hurried off to the opera to show off her slender figure, but the gossip broke out just the same. The attending physician, brought out from England by the Duke, was Dr Richard Croft, and when he committed suicide after mismanaging Princess Charlotte's pregnancy many years later, the stories of a Devonshire substitution broke out all over again. Only in our time have his letters to his mother surfaced, describing the birth of Hartington and the difficulty the young doctor had in getting paid by the lethargic Duke. It was all a very odd business and one can only ask oneself whether 'dearest Bess', obviously the prime mover of the trio, nourished a secret, maybe subconscious hope that her dear friend the Duchess and her child might die. What a future then for her little Augustus Clifford. Elizabeth Foster seems to have suffered from the delusion that a later marriage would legitimize previous bastards.

Mother and child did well, but Georgiana's debts had not been properly settled, and little Georgiana became seriously ill, delaying their return to England until August. When they did go, they took Caroline St Jules and Charlotte Williams with them to become part of the Devonshire House nursery. There was an outraged exchange of letters between Selina Trimmer and Lady Spencer, and Georgiana wrote her mother an unusually firm letter defending Bess and warning that she would not tolerate a situation where Miss Trimmer reported behind her back to her mother. But in the end she had to. She was hideously aware of her own shortcomings, loved her children deeply and was sure that Miss Trimmer was good for them, as indeed she was, providing such stability and moral framework as they had. In the end, Georgiana was reduced to lying to her mother in a letter defending the Duke and Bess which must have been extremely painful to write. She was helpless, and besides she too loved Bess. Little Augustus Clifford was quietly added to the nursery party soon afterwards, along with a French refugee Corisande de Grammont, who was the same age as Harryo, and Caroline.

Georgiana was thirty-three in 1790. She had borne her husband his heir at last and she had borne a great deal else. She truly loved her friend Bess, but it cannot have been easy or pleasant to watch her gradually take first place with the Duke, who also visibly preferred Bess's two children to her own beloved three. She was not so well as she had been, nor so beautiful, nor so happy, and Charles Grey was still her faithful slave. She fell tumultuously into love. The Duke actually noticed that something was going on and threatened a separation, but Bess pointed out that if the Duchess were exiled from Devonshire House she herself would have to go too, for lack of a chaperone. This silenced the Duke for the moment and he made a dignified, if sulky retreat to Chatsworth. The result was inevitable. His wife fell into Grey's arms for a brief spell of intense happiness in which she forgot everything else. Bess and Lady Melbourne, watching and commenting like a Greek chorus, were appalled, the public talked, and the Prince of Wales was furiously jealous.

When little Hartington was christened with full pomp and ceremony on May 21st, 1791, his first birthday, his mother was just pregnant by Charles Grey. An anonymous letter alerted Lady Spencer soon afterwards and she came up to London like an avenging angel to put a stop to the affair. She succeeded where Georgiana's two friends had failed. Agreeing to give Grey up, Georgiana did not even insist on a last interview. 'He is gone,' Bess wrote Lady Melbourne. 'She distracts me by working herself up to think she is more attach'd to him than I know she can be.' How did she know?

Georgiana retreated to Bath with her sister Henrietta, who was gravely ill after a matrimonial disaster of her own, and faithful Bess. Lady Melbourne acted as go-between in the correspondence Georgiana carried on with Grey, who had swiftly turned from adoring suitor to demanding lover, his appropriate codename Mr Black. An ambitious young man, he gradually backed away, writing her increasingly tetchy letters. He married a cousin of hers three years later, had fifteen children, and his moment of triumph, for which Georgiana and Fox had helped to train him, came in 1832, when he saw the Reform Bill through Parliament as Prime Minister.

By the autumn, the rumours about his wife had reached the Duke at Chatsworth and roused him from his inertia. He descended on the Bath party and issued an edict of banishment. Conniving doctors ordered Henrietta Duncannon abroad for her health; Georgiana could go into exile, respectably, as her companion. Lord Duncannon, their daughter Caroline Ponsonby, Lady Spencer, Bess, Caroline St Jules and Charlotte Williams all went too, and the inevitable horde of servants. It must have been an odd party, its problems exacerbated by the fact that the Duke was slow in sending the necessary funds. Eliza Courtney was born in secret, in the south of France in February 1792 and smuggled into Grey's own family at Howick to be brought up as his sister. Later, Georgiana was able to see her sometimes when the Grey family came to London. But for now the exile continued, money went on being tight, her debts got worse, she wrote loving weekly letters to her children at home, begging them not to forget her and putting in little pleading sentences for her husband's eye. A year later, in May 1793, perhaps galvanized for once by the outbreak of war with France, the Duke relented and sent for her.

Devonshire House welcomed her with open arms, but there were no more babies. She was still only in her thirties, but where Bess stayed slim and elegant Georgiana was eating and drinking for comfort. She was also gambling as much as ever and her debts got worse as well as her eye trouble. After enduring hideous operations, supported by Henrietta and Bess, she died, only forty-eight, in 1806, still plagued by debt. Her last letter to her mother asked for a loan of £100, which Lady Spencer was unable to send. After her death, the surprisingly disconsolate Duke said, 'Was that all? Why did she not tell me?' And presently he married Bess.

* * *

When Georgiana was allowed home at last in 1793, her sister Henrietta did not go with her. Her illness had been genuine enough; their travels can hardly have been restful and she was still coughing blood. Her husband was another dull, quiet man with a title. He was no politician, contenting himself with collecting rare prints and doing a little sketching. In ten years of marriage his wife had borne him four children, three of them boys. When the brilliant young dramatist and politician, the Prince of Wales's friend Richard Brinsley Sheridan, joined the Devonshire House set, Henrietta found someone she could talk to. Soon their relationship was so close that Sheridan's wife Elizabeth, with whom he had made a romantic runaway match eighteen years before, now seriously considered accepting a proposition from the young Duke of Clarence. More serious still, Lord Duncannon threatened divorce and a suit for criminal conversation that might well have ruined Sheridan.

Henrietta was very ill for a while, possibly as a result of a miscarriage, or even of an assault by her usually phlegmatic husband.

They must have made it up before she left England with her sister in the autumn of 1791, for unlike Devonshire, Duncannon went too. But he had to return to England early in 1793, when his father died and he became the third Earl of Bessborough, inheriting an estate burdened with debt. His wife went south for her health in the spring of 1793, where at Naples she met Sir William Hamilton and his amazing wife Emma, and a charming young man, Lord Granville Leveson Gower, who was making as much of the Grand Tour as one could, granted that war with France had just started.

Granville was the second son of the Tory Marquis of Stafford, the adored only child of his third wife. Born in 1773, Granville grew up in a largely feminine household, since his much older half-brother had married when Granville was twelve. He was almost too handsome, with deep blue eyes and a dangerous skill with women. When he met Lady Bessborough, as she now was, in Naples, he was twenty-one and she was thirty-three. They were to correspond for the rest of their lives. At first, even his anxious, devoted mother seems to have approved. Lady Bessborough might be a Whig, but she was high society and brilliant, the ideal older woman to mould a young man. It became an *amitié amoureuse*, the respectable devotion of the young man for the older married woman, but the fact that they started corresponding after that first meeting tells one a great deal.

When Henrietta got back to England, in 1794, apparently cured, Granville got leave from his militia duties at once and rushed to see her. He was Member of Parliament for Lichfield by now, taking his first steps in the political world under the influence of George Canning, his slightly older Oxford friend. Canning himself was a protégé of Pitt and Granville was naturally drawn into the same Tory circle. His birth and his charm made him a natural diplomat. While Henrietta was nursing her sister through her first terrible bout of eye trouble, he was in Paris on Lord Malmesbury's unsuccessful peace mission, flirting with the French ladies and ordering Henrietta a wig from Madame Tallien's own *perruquier*. Henrietta was corresponding with his mother by now, sending her political news from town and agreeing with her that it was high time Granville made his maiden speech in the House. And her *amitié* was becoming rather more amorous. Sheridan's wife had died in 1792 and the playwright was still at Henrietta's feet, and teasing her outrageously about Granville, as she enjoyed reporting to that young man in her letters. Things were getting serious: in the same letter she asked for 'just a few lines every night'. Granville was in Lille now, on another unsuccessful diplomatic mission.

Somewhere about this time they became lovers and he turned from devoted young worshipper to jealous tyrant, getting into rages when he met any of Henrietta's other admirers at her house. She forgave him, and bore him a daughter, Harriet Emma Arundel Stewart, in deepest secrecy at her Roehampton house in 1800. Her husband and grown-up children must have known, but they remained a publicly united family. Henrietta's man was less of a catch than Georgiana's, but he turned out a better long-term proposition. He truly loved both his wife and his children. He may have been a dull dog, but in the end he was a faithful one. It is satisfactory to know that their financial problems were solved later, in 1810, when their scientist relation Henry Cavendish died and left them £100,000, ignoring his other cousin the Duke of Devonshire. In 1802, the long war with France came to a pause with the Peace of Amiens, and English society flocked to Paris. The Bessboroughs went, taking their seventeen-year-old daughter Caroline with them and also Lady Elizabeth Foster, a good friend of Henrietta's as well as Georgiana's. Now it was Henrietta's turn to write to her lover from abroad, and she had plenty to tell. Her kind of charm was very much to the French taste and she was soon discussing literature with General Moreau, being kissed above the elbow by Marshal of France Alexandre Berthier and wooed by the Algerian Ambassador. But she refused to meet the First Consul, Bonaparte, writing to Granville, 'How naturally I slide into opposition wherever I am.' By now, Granville was saving her brilliant, informative letters.

He was a younger son with his own way to make in the world, and they must have agreed that it was necessary for him to make a good marriage. Returning to England Henrietta found her lover busy courting the banking heiress Lady Sarah Fane, and wrote him letters full of advice about his wooing. Lady Sarah was a great financial catch. She was the grand-daughter of the immensely rich banker Robert Child, who had been so furious when his only child, another Sarah, eloped to Gretna Green with the Tory Earl of Westmorland's son John Fane that he left a most unusual will, entailing his fortune on female heirs only so that no Earl of Westmorland could ever profit by it. But Sarah was also being wooed by Lord Villiers and in the end decided in his favour. Son of one of the Prince of Wales's mistresses, Villiers became Earl of Jersey on his father's death in 1805. Lady

Sarah was to become a powerful figure in society, one of the fierce ladies who made the rules at Almack's assembly rooms.

Henrietta was soon warning Granville that his attentions to Pitt's niece, Lady Hester Stanhope, who was acting as her uncle's hostess, were causing comment. There was actually a paragraph in the newspapers, and when Granville tried to shrug it off she gave him some good advice: 'Is it quite honourable, Dear G., to encourage a passion which you do not mean seriously to return?' And on another occasion: 'You are a pretty Gentleman, to be sure,' with a list of six other ladies he was seeing. By the time Pitt settled things by sending Granville as Ambassador to Russia Henrietta was pregnant again. She was worried lest his gambling might damage his prospects there and a sharp note of his suggests that things were not entirely easy in their relationship: 'You began blabbing out at supper last night what I had been telling you just before about the means made use of to surprise the Boulogne ships.' He was in the great world now, and she must remember it. He took her younger son Willy along as secretary and wrote her avuncular letters about him. Granville did well in Russia, charming the volatile Tsar Alexander into alliance with Britain and writing to Henrietta that he spent his evenings with the delightful Princess Galitzin, always referred to as 'the Barbarian'.

Henrietta spent a quiet month in Hastings that autumn. Presumably George Stewart was born there and sent to join his sister Harriet in obscure comfort somewhere nearby. Baby farms were big business in those days, and Harriet and George were clearly well looked after, since when they later went to live with their stepmother, that remarkable woman gave glowing reports of them, especially Harriet. Like her sister, Henrietta was putting on weight, and made jokes about it in her letters to Granville; it presumably made the concealment of her latest pregnancy easier. But again her husband and children must have known. Nineteen-year-old Caroline was certainly with her at the time. Henrietta describes seeing her family off to a ball: 'It does me good to see them all as happy as they are, but I dread damping their good spirits by my low ones.' The note of gloom is most unlike her.

Back in London, having got away with it, Henrietta wrote Granville the usual long, entertaining letters that kept him in touch with English life. The King was suffering from cataract, but refused to be operated on. He had had another fit of madness and insisted that he would open his speech in parliament, 'My Lords and Peacocks.' He was better now but he and the Queen were quarrelling dreadfully and he was pursuing the seventy-two-year-old Lady Pembroke, one of her ladies in waiting. And his relations with his son the Prince of Wales were no better. Henrietta had charmed Canning, who had originally disliked her, into friendship, and was able to send political bulletins too, keeping Granville up to date about the impeachment of Lord Melville.

How did she feel when he wrote, 'I think of you morning, noon and night, and do long for the time of our meeting with an indescribable impatience.' And then went on in the next sentence: 'I go on passing my evenings with the little Barbarian.' Was it reassuring that he always called Princess Galitzin 'little'? He also wrote that, 'If it had been my lot to have been married to you, I should have passed a life of happiness such as is enjoyed by few people.' Is there a valedictory note about this? Granville's mother died while he was in Russia and perhaps he was beginning to turn his mistress into a substitute for her. In return, she regaled him with tales of the men who went on obstinately pursuing her. Sheridan, particularly, made such a nuisance of himself that she had to forbid him the house. She enjoyed sending back to Granville the glowing reports she heard about how well he was doing in Russia. It was no wonder he did not want to lose her as a correspondent. But from now on it was to be friendship, not love. He was thinking seriously about the Princess Galitzin, but he was also asking to be recalled to England.

It took him a while to get there. In that autumn of 1805, Napoleon gave up his plan to invade England and marched dramatically east against Russia. Thus attacked, the Tsar Alexander chose to lead his own army against the French, and his court, of course, went too. Granville found himself in dangerous flight after the surrender of Ulm and the disastrous allied defeat at Austerlitz that December. He was born lucky and was not snapped up by the advancing French. It had been a tense summer in England too, with a French invasion expected daily, but Henrietta went down to Hastings that autumn just the same. Their two children were probably living there. Her legitimate children were grown up now, and both her oldest son and her daughter were married that summer. She told Granville that she did not like Caroline's choice of Lady Melbourne's son William Lamb. 'I dislike the connection extremely; I dislike his manners, and still more his principles and his creed, or rather no creed.' But the young couple were passionately in love, and she gave way.

It was a bad time. Nelson was killed at Trafalgar, Pitt died in January 1806, and then in March the Duchess of Devonshire also died. Henrietta Bessborough was with her through her 'three day's agony', and then took her bereaved daughters and son-in-law back to Roehampton with her. For her, nothing would ever be the same. She had lost, she said, the friend to whom her whole heart was open. It made her ill, and Fox told her that, 'Our Russian friends will be startled if you look so.' Granville and Willy got back at last in August 1806. There was an evening when Henrietta sent her husband and son to dine at Devonshire House promising to join them later and never turned up. 'Neither Lord B nor Willy knew that Lord G was in town,' wrote her niece Harryo, who knew all about the affair. But the affair was over. Henrietta Bessborough knew that Granville was thinking of marrying his Russian princess; he was thirty-three now, it was time he settled down. And she was fat and forty-five, the mother of six children, two of them illegitimate. If it was to survive, the relationship must change, and, remarkably, they achieved this. Henrietta went on sending him essential details about Fox's death and the new Ministry that was to be called the Ministry of All the Talents because it had so few. She also gave him advice as to how to conduct himself in the general election that took place that autumn.

They were to go on with their loving, friendly correspondence until her death in 1821, on holiday with William and his family in Italy. She wore herself out at the deathbed of her grandson and died a week later. 'Comfort there can be none,' wrote her desolate husband. 'I wish to live to do what she would wish: settle her affairs and mine.' Granville and his wife were desolated too. She wrote that he was, 'Very calm and has with the most heartfelt grief, a command over himself, which for his sake I strive to imitate.' Granville had always had command over himself.

4
The Next Generation

THE DUCHESS OF DEVONSHIRE and the Countess of Bessborough married to please their families; not all their children were so biddable. The first to marry, Georgiana's eldest daughter, does seem to have yielded to some extent to parental pressure. When young Lord Morpeth began to court Georgiana on her first coming out she held him off for a while, but her father the Duke was all for the match, promising a lavish settlement, and she gave way. The marriage worked. She settled down with her humourless in-laws at Castle Howard in Yorkshire, faithfully bore her husband eleven children and remained the devoted friend and confidante of her sister Harryo. Their brother Hartington, known as Hart, never married. Growing up in close association with his slightly older cousin, Henrietta's daughter Caroline Ponsonby, he took it for granted that they would marry. He burst into hysterical tears and had to be dosed with laudanum when he learned, at sixteen, of her engagement to Lady Melbourne's son William Lamb. Later, as Duke, he made overtures for the Regent's daughter Princess Charlotte, was snubbed, and subsided into the comforts of bachelordom and a good friend, Lady Hunloke. Very deaf and very rich, he occupied himself with improving Chatsworth and was the patron of Crystal Palace Paxton.

When his sister Harryo was still a child, her aunt Henrietta had written to her lover Granville Leveson Gower, that, 'Little Harryo cries after you and wants a horse to ride after you and fetch you back.' It says something about his charm that it worked on small girls as well as grown women. It was a joke to Henrietta but not necessarily to little Harryo, who was to love him all her life. Hers was not an easy childhood in that crowded nursery, with the grown ups changing partners downstairs. The Duke liked Bess Foster's Caroline the best of his daughters, and Harryo the least, and showed it. She grew up a dumpy child with a sharp tongue. And the Duchess, who had enjoyed launching Georgiana into society, and had married her off successfully in 1801, had been worn down by debt, and the Duke, and lost love. She did not live to see Harryo's marriage, or that of her third daughter, Eliza Courtney.

When the children were small she and her sister had hoped for a match between Harryo and her cousin, Lord Duncannon. He went through the motions of courtship civilly enough until he met beautiful Elizabeth Villiers, sister of the Lord Villiers Lady Sarah Fane had married. The Villiers' mother, Lady Jersey, had been the Prince of Wales's mistress and Lady Bessborough disliked the connection. Duncannon gave it up in deference to his mother's wishes, but when Harryo let it be known that she would expect him to give up his flirtations if they married, he said that, 'He would not bear rules to be prescribed to him by any woman living,' and engaged himself to Lady Maria Fane, another of Robert Child's rich grand-daughters, whom his mother had never met. Taken aback at first, Henrietta made the best of things and got her reward. On her wedding day, Maria, who had been brought up by a step-mother, told her that, 'I do not wonder at Lady Caroline being miserable at leaving you, for already I have received more kindness from you than I ever did from my own family.'

Meanwhile Harryo took a small fancy to a young diplomat called Charles Bagot, one of Canning's political set to which Lord Granville Leveson Gower also belonged, but nothing came of it. She knew all about Granville and her aunt, of course. 'Oh how many fair Germans, Poles, Hungarians, Livonians, Scavonians, etc etc. will rue this gay deceiver's soft looks and broken vows!' she wrote her sister Georgiana when Granville was appointed Ambassador to Russia. Harryo had a sharp mind and a sharp pen, a little suggestive of Jane Austen's, and like Jane Austen's her ironic remarks concealed a great depth of feeling. She could not help loving Granville Leveson Gower, and she could do nothing about it except say the occasional sharp thing.

When Granville came back to England in the summer of 1806, Harryo's life had been totally changed by her mother's death. She was twenty-one now, old to be unmarried, and quite old enough to act as her father's hostess, but she had to stand back and watch Lady Elizabeth Foster take what should have been her place at the head of his table. She could not move out since that would leave the unorthodox couple unchaperoned. Her grandmother and her aunt did their best to support her, but her position must have been almost intolerable. She had never liked Lady Elizabeth, hating her affectations and lisping endearments as much as her dubious position in the household. And now perceptive Bess was beginning to tease her about Granville. Harryo may even have been relieved when he was sent back to Russia in 1807.

He had a frustrating time there both politically and romantically. Russia declared war on England in October and Princess Galitzin quietly made it clear that she was no longer interested in marriage. He returned to England in January 1808 determined to find himself an English wife, with money. He was a younger son after all; besides, diplomats need suitable wives. Soon Henrietta Bessborough, who was rather reluctantly chaperoning her niece these days, was writing him wise advice about his simultaneous courtship of Harryo, codenamed 'The Pearl' in their letters, and the Beckford heiress Susan, known as 'The Sapphire'. Socially, Harryo was the better match, financially Susan was, since Harryo was entirely dependent on her unpredictable father.

It was understandably difficult to convince Susan Beckford that he loved her for herself alone, and her family had other plans for her. Granville called, was turned away, plunged back into politics and was appointed Secretary at War in 1809. Things were getting worse for Harryo that summer. So far she had managed to endure life with her father and his long-time mistress by dint of withdrawing herself as much as possible and going away for the long summer visits that were the custom of the age. But now, three years after her mother's death, it was becoming obvious that Elizabeth Foster was winding the slow Duke slowly towards matrimony. There were agitated family councils about what they would do, with Henrietta Bessborough taking her friend Elizabeth Foster's side against old Lady Spencer and her strait-laced daughter-in-law, the young Lady Spencer. It was Harryo's position that would be the worst of all, and Elizabeth Foster wanted her out of the way just as much as she wanted to go. Did Elizabeth conspire with her old ally Henrietta Bessborough? And did Henrietta give Granville permission to marry his 'Pearl'? It seems likely, but he still took his time about it. When his sister Lady Beaufort invited Harryo and the Morpeths to Badminton that September, everyone knew what it meant. Henrietta certainly did, writing to Granville that she wondered if, 'One week's stay at Badminton will be sufficient for so serious a decision as you talk of.'

Naturally, Harryo knew too. It must have been a hideous visit for her. She had loved Granville hopelessly for years. Now she had to wait for him to propose, with everybody agog, watching. Her half-sister Caroline St Jules was there too, writing reports to Lady Elizabeth, and as always Granville was writing to her Aunt Henrietta. Harryo herself was writing to Selina Trimmer, always a reliable confidante. Granville could not bring himself to the point. While the gossips watched, the nearest the two of them got to an intimate conversation was when he urged her not to quarrel irrevocably with her father over his expected marriage to Lady Elizabeth. When she told him she had no intention of doing so, he was delighted. A practical young man, he doubtless had her dowry in mind. A letter from Canning describing his idiotic duel with Castlereagh may have hardened his resolve. It meant that Canning had to resign, and Granville felt he had to go with him. It was high time to think practical thoughts.

But still he did not hurry himself. The watchers watched in vain. Harryo returned to Devonshire House as disengaged as ever, and had to endure her father's marriage that October unsupported. The family behaved with dignity about it in the end and Granville finally proposed a month later. Everyone was delighted, though the Duke only gave Harryo £10,000, a third of what he gave Georgiana and Caroline St Jules. If Granville was disappointed, he managed to hide it. The engaged couple had a long conversation about Henrietta Bessborough, in which Granville may have admitted to their two illegitimate children though Harryo probably knew all about them already. He promised the Duke that he would give up his flirtations and seems to have kept his word. He did not quite give up his gambling, but his wife doubtless preferred it to women. They were married in January 1810 and she had her first child, a girl, in October.

She must have had enough love for both of them. Her letters to her sister describe a remarkably happy marriage. 'That angel of kindness and goodness, my husband,' she writes, and 'Granville, adored Granville, who would make a barren desert smile.' They were not rich, could not afford a house of their own, and spent a good deal of time staying with friends, most particularly his two well-married older sisters, Lady Beaufort and Lady Harrowby. When the Duke of Devonshire died in 1811, her brother the new Duke made up her dowry to the £30,000 her sister and half-sister had had. After that, they could afford their own house. She was to have one more daughter and three sons, one of whom, William, was never mentioned, though he lived, quietly looked after somewhere, to be seventeen. Once they were settled in a house of their own Harryo adopted first her husband's daughter by Henrietta Bessborough, and a year later their son. The two children had been well brought up and settled easily into the happy household.

Granville's correspondence with Henrietta Bessborough continued for the rest of her life, unchecked and apparently unchanged, though the letters written in the short interval between his engagement and marriage do show him quietly adjusting the rules of their relationship. They are full of firm but civil reasons for not coming to call on his mistress turned aunt. And she, for her part, had a new conquest to report to him, and made it a good story. The Prince of Wales was outraged by the news of Granville's engagement and made a great scene: 'Mixing abuse of you, vows of eternal love, entreaties and promises of what he would do — he would break with Mrs F [Fitzherbert] and Lady H [Hertford], *I should make my own terms*!!' The Prince, 'Threw himself on his knees . . . kiss'd my neck . . . I screamed . . . that immense grotesque figure flouncing about half on the couch, half on the ground.' It has been suggested that this was kindness of heart, or just good manners, on the Prince's part, but he always did like older, larger ladies.

Henrietta Bessborough must have breathed a sigh of sad relief when her two illegitimate children were quietly absorbed into her niece's household. She had seen her sister's daughter by Lord Grey when she was on a visit to Howick, writing to Granville: 'It goes to my heart to see her — she is so evidently thrown into the background, and has such a look of mortification about her . . . Lord B has this moment ask'd me whether she is not the Governess.' Her own two bastards were much luckier.

Once the Leveson Gowers were settled in their own house, the Bessboroughs became regular visitors, and happy Harryo could find it in her heart to be sorry for Lord Bessborough, that quiet cypher: 'Poor Lord Bessborough *me pèse sur le coeur*,' she wrote to her sister. The Bessboroughs had a horrible, stinking, beloved dog, too, which must have added a touch of black comedy to their visits. But when Lady Bessborough died in 1821 Harryo joined her husband in real grief.

Their cheerful social life of visitors and visiting, Chatsworth and the Pavilion, came to an end after Castlereagh committed suicide in 1822 and Canning succeeded him as Foreign Minister. His old friend Granville soon found himself Ambassador, first at the Hague and then in Paris. Harryo disliked Paris at first, telling her sister that the Frenchwomen she had to entertain had 'not so much mind as would fill a pea shell.' But she applied herself to the business of being an Ambassador's lady, learned how to dress up to the exacting French standards, borrowed the family diamonds from Hartington, and made a success of the job. Canning was a little brisk with his old friend about the standard of his despatches at first, but for the next twenty years or so, when the Tories were in power, the Granvilles were in Paris. Granville was made an Earl in 1833, had to resign after a stroke in 1841, and died in 1846. 'You understand the utter and hopeless breaking of my heart,' wrote Harryo to her brother.

She was indeed desolate, but not destroyed. Selina Trimmer's influence had stayed with her and she had become evangelical in tune with the new century. She lived piously for another twenty years, loved by generations of her family, but her brilliant, entertaining letters were a thing of the past. She kept a commonplace book now, full of extracts from divines like Keble and Wesley. 'Such a little love of a queen!' she wrote of Victoria, and died, in 1862, a good Victorian.

* * *

Harryo married for love; so did her cousin Caroline Ponsonby, Henrietta Bessborough's daughter, but the outcome was to be very different. Always a liar, Caroline fantasized a childhood of total neglect, but in fact it had been bad enough. While her cousins Georgiana and Harryo were left behind with Miss Selina Trimmer in the safety of the Devonshire House nursery, she and Caroline St Jules were dragged around Europe during the Duchess's exile. Caroline Ponsonby learned early in life that hysterical tantrums would get her attention, and her own way. The doctors her mother consulted advised little discipline and less education. Back in England at last her mother did try putting her into one of the girls' boarding schools that were proliferating at the time, but it was a disaster, and at ten she was absorbed into the Devonshire House nursery with her cousins, legitimate and otherwise. She went on having tantrums, but Selina Trimmer's influence told, and when she was confirmed, along with Harryo and Caroline St Jules, in Westminster Abbey in 1799, she took it seriously. She had found something to hang on to. She needed it. Her mother's illegitimate daughter was born next year, in secret at the family's Roehampton house, and Caroline must have been part of the conspiracy of silence. It is hard to tell just how much the group of children who had grown up under Miss Trimmer's eye at Devonshire House knew about each other's origins. Caroline St Jules thought herself an orphan until her half-brother, Hart, told her the truth after the death of their father the Duke. Georgiana and Harryo had known long before, so Caroline Ponsonby very likely did too. But that was a long time ago. Now it was her own mother's name at stake.

It was probably a relief to get away to the familiar society at Devonshire House. Lady Melbourne's sons the young Lambs were constant visitors there since Lady Melbourne was a good friend of the Duchess, though not of Lady Bessborough. The Lambs were a tough, noisy lot, devoted to practical jokes, amateur dramatics and their formidable mother. Perceptive young Harryo described an Assembly at Lady Melbourne's: 'Not pleasant . . . William very *drunk*, and . . . talked to me in a loud voice of the danger of a young woman's believing in *Weligion* and *pwactising mowality*.' The Lambs' speech mannerism was famous. William was six years older than Caroline, handsome and intelligent, where she was fey and brilliant. They noticed each other. She came out in 1803 and took society, and him, by storm. He proposed and was refused. He was a younger son and she only nineteen with the world before her. Next year, her mother had her second illegitimate child, a boy this time, and again Caroline certainly knew.

In January 1805, William's older brother Peniston died, leaving him heir to the title. He proposed in May and they were married in June. His mother had wanted the match all along; hers was doubtful at first but her tempestuous daughter was passionately in love, perhaps it was just what she needed. Henrietta gave way. Caroline was hysterical before the marriage, and shocked by the physical side of it. Her mother wrote to Granville that, 'Really, being married is a state of great sufferance to a girl in every way.'

Knowledge of this correspondence must have been an extra pressure on Caroline, and so must the fact that the two mothers-in-law did not get on. Lady Melbourne told Lady Bessborough that she hoped Caroline would be a better wife than her mother had been, and Lady Bessborough, reporting this to Granville, referred to Lady Melbourne, as usual, as 'The Thorn'.

If Caroline had been attracted by the feeling of family solidarity amongst the Lambs, she may have got more of it than she bargained for. She and her new husband set up house on an upper floor of Lady Melbourne's Whitehall mansion. This habit of the time must have done a good deal to exacerbate any problems a young couple might have had. At first it was all honeymoon. Unlike the Duke of Devonshire, William Lamb liked to have Caroline sit on his lap and tell him how she adored him. But he soon set about disabusing his young and highly-strung wife of her old-fashioned notions. Religion was a bore and church on Sunday a waste of time. Lazy, intelligent and amoral himself, he meant to have a wife to match, although, to do him justice, having succeeded in destroying what moral grounding Selina Trimmer had given her, he stuck by his wife throughout the notorious consequences. At first Caroline was happy being her own mistress and designing frivolous costumes for her troop of pages, with one to fit her when she decided to dress up as a boy. Living in her mother-in-law's house, she must have had even fewer domestic duties than the average married woman of her day. Boredom threatened, and she planned a course of self-education that would make her a fit companion for her husband. He probably teased her out of it. Even her mother wrote in loving mockery: 'I know your happiness cannot be compleat [*sic*] without Rollin's Ancient History, that dear beautiful, light, amusing book.' Charles Rollin's *Histoire Ancienne* was in twenty-four volumes.

At one point William had dabbled in the law and Caroline proposed going on circuit with him disguised as his clerk, but now that he was heir to the title it was time to enter Parliament. Even a safe seat needed some attention and he could no longer spend all his time with his wife. She had an early stillbirth in January 1806, just when he was being elected for Leominster. And she was just pregnant again in December of that year when she dressed in his clothes and smuggled herself into the House to hear him make his successful maiden speech. Her son Augustus was born in August 1807 and the Prince of Wales stood godfather at a party that lasted all night. Caroline nursed the big healthy baby herself and it took a long time before she would admit that while her son's body developed, his brain did not. She had a baby girl in 1809, but the child only lived a few hours. That was the end of her child-bearing.

From now on Caroline had much too much time on her hands, while her husband throve in the congenial atmosphere of the House of Commons. He was doing well, moving steadily into the inner counsels of the Whig party. Inevitably, he spent more time away from her, while she plunged into society, making older, faster friends, like Lady Oxford and Lady Wellesley, and conducting a brief, publicly flaunted affair with dull Sir Godfrey Webster. She was also in touch with the literary world. Her friend Samuel Rogers sent her the proofs of a highly romantic, semi-autobiographical poem called *Childe Harold* by an unknown young poet, Lord Byron. Knowing Lady Caroline's reputation, Rogers told her Byron's own romantic story and swore her to secrecy. He and the publisher, John Murray, had hit on this ingenious method of getting some advance publicity for the poem. It worked. 'I awoke one morning and found myself famous,' said Byron.

Caroline was all agog to meet the new lion. 'He has a club foot and he bites his nails,' Rogers told her. 'If he is as ugly as Aesop, I must see him,' she replied. But the first time she saw Byron he was so surrounded by adoring women that she turned her back on him, summing him up as 'mad, bad, and dangerous to know.' Byron had heard about her too, and he noticed this. The next stage was inevitable. It is hard to tell how much actual sex there was in their immensely public affair. Society was enthralled; *Childe Harold* sold; William shrugged his shoulders and got on with his career. He had told his wife once that she was too chilly to be a success with a lover. It would be good to think that Byron made her really happy for a while, because it all turned sour soon enough.

Byron felt he had a right to hate women. His mother had been a drunken, half-mad shrew. As an adolescent, he had fallen in love with a cousin, only to hear her say, 'Do you think I could care anything for that lame boy?' He had homosexual leanings, too, left over from Eton and his Greek adventures. Even innocent Caroline noticed that he liked her better in page's costume than when she changed back to more conventional dress. And downstairs lived her mother-in-law, Lady Melbourne, still attractive and self-confident at sixty-three. When Byron's attention began to stray and Caroline started making jealous scenes, he took refuge in the comfortable ground-floor apartments where Lady Melbourne was always ready to supply the flattery he throve on, combined with a spice of malicious gossip about the Devonshire House set. By now, her younger son George had made a love match with the Duke's illegitimate daughter Caroline St Jules but had failed to consummate the marriage. There were two Caroline Lambs now, known as Caro William and Caro George, and frustrated Caro George was carrying on an affair with the ugly, brilliant politician Henry Brougham. Lady Melbourne was not pleased. She must have been a formidable mother-in-law. Her son Frederick very sensibly did not marry until long after she was dead, when at sixty he made a successful match with an Austrian countess of twenty, who saw him lovingly through old age.

Byron himself summed up their situation. 'Man's love is of man's life a thing apart, 'Tis woman's whole existence.' Caroline thought she had found the great love of her life; for him she was just another diversion. He was being lionized by society, and he had started an affair with her friend Lady Oxford, retiring to stay with her at her Herefordshire house when London, and Caroline, became too exhausting. Caroline thought they were just friends, but resented his neglect and made worse and worse scenes. He probably enjoyed them at first. It was flattering. She dressed in page's costume to smuggle herself into his rooms; she threatened him, and herself, with knives and scissors. One evening, after being rebuked by her long-suffering father-in-law, she rushed out of Melbourne House into Whitehall and disappeared. Her family panicked and her mother had a stroke, and it was Byron himself who found her and brought her back to Melbourne House. But the story was all over town.

William's career had run into the doldrums at this point. He had refused office, lost his seat and relapsed into inertia. Now he roused himself enough to go on a trip to Ireland with Caroline and her parents while the scandal died down. Byron breathed a sigh of relief. He had inherited no money with his house and title and the proceeds of *Childe Harold* far from matched his extravagant lifestyle. He was deep in debt and thinking about a good marriage. At Lady Melbourne's house he had met a rich niece of hers. Annabella Milbanke was up from the country for a visit, a high-minded girl with a gift for mathematics. She was totally different from Caroline Lamb, and he was intrigued. He approached her through Lady Melbourne, while carrying on a public affair with an Italian diva. He kept it light. He would like to marry Annabella, he told Lady Melbourne, 'If only for the pleasure of calling you *aunt*.' When Annabella very sensibly turned down this oblique proposal, he shrugged it off. 'I thank you again for your efforts with my *Princess of Parallelograms* . . . we are two parallel lines . . . never to meet.' At this time, he was carrying on correspondences with both Lady Melbourne and Caroline, telling Caroline that he loved her still and Lady Melbourne that it was all over. In the end, he retreated to Lady Oxford's house and left Caroline to learn the truth about that affair. Caroline tried to kill herself, failed and came back from Ireland thin as a skeleton, vowing revenge but probably not quite meaning it. After much pleading,

Byron agreed to one meeting which achieved nothing, and she made another of her outrageous scenes at a ball at Lady Heathcote's. This time she had gone too far and the town was on Byron's side, but her husband stood by her as usual.

Byron's affair with Lady Oxford began to cool after he made advances to her schoolgirl daughter, but he was shocked when she suddenly went abroad with her husband without telling him. He turned for comfort to his half-sister Augusta Leigh, who had been abandoned with three small children by her hopeless husband. Brother and sister had not grown up together and became instant loving friends when they met in their teens. Now they became more. She had a daughter in 1813 and called her Medora after the heroine of his poem, *The Corsair*. He sent her £3,000 and wrote to Lady Melbourne that, 'It is not an Ape, and if it is that must be my fault.' He spent the summer at Hastings with Augusta and her children, but went on corresponding with Annabella. In September he wrote her a half-hearted proposal and was appalled when she accepted. She meant to reform him; he hoped to get out of it. There was less money than he expected and they spent the honeymoon at her family house, Halnaby Hall in Yorkshire. He was on her ground, not his, and disliked it. He quarrelled with her in the carriage, ignored the family servants drawn up to greet them and wrote that he, '*Had* Lady B on the sofa before dinner.'

The marriage was doomed. He was nervous about what Caroline would do when she heard about it, disappointed when she behaved like a lady, and outraged when he heard that she was in Paris, after Waterloo, setting her cap at the new hero, Wellington. It did not bode well for Annabella.

Caroline had not really forgotten. She broke up the furniture in their hotel room when her husband refused to stay on in Paris on hearing a rumour that the Byrons were coming. She found a new occupation in writing a novel, *Glenarvon*, which was to be both her self-justification and her revenge on her husband, Byron, and society. It is high melodrama, unreadable today but an instant success in 1816. William appears, thinly disguised, as the heroine's cynical husband who destroys his young wife's faith. Glenarvon himself is a hero villain on the grand scale, ancestor of Rochester and countless others, so it was easy for Byron to shrug it off. 'Kiss and tell, bad as it is, is surely somewhat less than f . . . and publish,' he wrote to John Murray, who had refused the book. The portraits of Lady Oxford, Lady

Melbourne and Lady Holland helped *Glenarvon* to its scandalous success and the Lambs were outraged. Caroline claimed that her husband had read and approved the book, but this was another of her lies. 'I wish I were dead,' he is reported to have said. His family thought this was the moment to get rid of her, but when they had got him to agree to a deed of separation they found her sitting on his lap feeding him bits of bread and butter and the whole thing was shelved. She did have charm.

While she was writing *Glenarvon* Caroline had let herself be drawn into the disaster that Byron's marriage had become. Annabella had a daughter, Ada Augusta, in December 1815. She went to stay with her parents in January, parting with Byron on apparently friendly terms, but never returned. Away from him, she may have had space to decide that his sexual practices were intolerable. She was soon in a strange alliance with both Caroline and Augusta Leigh, and the outcome was a scandal that drove Byron out of England. He was abroad when *Glenarvon* came out, making friends with the Shelleys in Switzerland. Yet he was launched on his career as poet, womanizer and, finally, political hero, while Caroline was almost finished.

She wrote two more novels and for a while her marriage with William continued. They loved each other, in their fashion, and there was Augustus, growing up a permanent child at Brocket, their country house in Hertfordshire, where his now senile grandfather Lord Melbourne was also housed after Lady Melbourne died in 1818. Caroline and William were devoted parents, and their marriage might have been different, with different children, but neither Caroline's build nor her temperament were suited to child-bearing. When Lady Bessborough died in 1821 they added a protégée of hers to their nursery. Susan Harriett Elizabeth Churchill was the daughter of Harriet Spencer, a cousin of Lady Bessborough's. Harriet's idle, amusing parents had separated when she was quite young and there was no one to watch over her. She got involved with a group of young men, including her cousin, Lord Blandford, the Marlborough heir. When she found herself pregnant, almost certainly by him, in 1817, there was no one to turn to, to help her arrange the essential secret birth. Her plight became a public scandal and she was lucky when her parents did manage to arrange what turned out to be a happy enough marriage with a German cousin. Lady Bessborough took the baby, and the young Duke of Devonshire gave a ball to celebrate her marriage and re-establish her in London society before she left for

Germany. It hardly worked. Wellington's friend Mrs Arbuthnot described it in her diary as, 'This grand ball . . . As no one spoke to her, I do not see that it will assist much in patching up her broken reputation.' By then, little Susan had been with Lady Bessborough for two years, and next year, on her patroness's death, she moved to Brocket where she was to live for seven more years, a loving companion to her backward cousin Augustus. After Caroline's death, her husband looked after young Susan, sending her to Switzerland and helping her to a happy marriage.

Caroline was drinking too much, taking too much laudanum, taking lovers ranging from her doctor to Bulwer Lytton, in the hope, perhaps, of proving something to herself, to her husband, or to Byron. When Byron died, a hero, in 1824, she learned for the first time just how savagely he had spoken of her. She had once written, 'Remember me,' in his copy of Beckford's *Vathek*. Below it, he wrote:

> Remember thee: remember thee!
> Till Lethe quench life's burning stream
> Remorse and shame shall cling to thee
> And haunt thee like a feverish dream.
> Remember thee! Ay, doubt it not,
> Thy husband too shall think of thee,
> By neither shalt thou be forgot,
> Thou *false* to him, thou *fiend* to me.

In a relationship with a poet, the poet does tend to have the last word. By next year, Caroline's husband could bear her manic behaviour no longer. He banished her from Brocket for a while, but relented in the end and let her come back to share her ravaged last few years with her senile father-in-law and her defective son. When she died in January 1828 he was in Ireland beginning on the political career that was to make him Queen Victoria's beloved mentor. He was also involved in the first of two affairs that were to land him in the criminal courts.

5
Love against the Rules

L ADY CAROLINE LAMB defied the unwritten rules of the day by flaunting her affair with Byron, and even her husband's continued support could not spare her a large measure of social ostracism. Society bought her books but did not invite her to its parties. Born forty years earlier, Lady Sarah Lennox was much more ruthlessly treated. Her marriage prospects had been damaged by her royal jilting, and so had her self-confidence. Her sisters had all made brilliant marriages. It was true that Caroline had married young Henry Fox against her father's wishes, but Fox had turned into a more successful politician than her father, rising to become rich Lord Holland. Caroline was forgiven. Emily had married Lord Kildare, later the Duke of Leinster, the senior peer of Ireland, and Louisa had married Thomas Conolly, an immensely rich Irishman, whose money made up for his lack of family tree. Caroline had to wait until she was twenty-one to marry Fox because of her parents' opposition, but Emily and Louisa both married at fifteen.

Sarah, the youngest, was fifteen when she went to live at Holland House and the Prince of Wales first saw her, and coming up for seventeen in 1761 when he announced his engagement to Charlotte of Mecklenberg Strelitz. She might pretend that she was more concerned for the welfare of her pet animals than the King's affections, but the affair had been all too public. She was damaged goods. Her sister Caroline, who had hoped to catch the young Duke of Marlborough for her, now produced a dull Lord Erroll, whom Sarah called Ajax and refused. So when handsome young Charles Bunbury began to haunt Holland House that December of 1761 no one minded that he was merely the heir to a baronetcy, and far from rich. Caroline decided to approve of him, describing him as a scholar and a poet. Sarah enjoyed having him write poems to her, and flirting with him, but it was not a passionate courtship. When Bunbury put off the wedding for a week at the last moment, Caroline wrote to her sister Emily: 'I feel exceedingly peevish with him . . . happily she is not the least in love with him.' They were married the following week, in June 1762, the year the Prince of Wales was born. George III had a brief illness that year which may or may not have been an early warning of the porphyria that was to make him mad.

Charles and Sarah had no honeymoon. He was eager to get back to his Suffolk house, Barton, and his stables, and she had brought only £10,000 to the match; they were not going to be wealthy. After the wedding night, she wrote to Emily: 'I was not so frightened as Louisa was yesterday, but . . . I am ten thousand times more terrified now than she was the second day. Hers was shyness at first which one only always gets the better of; but real dislike I am sure is not so easy to get over.' She was right, and the physical distaste was mutual. Bunbury stopped writing poems for her and turned back to his horses and hounds, his greatest ambition to train a Newmarket winner. It was just bad luck that the Derby was not named after him. At first, Sarah made the best of things, planning gardens, inviting the family to stay, joining in the general pretence that all was well. 'Pray now who the devil would not be happy with a pretty place, a good house, good horses . . . and £2,000 a year to spend,' she wrote her cousin and friend, Susan Fox-Strangways.

Susan had fallen in love with an actor, William O'Brien, and Sarah was involved in their elopement in 1764. It began a tide of gossip that was to engulf her in the end. Susan and her husband were banished to New York, since the family would not countenance his remaining on the stage, where he could support them. Sarah went on writing to Susan about her happiness with Charles Bunbury, who spoiled her, she said, but on a trip to Paris she and her childless sister Louise went to St Cyr and prayed for children. It had worked for the Dauphine, Marie Antoinette, perhaps it would for them. It was all very well to write enthusiastically about 'little loves' of horses, the central failure of her marriage meant no hope of children. Without them, there was simply not enough in life with Charles Bunbury to occupy her, and it began to show.

On another trip to Paris she caught the eye of a known womanizer, the Duc de Lauzun, and when he followed her home to Barton, her husband went off to Bath for his health leaving the two of them alone. This affair did not last, but the gossip did; and then she met Lord William Gordon at her brother's house, and he too visited her at

Barton in Bunbury's absence in the spring of 1768. By summer she was pregnant, and everyone, including Bunbury, kept up a gallant pretence that it was his child. Everyone was relieved when a daughter, Louisa, was born in December. An heir to the baronetcy, to which Charles Bunbury had now succeeded, would have been more of a problem. He was perfectly prepared to accept little Louisa as his, so long as Sarah gave up Lord William. Instead, she eloped with him, and the scandal was out. Bunbury (now Sir Charles) sued for a separation, and in the end for a divorce, though he and his family went on treating little Louisa as his child.

The elopement and Bunbury's successful suit for separation in June 1769 left Sarah at the mercy of the press. Everything was raked up, her royal blood and royal jilting, even her husband's preference for horses. A reporter who pursued the runaway couple to Scotland was astonished to find them glowing with happiness, apparently glorying in 'having risked all for love'. But it did not last. Gordon had to give up his commission because of the scandal, they had no money and no future. By December Sarah had yielded to family pressure and taken little Louisa to Goodwood where her brother, the Duke of Richmond, installed her in a house on his estate and laid down the rules of her penance. She was to live in modest comfort with her child, seeing her family and no one else. If guests came, she must vanish. She could visit Holland House and Richmond House in London, on the same terms. She was twenty-four. There was talk of a reconciliation, and a friendly meeting with her husband when she asked his pardon and felt better, but nothing came of it and Bunbury got an uncontested divorce in 1776. This gave her back the income from her £10,000, and she resumed her maiden name, but little Louisa went on being Bunbury.

Sarah's other brother, Lord George Lennox, and his wife, another Louisa, lived near Goodwood. He was commander of the 25th Foot Regiment and the Lennoxes seem to have felt that the officers who frequented their house could safely be exposed to a fallen woman like Sarah. She was soon good friends with a career officer called George Napier and his wife. He was yet another impecunious Scots younger son, with Irish connections, a handsome man, not brilliant, but methodical and serious, and above all a soldier. He and his wife had two children and when he and Sarah fell in love the situation was serious. The Lennoxes intervened and persuaded him to leave the 25th Regiment for the 80th where, doubtless with their help, he got his own company. Most important of all, from their point of view, the 80th had been ordered to America, where the revolutionary war was raging. The Lennoxes must have hoped to have seen the last of him. Like all good Whigs, they were passionately in favour of the embattled colonists. Back in 1776 Sarah had written to Susan: 'I am sure I can thank God very sincerely I am not Queen, for I should have quarrel'd with his Majesty . . . and my head would have been off probably. But if I had loved and liked him and not had interest enough to prevent this war, I should certainly go mad, to think a person I loved was the cause of such a shameful war.'

Sarah kept in touch with the Napiers. She knew that when the family got to New York in 1779 they all succumbed to the fever that was raging there. Presently Napier had to go south to the siege of Charleston, where he recovered, but his wife and one of the children died. By 1781 he was back in England with his remaining daughter Louisa, proposing to Sarah. Her sisters were in favour of the match, even though Napier had no money and few prospects, but her brother the Duke opposed it, insisting that she was very well off as she was. She had moved into the nearby house at Halnaker that he had built especially for her and he doubtless thought it ungrateful of her to want to leave. She was twenty-six, and could look forward to years of dull safety, with few friends and less entertainment. She would not even be able to bring out her own daughter, but would have to rely on her husband's female relations and her own. And here was George Napier refusing to be mortified about her 'character' and laughing at every objection. Her one fault, he told her, was delay. Sarah merely waited until her brother was away, to spare his feelings, and then they married quietly, in 1781, in Goodwood parish church, her rank presumably outweighing any scruples the clergyman may have had about her divorce. It was the start of a long, impoverished, productive and happy life.

Sarah had loved horses when she was married to horse-mad Bunbury, now she loved Napier and the army. Like Gordon, Napier had had to sell his commission, but she was sure her family would find him something. Her brother the Duke and her cousin Charles James Fox were both prominent in the Whig party, but it was not the Whig party's hour. When Pitt came into office in December 1783 the Napiers' hopes of affluence faded. Sarah had an annuity of £500 a year, wrested from Bunbury by her brother the Duke, who was her trustee, but she quarrelled with him because he would not hand over the trusteeship to her adored husband. This may have tempered the Duke's enthusiasm for finding work for his new brother-in-law. When he did get Napier a position in the ordnance department at Woolwich, Sarah grumbled that it was not a good enough one. Her rich sisters helped them a good deal and in the end they moved to Ireland to be nearer Emily and Louisa and to live more cheaply. Once they were settled in a 'new, dear, cheerful, comfortable, pretty house', their family rapidly increased. They had eight children by 1791, five boys and three girls. When their first daughter Emily was born in 1783, Sarah's still childless sister, rich Louisa Conolly, offered to adopt her, pointing out that Sarah obviously liked boys best. Demurring at first, Sarah soon gave way. One less mouth to feed had to be a consideration.

Napier had various jobs in and around the army, and saw active service in Lord Moira's short, disastrous 1794 campaign in Holland, but when he died in 1804 he was still a mere Controller of Army Accounts in Ireland. This was when Sarah made her appeal, through Queen Charlotte, to her old friend and fellow sufferer from poor eyesight, the King. He gave her a badly needed pension of £800 a year. She lived on until 1826, much loved, a great correspondent, still on the fringes of unrelenting society. Her own daughter Louisa Bunbury had died young of consumption, but Napier's Louisa was a devoted stepdaughter and became her secretary and reader when Sarah's eyesight failed her. But her five sons were the joy of her life: three upstanding army officers (one of them the historian of the Peninsular War), a naval captain and a successful barrister. She had every right to compare them favourably with George III's obstreperous brood, and looked on them as her justification in a world where some doors would always be closed to her. They made it all worth while.

* * *

Another woman who broke the rules was Mary Nisbet, a Scottish heiress who was twenty-two when she married Thomas Bruce, seventh Earl of Elgin. He was eleven years older than her and had tried the army before deciding on a diplomatic career. In 1799 he was appointed Ambassador Extraordinary to the Ottoman Empire after the Turks were driven to war with France by Napoleon's surprise landing in Egypt, then under Turkish control, as was most of the Middle East. It was in fact George III who suggested Elgin apply for the job. When he got it he made another proposition to the government: he wanted funds for a team of experts to collect patterns and moulds of the famous Greek antiquities of which travellers were bringing home such tales. Like Egypt, Greece was under Turkish control and as Ambassador he would be in a good position to get permission for this. The government liked the idea, but not the expense, but Elgin went ahead commissioning experts just the same. He approached a twenty-four-year-old painter called J.M.W. Turner, but Turner wanted £400 a year, and Elgin was only offering £30 so nothing came of it. In the end he found some experts in England and decided to pick up the rest in Sicily, where he heard they were going cheap.

Ambassadors need wives and Elgin had recently met a childhood friend in Mary Nisbet, a lively young beauty who was also her rich father's sole heir. When Elgin proposed, she hesitated at first. A good deal older than her, and a proud, cold, frugal man, he suffered badly from rheumatism, which may have affected his temper. He seems to have made enemies more easily than friends, but it was a splendid match, and her doting parents approved of it and promised to come and visit her in Constantinople. Mary decided to be in love and accept him and was already pregnant when they started on the long journey east, which she chronicled in lively letters home. She was horribly sick at sea, partly no doubt owing to her condition, which she did not mention to her parents. Lisbon stank. General O'Hara at Gibraltar was, 'The man for me! If he were forty years younger what a scrape Eggy [she was presently to stop calling her husband this] would be in.' In the Mediterranean she was 'shockingly bit by the Miss-Kitties,' but liked Palermo, though the wife of the Ambassador, Sir William Hamilton, presented her with a social problem, with which she seems to have dealt tactfully. Mary was the first person to call Emma Hamilton 'a whapper' and she drew a careful social line around her, remarking that she had made Nelson 'do many very foolish things.' The fledgling Ambassadress may have been a lively young woman, but she was no fool.

Reaching the Dardanelles, Mary had her first taste of Ambassadorial splendour in a lavish welcome on the Captain Pasha's ship, and went ashore with Elgin to explore the ruins of ancient Troy: 'Ruins it is, for there are not two stones left one upon another . . . only think of my riding twenty-two miles on a Turkish saddle.' It was dark when they got back to the ship and the surf was so high they thought it would swamp the boat. 'I feel better today than I have done since I saw you,' she wrote home. Adventure suited her.

In Constantinople their palace (which had been the French Ambassador's) was splendid, their welcome sumptuous, all she wanted was a visit from her parents to make life perfect. When Elgin was summoned to audience with the Sultan, Mary went too, in the costume of a dragoman, her husband having warned the Sultan and his Vizier that she was going to do so. She told her parents that she wore her habit. She was introduced as Lord Bruce, which would be her son's title, and stood behind her husband's chair to watch the whole ceremony. She admired Elgin's speech, and was given a magnificent sable pelisse, made specially for her on the Sultan's orders. She was soon busy giving balls and suppers and making friends with the Russian Ambassador's wife. Her letters make only glancing references to a problem her husband had with the man he was succeeding. John Spencer Smith was the powerful Levant Company's representative in Constantinople and had been handling British affairs there for the five years since the last Ambassador left. He and his brother, the volatile, brilliant Admiral Sir Sidney Smith, had been managing extremely well, and resented Elgin's arrival. They refused to co-operate and Elgin was not a man for conciliation. The result was a deplorable muddle about the treatment of French prisoners which prolonged the war and left Napoleon with a prejudice against Elgin.

But on the surface, everything was going swimmingly, aside from the continuing anxiety about money. They received expensive presents, but must give them too, and Mary must entertain lavishly. She had her own salon, and, 'Sixty people to feed every day . . . I am rather annoyed about our expenses.' It was not just the cost of living in Constantinople. Lord Elgin had engaged his experts in Sicily and their work in Athens had extended itself to the salvage of antiquities they felt to be under threat from neglect and vandalism. British success in Egypt, and the Elgins' success in Constantinople, ensured that Elgin got the permission he needed for the work, though its terms may have been stretched a bit by on-the-spot bribery. At all events, what were to become known as the Elgin Marbles were soon being taken ruthlessly down and loaded on board British ships for transport to England. The transport itself seems to have come free, courtesy of the British Navy, but the whole operation cost a fortune that Elgin did not have. He surprised the staff he had engaged in England by breaking it to them, only after they had sailed, that he did not propose to pay them until the end of the trip, when he would himself be paid, but he was not always such a ruthless economist. It is interesting that his wife wrote all the way home to Scotland to ask her mother for advice about tipping.

Their son George Charles Constantine, Lord Bruce, was born in April 1800. 'I was very ill . . . but it is quite astonishing how well I am now.' Mary never mentioned that the beloved little boy was subject to epileptic fits, perhaps a result of the adventurous journey. He was to die at forty, failing to succeed to his father's title.

His mother was back into society at once. 'I am writing with no less than 15 beaux in the room, so don't wonder if there are a few blunders.' Her parents did come to stay with them for a happy year or so, and dropped in to look at the work going on in Athens on the way home. 'Elgin,' Mary wrote to them, 'was quite charmed at your entering so heartily into his cause.' But she missed them badly and had a great fit of her 'chokings' after they left. She was presumably asthmatic. The prolonged war with the French in Egypt had come to an end at last and Mary was afraid Elgin would be criticized about the terms of the peace treaty, although he was not responsible for them. This turned out to be prescient of her.

She had a daughter, also Mary, in August 1801, and had her inoculated against smallpox at seven days old. The example of vaccination that she set was beginning to be widely followed. There was trouble at this time about the way the French defeat in Egypt was being reported and Mary begged her mother to write and tell her what was being said about it in England. In Constantinople they planned illuminations to celebrate the victory, but found that every lamp in the city had been bought up. The British were so popular there as a result of their Egyptian triumph that Mary was finally invited to visit the Sultan's mother, the Valida Sultana, an honour she had longed to receive. It was a splendid occasion and caused jealousy among the other Ambassadorial ladies. 'The Valida had not an immense quantity of diamonds, but what she had were thumpers.' And of course Mary and her retinue all received lavish presents. She was being a success, and enjoying it, and she also persuaded the Valida's favourite to have her child inoculated.

The peace of Amiens with France in 1802 meant that her parents were planning a trip to Paris and she begged her mother to send her a 'dashy gown' from there, even entertaining some hopes of being Madame Ambassadrice there herself. Elgin had achieved a great coup in persuading the Sultan to release the Maltese prisoners he had held as slaves, some of them for as much as forty years, and they were thinking of making a trip to Egypt, but then suddenly there was trouble with the volatile Turks. 'If we should go to war with the T—s, know that I think all will end well.' But it blew over and the British Government was pleased with Elgin's handling of it.

Instead of Egypt, they went to Athens, taking the children and their Turkish nurses, known as *paranamas*. It was a venturesome journey with the threat of pirates and a night in a cave guarded by their escort of janissaries. After that, it was two day's hard ride to Athens with a night in a village *han* where they were eaten alive by fleas. She celebrated her arrival in Athens by a visit to the Turkish bath: 'The dancing was too indecent, beyond anything – Mary shall not go to a Turkish Bath!' They visited the monastery at Daphne but she did not go with her husband to Thebes. Elgin was pleased with the progress his workmen had made, hoping to be able to show a 'complete representation of Athens.' They left the children and their nurses in Athens and made a tour of antique sites that reads like the brochure of a Swan cruise: Salamis . . . Eleusis . . . Megara . . . Corinth. At Corinth they saw 'several columns of the Doric order,' on the way to the Bey's Palace, where all the ladies of the two Beys' harems had come in from their country houses to greet them. 'They come in kind of covered boxes, two of which are slung across a mule like Gypsies panniers, with a lady in each. I was deluged with rose water, then perfumed . . . With my three or four Turkish words . . . I contrived to stay about twenty minutes with them.'

They went by Megara to Mycenae, where Mary crawled through a hole on all fours to see, 'The Treasury of the Kings of Mycenae . . . The stone which forms the architrave of the door . . . exceeds everything in magnitude that I had seen at Athens.' The Governor of Tripoli sent a magnificent escort to welcome them to his city, and Mary learned to ride in 'a "tarta-a-van" like the Turkish ladies. To get in you tread on a Turk, known as "the step".' There was a ceremonial reception and the usual presents at Tripoli and on the way back they found that the entrance to the Treasury of Atreus had been cleared for them. They visited Tiryns with its walls, 'supposed to be built by the Cyclops' and went on to Epidaurus where they saw 'the sacred Grove of Esculapius, and the Theatre . . . the most perfect . . . in Greece.' It was the 'most enchanting ride I ever took, quite in my stile [*sic*]; the road very dangerous and the mountains perpendicular.'

Back in Athens, she told her mother that she was glad she had done it, but, 'Extremely happy to find myself again at Athens with my dear

Babs.' Mary was a great, strong, healthy child, said their devoted mother, and Bruce a little torment who would not eat his vegetables. Elgin went off on another tour, but she stayed in Athens with the children and made herself useful in overseeing the loading of his treasures on board ship. 'How I have fagged to get all this done,' she wrote to her husband. 'Do you love me better for it, Elgin?' She went on, perhaps not altogether tactfully: 'I am now satisfied of what I always thought – which is how much more Women can do if they set about it, than Men . . . Mind Elgin you do not drop this letter out of your pocket. I wonder whether you will be at the trouble of reading it . . .'

On their way back to Constantinople they visited Sunion where she thought the temple of Minerva very much like that of Theseus in Athens. It is now known as the Temple of Poseidon. Off Delos they were attacked by Maniot pirates but no one was hurt, 'Tho' many balls struck the deck, guns, etc.' Delos was 'quite a desert,' though Elgin 'brought an altar on board . . . round and ornamented with festoons of fruit and flowers pendent from bull heads.' But at Smyrna (Izmir) they found that slanderous stories had been circulated about Elgin and there was no ship to take them through the Dardanelles to Constantinople. The Smith brothers had been at work. They would have to go overland but when the preparations for the journey were complete Elgin was not ready to leave. There was whooping cough in Smyrna and a threat of the plague. Mary decided to go on without him: 'Pray tell my Father I manoeuvred the troops consisting of 50 people for five days; the fifth day Elgin joined our party.' They were threatened by robbers and overturned two or three times on this journey and she found the views disappointing.

Mary and her children were safe back in their country house outside Constantinople early in September, and her second daughter, Matilda Harriet, was born in mid-October. It was no wonder she had been in a hurry to get back to comparative civilization. One does begin to have a few doubts about Elgin as a husband. Plagued with ill-health himself, he presumably thought his young wife indestructible.

Elgin had asked to be recalled, and the frigate *Diana* had been sent to fetch them. It was just as well as there was plague in Constantinople. Mary and the children stayed at their country house and Elgin went through an elaborate process of fumigation every time he came to join them. They sailed at last in January 1803, calling at Athens to see how Elgin's works were progressing. At Malta the family had to endure some days in quarantine, and then called at

Sicily, Naples and Rome, where they decided to send the children home by sea and go on by land themselves. They may have had serious hopes of succeeding Lord Whitworth who was Ambassador in Paris, and of course Mary was always sick at sea.

They persisted in this decision though all the talk in France was of a fresh outbreak of war. Elgin was convinced that his status as Ambassador would protect him whatever happened. War was declared when they were in Lyons, but everyone assured them it would be safe to go on to Paris. They learned their mistake when Napoleon, now First Consul, ordered the arrest of every male English traveller of military age in France. It was a flagrant breach of the contemporary code of warfare, but that was small comfort to the *détenus*, as they were called. Writing from Paris, Mary did her best to reassure her mother, but it was not easy. From being Their Excellencies the Ambassador and his Lady, they were a prisoner of war and his wife, dependent on the whim of the French authorities. Diplomatic friends did their best to help the Elgins, but it was all confusion, and they were totally in the dark as to what was going on. At first they lived in some comfort at the Hôtel de Richelieu. 'We kill time by going to plays and Operas, this is a curious life!' But at least they heard that their children were safe with their grandparents. A letter from her mother about their arrival broke the calm Mary had managed to maintain. 'What comfort it has given me dearest Mother. I cannot write – your letter has put me into a tremor, my hand shakes.'

In the confused situation, Mary hoped for a while that she would get leave to pay a short visit to England, but this hope deferred brought back her chokings, and Elgin was ill too. His rheumatism continued to plague him and a skin disease caught at Constantinople had eaten away his nose, or so Mary said. He cannot have been an easy companion in misfortune, but Mary never grumbled in her letters home. Instead, she wrote to her mother at length about the children, whom she missed horribly and wanted brought up to be hardy. The English internees were ordered out of Paris in July and the Elgins applied for leave to go to Barèges in the Pyrenees, for the waters. But permission to go there meant that all hopes of Mary's getting to England were at an end. And the journey was worse than 'my Grecian expedition. Such a journey to jumble down a disappointed heart.' But Barèges was agreeable, with society and whist and the waters doing Elgin good. They had asked for leave to go north to Pau for the winter and return to Barèges in the spring and Mary once again hoped for leave to go to London. 'Do you give the Bratts [*sic*] boiled rice before their meat, it makes the skin fine.' And, 'Have you taught them to eat vegetables yet? That I could never accomplish.' But there was only one ride at Barèges, and she became hideously bored.

Winter came, the weather broke, everyone else left Barèges and life became increasingly wretched. At last they received permission to go to Pau, a delightful place in the foothills of the Pyrenees, where they took a house and were as content as prisoners of war could be. But still she got no passport for England and 'the Father and Mother that she loves dearly and three little Bratts [*sic*] she would give the world to kiss.' Meanwhile a new menace was looming. A rumour began to circulate in France that Elgin had been involved in the Turkish mistreatment of French prisoners of war. It was untrue but deeply damaging.

Mary went to Paris in November on being given hopes of a passport for England, but yet again her wish was denied as a result of what seems to have been a bureaucratic muddle. And then, in December, she learned that Elgin was in real danger. A French General Boyer had been captured by the British in the West Indies. There were rumours that he was being ill-treated in captivity, and Napoleon planned to use Elgin as a pawn to ensure his release. If the British Government did not agree to an exchange, Elgin would be incarcerated in a fortress for the duration of the war. Mary was in despair: 'Lourdes, where he is now confined . . . is a complete ruin . . . Lose no time, dearest Mother. The First Consul has agreed to this exchange in consequence of my application.' She also wrote to Lord Hawkesbury (the Foreign Secretary, later Lord Liverpool) and begged her mother to speak to the King. She had managed to charm the powerful Foreign Minister Talleyrand, and persuade him to act as her intermediary with Napoleon. 'How fortunate that I came to Paris, nobody could have done what I have for Elgin.' Mary was using all her charm and all her diplomatic skills on her husband's behalf. Meanwhile he was having a very unpleasant time in Lourdes, where attempts were made to implicate him in spurious plots against the French state.

The British Government refused to agree to the exchange with Boyer, since this would set the dangerous precedent that a *détenu* could be exchanged for a genuine prisoner of war. But a personal letter Mary wrote to Napoleon seems to have done the trick: 'I am just now in great vogue at Paris, since the First Consul was so amazingly captivated with my letter. He really behaved very handsomely . . . the order was immediately given and instantaneously executed.' Elgin was soon back at Pau, but Mary stayed on in Paris, still hoping for a passport for a visit to England. She was worrying about money: 'I wish E. would think a little more about money. I would give the world to be able to comprehend the real state of our affairs.' And then, a significant conclusion: 'I cannot say I have had much happiness since I left my dear dear Father and Mother's house, tho' I give you my word of honour nothing can equal his kindness to me.' She was getting scolding letters from her parents, both about the disastrous decision to visit France and about their debts. 'Don't believe all you hear. E. has got so many enemies . . .'. She longed, 'To clear off all debts . . . and know to a fraction what we can spend.'

She was pregnant again and did not dare go to join Elgin at Pau or even at Orleans because of the appalling state of the roads. Her second son, William, was born in March 1804 and she and her husband were back at Barèges together that summer, and then at Pau for the winter. Elgin was getting scolding letters from his widowed mother too. It must have been maddening to have their parents assume that their detention was all their own fault, particularly as, to some extent, it was. Mary wrote to her mother that autumn that their *détenu* friend Robert Ferguson of Raith was hoping for leave to go back to his estate in Scotland. 'I am sure a quiet confab with him will thoroughly convince you what an erroneous idea it was, that ever I have missed an opportunity of getting home – no one knows that history better than him.' The Elgins had met Ferguson, a childhood friend of both, in 1803 when they were first detained in Paris, and he had supported Mary while she was appealing to Napoleon through Talleyrand.

Napoleon made himself Emperor in 1804. Mary was studying Plutarch and Herodotus that winter at Pau and taking an interest in the fate of the manuscripts that had been collected at Athens by the Reverend Joseph Dacre Carlyle, one of Elgin's experts, now dead. But their delight was little William: 'He has such a merry little intelligent face of his own . . . He is the life of the whole house.' He was also the back-up heir to the title, since his older brother, Lord Bruce, was epileptic.

In April of 1805 they both received permission to travel to Paris, where Mary had real hopes of obtaining a passport for England. 'I am perfectly persuaded, as Ferguson says, that if my demand was made known to the Emperor, he would give me a passport.' Two weeks later, a short desolate note from Paris announced little William's sudden death: 'My William, my adored William is gone . . . gone . . . and left me here.'

Her son's death got Mary the longed-for passport at last. She was allowed to take the child's body back to England for burial there, and Robert Ferguson, who was released at about the same time, helped her with the arrangements. Mary was in fact pregnant again when she travelled back from France, and her daughter Lucy was born in January 1806. She must have been conceived at about the time of her brother's death, Elgin no doubt desperate for a replacement heir. Announcing Lucy's birth in a letter to her husband, still in France, Mary wrote that she had suffered so much from 'this event' that she 'would never subject herself again to that intercourse with him which might be productive of such effects.'

This digest of her letter was later to be produced in court. They were bold words from a wife to her husband in those days, but a later letter of Mary's to Ferguson shows that Elgin took them seriously and promised to leave her alone. It seems likely that Lucy's conception had been a case of rape within marriage. It ended the years of compromise and pretence. And Ferguson was at her side now, an old friend and supporter. Some time in the course of that winter, which she spent first with her parents in their Portman Square house and then by herself in Baker Street, Mary and Ferguson became lovers. 'You must exasperate him,' Ferguson wrote to her after Lucy's birth. 'You must consider his approach as a violation of your person, and force him to a separation.'

Released at last in the summer of 1806, Elgin came home to find, to his surprise, that his wife meant to stick by everything she had written. She wrote to Ferguson describing one of the resulting scenes: 'He was very much agitated indeed, but he said nothing . . . Went into his room for a couple of hours. He coughed dreadfully which he always does when he is annoyed . . . I must do him the justice to say he has taken upon himself to keep his promise, but I hardly think it possible he can go on with it . . . What a desperate horrible idea that nothing but death can make us free. I shudder when I dare think of it and too thoroughly I feel I cannot live without you.'

The letters she wrote to Ferguson at this time themselves produced the drastic solution. Elgin got hold of them and used them as evidence for divorce. He sued Ferguson for criminal conversation in London in December 1807, and Ferguson, denying adultery in Paris (thus establishing Lucy's legitimacy) admitted it in London and had to pay

£10,000 in damages. Instead of going to the Lords for a divorce, Elgin then sued in Edinburgh on the grounds of his wife's adultery. Her lawyers decided to fight the case, and lost it. The details of servants and bedrooms provided even more of a field day for the gutter press than had the London trial. However Elgin did not get his hands on Mary's fortune, though of course he had custody of the children. After she married Ferguson, Elgin let them go and stay with his mother in Scotland so as to see Mary there. Old Lady Elgin had experience with the children of divided parents. She had been in control of the Prince of Wales's daughter Charlotte's nursery for the first eight years of her life, until she resigned in 1804. Charlotte seems to have been fond of her. One can only hope that the old lady made life easy for her grandchildren, whose father soon married another Scottish woman and had eight children by her, including an heir to replace the epileptic Lord Bruce.

The scandal of the divorce seems to have hit Elgin quite as hard as it did the Fergusons. He never got another diplomatic appointment and even lost his seat as a Scottish representative peer in the Lords in 1807. He became the butt of satirists from the halfpenny press to Lord Byron, and he never recovered from the burden of debt in which he had embroiled himself. In the end, he sold his collection of marbles to the Government for an absurd £35,000. It must have enraged him to see Ferguson stand successfully for Parliament as a Whig. Mary outlived both her second husband and her son, and when she died in 1855 there was no one to put her name on her gravestone. This shocked her daughter Lucy's grandson into publishing her letters, which showed, he said, her devotion to her parents.

* * *

Lady Hester Stanhope was the daughter of a love match. Her father, Lord Mahon, the brilliant Stanhope heir, had married the elder Pitt's daughter Hester and four years of happy marriage had produced three little girls, of whom Lady Hester was the outstanding eldest. When his wife died after the birth of her third child, Lord Mahon was desolated, thrown off balance – and married again in six months. His second wife, a cool Louisa Grenville, capably produced three little boys and then lost interest in her family and plunged back into society, leaving them behind at Chevening in Kent. Her step-daughter, Lucy Stanhope, later said that she doubted if she would have recognized her if they had met in the street. This left the six children in the hands of governesses and of their increasingly eccentric father. Hester was the only one of his children who was not terrified of him. She stood up to him in defence of all of them, and he recognized a kindred intellectual spirit in her and used to call her into his study for philosophical discussions.

A brilliant but frustrated inventor, he submitted a design for a viable steamship to the Admiralty in 1793. It might have changed the course of the war that had just broken out but they turned it down. This may have been partly because he was a fierce republican, renaming his house Democracy Hall and sending his daughter to keep turkeys on the common. He meant his children to grow up as commoners, but when his daughter Lucy obliged him by eloping with the local apothecary he was not pleased. Hester, a brilliant rider and talker, later told her faithful friend Dr Meryon how she took her life into her own hands, at twenty, in 1796. When her father forbade her to attend the royal review at Lord Romney's house nearby, she pretended she was visiting a friend and drove herself over to join the party without so much as a maid to support her. Tall like all the Pitts, and handsome rather than beautiful (she described her looks as 'homogeneous ugliness') she cut a striking figure and was soon surrounded by men of whom she was not afraid. The King heard the roars of laughter, asked what was going on and took a fancy to her. 'My dear,' he said to the Queen, 'Lady Hester is going to ride bodkin with us. I am going to take her away from Democracy Hall.'

The Queen did not let him, of course, but Lady Hester was launched in society. After this triumph her father could not keep her at home and she was soon making numerous male friends, from Beau Brummel to the Royal Princes. She did not care for women, or the Prince of Wales, but the Duke of York was a loyal friend and correspondent over the years. When her father denied her brother Lord Mahon an education, she contrived his escape, in 1801, to the University of Erlangen, with the help of such friends as radical Sir Francis Burdett and Francis Jackson, a successful diplomat. Both her sisters were married by now, all Hester had was friends, none of them women. Although men enjoyed her lively company, she was probably too masculine to be considered as a possible wife. An acute Frenchwoman, the Duchess of Gontaut, described her at a fancy dress ball as tall and slim, in 'a costume that had nothing feminine about it except the mask.'

Hester almost met her match in her cousin, another eccentric Pitt,

Lord Camelford. He had had a lonely, secluded childhood at his family estate in Cornwall, and had grown up quite as odd as Hester's father, given to fighting duels and secretly helping London's desperate poor. They first met in 1800 and felt an instant sympathy for each other and maybe something more for a while, but nothing came of it. When he was killed in a duel in 1804, she could write coolly enough about his, 'Untimely end. He had vices, but also great virtues.' They had both been abroad during the short peace of Amiens, he, apparently, trying to assassinate Napoleon, she doing the Grand Tour, just like a man. She spent the winter of 1802 in Naples, flirting outrageously at that outrageous court, but had to hurry home by way of Germany, when war broke out again in 1803.

The doors of Chevening had been closed to her since she helped her brother escape, and now her beloved grandmother, Pitt's widow, Lady Chatham, with whom she had been living at Burton Pynsent, had died. Hester had no home. Society was amazed when her forty-four-year-old uncle, William Pitt, invited her to live with him. He had never married, preferring his career to Lord Auckland's daughter Eleanor Eden, and his hard drinking had already damaged his health, but they had a happy few years as bachelors together. He was out of office when she went to live with him at Walmer Castle in Kent, but when he became Prime Minister again in 1804 she throve as a political hostess, and was soon acting as unofficial adviser and go-between for him. Through Pitt, she met his protégé, the 'gay deceiver' Lord Granville Leveson Gower, and fell in love with him. When Granville slid away to Russia she was desolated, may have had a miscarriage, and wrote to a friend that 'my heart points, like a compass, to the North.' She retired to Walmer Castle to distract herself by making a garden for her uncle. Lacking labourers, she put whole regiments of soldiers stationed at Dover to work. Pitt was delighted, but he was drinking and working himself to death.

When he died in 1806 it was as grave a blow to Hester as to the country. One of his last acts had been to ask for pensions for her and her sisters and these were actually granted. She now had £1,200 a year, but once again no home. Jane Austen's Edmund Bertram might plan to live comfortably as a country clergyman on £700 a year, but £1,200 was pitifully little for an aristocratic lady in London. She could not afford a carriage and the streets were too dirty for walking. Besides, ladies walking alone in London were apt to be taken for prostitutes. 'A poor gentlewoman is the worst thing in the world,' Hester once said. Many of her glittering friends abandoned her, but some were faithful. Among them was Sir John Moore, a friend and admirer of her uncle's, who had been campaigning in Sicily at the time of Pitt's death. Hester later told Meryon that she had helped to get Moore the command of the expeditionary force that was sent to Spain in 1808, and they had probably agreed to get engaged when he came back. He never did. He and her brother Charles were both killed at Corunna. 'Stanhope, remember me to your sister,' Moore said to her other brother, James, and died.

She was alone again, and in despair, but she fought it. She tried a Welsh retreat, like the Ladies of Llangollen, but it bored her into illness. Granville Leveson Gower had married Harriet Cavendish that winter of 1809. Lady Hester was thirty-three and still single. Sir Walter Farquhar, the great society doctor, ordered a change of air. She would travel again. There were not many places she could go to in 1810, with Napoleon's armies straddling Europe, but her brother James was due to rejoin his regiment at Cadiz. She would go there with him and then on to Sicily and beyond. She engaged a young doctor called Charles Meryon as medical companion, imperiously demanded transport from the Royal Navy, and got it. It took them a hazardous month to get to Gibraltar, where James left her to rejoin his regiment. Hester, the great Pitt's niece, was fêted by society, and made a new friend. His name was Michael Bruce and he had been sent on the Grand Tour by his very rich, very devoted father, an Indian nabob, Craufurd Bruce. At twenty-two Michael Bruce was twelve years younger than Lady Hester, but he was highly educated, charming and, said Meryon presciently, 'Handsome enough to move any lady's heart that is not, like my poor lady's, too much a valetudinarian . . . for love.'

Lady Hester was recovering. When she moved on to Malta, Bruce followed her, and they became lovers, his experience of sex balancing hers of life. From now on, they would travel together, flouting convention as was Lady Hester's habit. But this could have serious consequences, and she knew it. There was Michael Bruce's loving father to be considered, partly because he was a loving father, but also because his son was entirely dependent on him for funds. Lady Hester sat down and wrote Craufurd Bruce a remarkable letter. Full of loving praise for Michael, it also contained a solemn promise: 'At this very moment (while loving him to distraction) I look forward to the period when I must resign him to some thrice happy woman really worthy of him.'

Michael wrote too and the happy couple set off for Constantinople, since Sicily, where they had thought of going, was under too serious a threat from Napoleon's advancing armies. On the other hand England and changeable Turkey had signed a new peace treaty in 1809. On the way, at Athens in 1810, they met Michael's friend and one-time travelling companion the Marquess of Sligo, and a friend of his, Lord Byron. Hester thought nothing of the still unknown Byron: 'It is easy enough to write verses,' she said, while he described her as, 'that dangerous thing – a female wit.' But she shocked Sligo by her ignorance of antiquity. One Greek statue was very much like another to her. She preferred to talk politics, reminisce, and be listened to.

The British Navy obligingly got them as far as Zakynthos, but from there on they had to rely on local polaccas and feluccas for transport and had an exciting time of it. Reaching Constantinople at last in October 1810 they finally received answers to the letters they had written to Craufurd Bruce in June. Considering all things, it seems a remarkably speedy exchange. Two letters from her lover's father came for Hester in quick succession. The first welcomed her enthusiastically as aristocratic patroness, lover and educator to his son, but the second, sent to Michael, spelled out some of the harsh realities of their relationship, pointing out that Hester was the one who would suffer in the end. Answering it, Hester went to the heart of the matter: 'A man in no age has ever suffered in the public opinion by his intimacy with a woman who had his real interests at heart . . .'. As for her, she promised that she would from then on, 'Most scrupulously avoid ever setting eyes upon a modest woman. I will never give an opportunity to those fair ladies [who have] married for a title, a house and fine diamonds, having previously made up their minds to be Faithless Wives, to sneer at me.' Can she have been thinking of Mary Elgin who had shone in Constantinople ten years earlier? Michael was writing at the same time to say that, 'I have gained more knowledge in these six months from my conversations with Lady Hester than I have acquired for the last ten years of my life . . .'. Craufurd Bruce was satisfied, and the money for their travels secure.

Meanwhile Lady Hester had made friends with Stratford Canning, the twenty-four-year-old diplomat who was in charge of the British Embassy at Constantinople. Her high birth and political connection seem to have comfortably outweighed her scandalous position in his eyes. He was unmarried, which simplified matters. She knew his cousin, George Canning, one of Pitt's bright young men, and could tell him tales of the great Pitt himself. The few ladies of the English community perhaps proved less friendly, and were dull, Hester said. She applied herself to finding out about Turkish society. She liked what she saw, and the Turks were fascinated by her. While their women stayed cooped up in the harem, she thought nothing of riding by herself through Constantinople, and on one occasion encountered the formidable Sultan Mahmoud and his retinue. The crowd around her bowed to the ground, she sat her horse, which she rode astride, cool, undaunted and unveiled. Anything could have happened, nothing did. Sultan Mahmoud II was a clever man, and neutral Turkey needed its new British allies, threatened as it was by both France and Russia. But Hester learned a lesson that was to stand her in good stead in her dealings with the Islamic world: never show fear.

Michael and Sligo went off on a trip to Smyrna and when he came back Michael asked her to marry him. It was a handsome gesture and Hester handsomely refused him. She had given his father her word and meant to keep it. She may also have begun to notice some of young Michael's shortcomings, the weakness that underlay the charm. Refusing him, she must have realized how difficult it would be to return to England. Here, she was a public figure, there she would be an outcast. Michael was affronted. Had he counted on her influence as his wife in the diplomatic career he and his father planned for him? As a wife she could have been an asset, as a mistress, she was not. Inevitably, the rejected proposal changed their relationship, but it continued. It must have been a bad time, made worse by a bitterly disapproving letter from her brother James to whom she had written about their affair.

As a distraction, perhaps, that autumn of 1811, Hester thought of returning to England by way of France. Her plan was to meet Napoleon, study his character and return to England with ideas for defeating him. She arranged a secret meeting with a French representative to ask for passports, but the French Ambassador very sensibly refused them and the only result was a row with Stratford Canning who was justifiably furious at what she had done. It was time to go. They decided to go to Egypt, then under Turkish domination, but were dramatically shipwrecked on the way and ended up on Rhodes with only the clothes they stood up in. Hester kitted herself out in the becomingly flowing breeches of a Turkish gentleman, and wore them for the rest of her life. The Royal Navy came to their rescue in the end and took them to Alexandria on the frigate *Salsette*.

In Cairo, Hester had one of her successes with Mehemet Ali, an Albanian shopkeeper who had waded through blood to be master of Egypt, under the slack jurisdiction of the Sultan in Constantinople. Mehemet Ali was 'civiller to me than he ever was to anybody in his life,' Hester wrote proudly to Stratford Canning. He reviewed his troops for her, an unprecedented honour for a woman, and gave her two Arab horses. Was Michael affronted at getting only a sabre and a Kashmir shawl? After all, he was paying for the lavish presents that must be given in exchange. It must have been quite an exercise for the complacent young man to find himself so very much in Hester's shadow. She was talking about an old prophecy that she would become Queen of the Jews. But Jerusalem proved disappointing, the inevitable tension between Michael and Meryon was getting worse, and she was glad to accept an invitation to visit the Emir of the Druse, a wild Islamic sect who lived in the mountains between Sidon and Tripoli. The Emir sent her a cavalcade of twelve camels, twenty-five mules, four horses and seven foot soldiers and they set off through the rugged mountains. 'I have travelled for nine hours,' wrote Hester, 'and never found a place large enough to pitch a tent. The vineyards are like staircases and every little flat place stuffed with mulberry trees for the silkworms . . . and the people savage and extraordinary, the women wearing a great tin trumpet on their heads and a veil suspended upon it, and seeming very proud of these frightful horns.' They stayed a month with the Emir who had recently and surprisingly become a convert to Christianity. 'I can ask questions no other person dares to put to them,' she wrote. Meryon took a different view of the Emir. 'They say he is a very good man. He blinded his three nephews and had his prime minister strangled . . . but these things go for nothing in Turkey.' Hester seems to have been enjoying the adulation too much to notice the dark background. They travelled in immense style, spending lavishly and word had got about that she was an immensely rich English princess. It was doubtless what she felt she was and she was enjoying every minute of it. But Craufurd Bruce was beginning to grumble about the amount they were spending, and things were now so bad between Michael and Meryon that Meryon wanted to leave, writing secretly to his sister that Bruce had been 'Flattered and caressed [by his father] until the slightest opposition to his will makes him sulky and churlish.'

Hester did not want to lose Meryon and suggested that the party break up for a while. Michael could go to Aleppo, as he wished to do, while she accepted an invitation she had managed to get from the Pasha of Damascus. The Pasha stipulated that she must wear a veil, but Hester had her own ideas about that. As always, she sent Meryon on ahead, to make sure of a fitting welcome and arrange for lodgings. She did her adventuring in some comfort. When he came to meet her and advised that she enter the city veiled as the Pasha had requested, she refused, and got away with it. Then she refused to live in the house that had been allotted to her because it was in the Christian quarter — tantamount to a ghetto in this Muslim country. Established at last in one of the best houses in the best quarter of town, she rode about unveiled and was, she said, respected everywhere. It was a triumph, and she meant to better it. She would make the dangerous journey to Palmyra. Only three Englishmen had attempted it, and one of them had failed. She was being hailed as the great English queen now, and liked to compare herself with Zenobia, queen of Palmyra, a formidably energetic and beautiful woman who led a revolt against the Romans in the third century AD. She had been defeated in the end, and Palmyra destroyed, but Hester, dreaming of greatness and laughing at herself a little as she did so, ignored this.

This was a really dangerous journey and Hester was still trying to work out how to do it, when Michael came anxiously back from Aleppo having heard about her plans. He wanted her to travel in a tartaravan, the type of sedan chair hung between mules that was used by Turkish ladies and Mary Elgin, but she would have none of this. They were still arguing when Hester received an invitation to visit Mahannah el Fadel, the formidable sheik who controlled most of the desert around Palmyra. The invitation was brought by his charming son Nasar who admitted they robbed travellers but promised that Hester would be safe with them and offered to escort her to Palmyra. Michael was away; Hester accepted the invitation for the following spring, dressed up as the son of a Bedu chief, and charmed the formidable Mahannah into friendship. And she fell in love with Bedouin life, the feeling of freedom and the feeling of power. She saw it all, of course, from the high, masculine ground.

Since it was too late to go to Palmyra that year, they spent an uncomfortable winter in Damascus at the house of a 'very jolly Turk . . . with four wives here, and I believe, fifty women . . . they are all very good to me and less shut up than any women I ever saw in this country.' It poured with rain, the house leaked, everyone got ill, especially Hester's maid Mrs Fry, who developed pleurisy. One does wonder how she felt about it all. Meanwhile Dr Meryon was in the desert tending the great Mahannah, who was ill, and later that winter he got to Palmyra, which he found disappointing. But he organized accommodation for Hester in the spring, and in the meantime a long gloomy letter arrived from Craufurd Bruce. He was worried about money, but still more worried about Hester's position. It was too late now for her to marry Michael; the scandal was out; if they returned to England he would not even be able to invite them to his house, because this would involve his wife. It confirmed Hester in a decision she had been quietly making. When Michael went back to England, he would go alone.

At last, in March 1813, they set out for Palmyra, having paid Mahannah £300 protection money in advance. They were all dressed as Bedouins, even Mrs Fry. It was a formidable expedition, and crowds lined the roads to cheer it on, except for those who wailed because they were sure Lady Hester would be killed. And there were problems. Mahannah's son Nasar was their guide and he and Michael had taken an instant dislike to each other. Hester sensibly ordained that Nasar ride in front with her while Michael followed behind as rearguard, which he resented. A few days into the desert Nasar began to act up. On one occasion he and his men vanished suddenly, leaving the party unprotected. Hester remained totally calm, and they presently reappeared with an unlikely story of having repelled an attack. As they approached Palmyra Meryon went on ahead to confirm their lodgings and when he rejoined them it was to find the caravan being subjected to a terrifying mock attack, a last test of Hester's nerve. But when they neared the ruined city at last they found Palmyran girls replacing the statues of the ceremonial way as part of a tumultuous welcome. 'Without joke,' Hester wrote, 'I have been crowned Queen of the Desert.' From then on she styled herself 'Queen of the Arabs'. It was the high point of her career.

What did Michael think about it all? Was he relieved when they got back to Damascus and found a letter announcing that his father was seriously ill? It was the end of the affair. He must go home. She would not. But after Michael left, in October 1813, Hester and Meryon both fell ill and she nearly died. By January 1814 she was well enough to be moved to Sidon and face what the future held for her. In England, she would be treated as a fallen woman, here she was the rich princess. She decided to settle in the Middle East, and made herself a home in a disused monastery at Mar Elias, at the foot of Mount Lebanon near Sidon.

She wrote Michael long letters, but received only three from him in the eighteen months after he left. If she had hoped for the kind of correspondence her old lover Granville Leveson Gower had kept up with Lady Bessborough, she was to be disappointed. Michael had also promised to sort out her financial affairs for her and send her £1,000 a year, but he did neither. His letters were full of endearments, but she heard, gradually, about his wasted life and numerous affairs and, in 1818, his marriage to a rich widow with several children. As for the political career for which she had sacrificed herself, it never happened. She blamed his father, but it must have been a bitter blow to her.

It was a distraction to come on clues to a possible buried treasure in the desert. She got permission from the Sultan to look for it and asked for funds from the British, but they were refused. The treasure hunt, widely publicized, was a total failure. All they found was one huge statue which Hester ruthlessly had broken up for fear of being accused of smuggling antiquities. She had never been much of a one for antiquity. And the expedition, lavish as always, increased her financial problems. After Michael left, she had gone on living as if she still had his rich father behind her, counting on his promise of an allowance. It was not so easy to be a rich princess on her own income of £1,200 a year. She was getting into debt.

She was a tourist attraction now, visited by English travellers whom she entertained lavishly. She was also a political figure in the complex Arab world. When her old friend Mehemet Ali rebelled against the Sultan, she sided with the government, and her house became a haven for refugees in the savage war that followed. Mehemet Ali, having won his independence, said, 'The Englishwoman has caused me more trouble than all the insurgent peoples of Syria and Palestine.' He left her alone, but the refugees were expensive to feed, and her debts were mounting.

Lonely, ageing and increasingly unbalanced, she still ruled her household with a rather erratic rod of iron, applying the same ferocious interest to questions of politics, medicine and domestic economy. And she turned more and more to eastern superstition and eastern medicine. One way and another, Dr Meryon had had enough by 1817 and went back to England where he married but could not stop worrying about Lady Hester, whom he loved. He came back to visit her twice, and continued a faithful friend and, ultimately, memorialist. She moved to another deserted monastery, Djoun, a little further inland, and it was there that the burden of debt finally caught up with her. An Aleppo merchant complained to the British Consul about the £1,000 that she owed him. As always, she tried to carry it off with a high hand, but the resulting muddled long-distance row ended in her pension being withdrawn by the British Government. She still thought of herself as a powerful Pitt, and the Sultan's friend. But she had lived too long. Mehemet Ali was ruling Egypt and Syria now, and Palmerston was Prime Minister in England. She wrote furious letters to Wellington . . . to Palmerston . . . even to the young Queen Victoria. 'I shall not allow the pension given by your Royal grandfather to be stopped by force; I shall resign it for the payment of my debts, and with it the name of an English Subject.' The Queen did not answer. She probably never saw the letter.

This was no way to treat a Pitt. Hester wrote again. If they did not restore the pension she would wall herself in. But this was the 1830s. Pitt was no longer a name to conjure with. Her English maid had died, Lady Hester had lived too long alone, she was a little mad. She did wall herself up although, basically sensible to the last, she left enough space for her goats to get in and out. She died in June 1839, without a European beside her. The English Consul, arriving too late from Beirut, found her dead body and 'thirty-five rooms . . . full of trash.' But she became a legend, thanks largely to Dr Meryon and his *Memoir*.

6

Love, Blood & Money

WHEN IT WAS A QUESTION of stretching the matrimonial rules, money was almost as useful as blood. Poverty and pride destroyed Hester Stanhope in the end, and it was money that supported Maria Fagniani. Her mother, the rich Marchesa Fagniani, had had simultaneous affairs with George Selwyn, dandy and wit, and Lord March, a dissolute peer who later became famous as Lord Queensberry, or 'Old Q'. Selwyn doted on little Maria and actually brought her up, bribing her conniving parents to let him keep her. Both fathers left Maria money, and her official father, Fagniani, never disowned her. She was therefore a respectable heiress and respectably married Lord Yarmouth in 1792, after which they were fashionably unfaithful to each other. When Yarmouth found his friend the Prince Regent trying to kiss her he was said to have thrashed him so savagely that he had to stay at home with a 'sprained ankle', an occasion celebrated in cartoon by George Cruikshank and in verse by Peter Pindar, who concluded:

> So let us sing, Long live the King,
> The Regent, long live he;
> And when again he gets a sprain,
> May I be there to see.

Yarmouth, the original of Thackeray's Lord Steyne, seems to have minded less the Prince Regent's relationship with his mother, Lady Hertford.

Money also shaped the lives of the three charming Misses Coutts, daughters of Thomas Coutts, the banker who was friend and adviser to the Duchess of Devonshire. He had married his own brother's nursemaid, but society bore with her and their daughters because of his money. Good looking and well brought up, the three sisters were painted by Angelica Kauffmann as the Three Graces and introduced into the world by their father's grateful clients. There were only three years between them, and Sophia, the youngest, made the first of their good matches. After a tempestuous courtship, she married radical Francis Burdett in 1793, but their honeymoon was saddened by news of the tragic death of his brother Sedley and his friend Lord Montagu in an almost suicidally foolish boating accident. The oldest Coutts girl, Susan, had been engaged to Montagu and Fanny had been in love with Sedley. Mourning their lost loves the sisters must have wondered why they had thrown away their lives so gratuitously. In the end, Susan and Fanny recovered and married the Earls of Guilford and Bute respectively, though Fanny took so long about it that her parents began to worry. All three marriages produced problems as well as children, but Sophia's was the stormiest. She had been nineteen and Burdett twenty-three when they married, and while she was bearing her first five children and sliding into gentle invalidity he was becoming more and more passionate in the cause of reform. Several deaths in his family made him rich in his own right and he drifted away from his ailing wife into the open arms of Lady Oxford, maybe even contributing to her Harleian Miscellany of children.

When Burdett's flamboyant espousal in Parliament of what we would look on these days as basic civil rights led the Government to issue a warrant for his arrest in 1810, Sophia stood by him through a four-day siege of their Piccadilly house by the authorities. A late afterthought daughter, Angela, was born in 1814 and grew up to find herself heir to her grandfather Coutts' immense fortune. He had left entire control of it to the actress Harriot Mellon who had comforted him through his wife's years of senility, married him after her death, and married the Duke of St Albans after his. Coutts made his will well; Harriot kept control of his fortune, doubtless to the disappointment of the Duke of St Albans as well as of the family. She watched the grandchildren growing up, and when she died in 1837, Angela found herself Angela Burdett-Coutts, probably the richest woman in England next to the Queen, who came to the throne in the same year. Angela handled the responsibility well, becoming a formidable figure in the field of Victorian charity. She was friends with Queen Victoria and the Duke of Wellington, to whom she actually proposed, but outraged both Queen and public when at sixty-seven she married for love. Her husband Ashmead Bartlett was a protégé of hers, and thirty-five years younger. Angela survived both the outrage and the Queen, dying universally mourned in 1906, her husband at her side.

Both love and money played important parts in the Prince of Wales's long relationship with Maria Fitzherbert. She was a beautiful, well brought up young woman, but nobody ever called her brilliant. She did not need to be. Many men fear brilliance in a woman, and she had something more important, the charm that comes from a warm heart. Altogether she was a surprising figure to come so near to causing a constitutional crisis. She was also a devout Roman Catholic, which must have been an added strength when it came to dealing with the volatile Prince of Wales.

Born Maria Anne Smythe in 1756, she was the daughter of an old Catholic family, and convent educated in France. Back home, she dutifully married at nineteen a much older, very rich man, but he died the same year without making the promised will in her favour. Her next husband, another wealthy, older Catholic, Thomas Fitzherbert, died in 1781 after only three years of marriage. This time she was left a comfortable income and a house in Park Street, Mayfair. After a suitable period of mourning, the young double widow moved to town in 1783 and appeared in society under the wing of Lady Sefton, whose husband, the first Earl of Sefton, a connection of the Fitzherberts, had conformed to the rites of the Church of England in 1768. By 1784, the *Morning Herald* was reporting that, 'The Widow of the late Mr Fitzherbert has in her train half our young nobility.'

Her golden hair and wild rose complexion, not to mention her wealth, must have outweighed the drawback of her faith. In those days Catholics were still looked on with suspicion and could not be officers in the Army or Navy, nor enter Parliament. The ferocious anti-Catholic Gordon Riots had taken place only four years before Maria Fitzherbert came to town, but memories seem to have been short. She was constantly surrounded by admirers when she appeared in Lady Sefton's box at the opera or drove her phaeton in the park. The Seftons were Whigs and she soon caught the eye of the Prince of Wales, who had come of age the year before and plunged gladly into the social whirl. Maria was twenty-eight. Her new admirer was six years younger but infinitely more experienced. Their conniving tutors had smuggled women into Windsor for him and his brother Frederick, Duke of York, when they were still immured there, and since then there had been various relationships, including a notorious public affair with Mary Robinson, a married woman who had been driven on to the stage by the financial incompetence of a worthless husband. She was having a great success as Perdita in *The Winter's*

Tale in 1778 when the Prince saw her, fell in love, wrote her a series of passionate letters signed Florizel after the hero of the play, and won her at last. She had a legitimate daughter to support as well as her leach of a husband. When the Prince tired of her, necessity drove her to blackmail and she was expensively bought off by his disapproving father the King. Later she turned author and feminist in the heady 1790s.

The Prince had also had his successes on a higher level. The gossips talked about his relationships with the Duchess of Devonshire and the Countess of Bessborough and said that he was the father of Lady Melbourne's son George, born in 1784, and in this at least gossip may well have been right. Now he fell in love with all the 'boiling passion' his father had felt for Lady Sarah Lennox. He was always to prefer older women, and it must have been a delight for Mrs Fitzherbert to have him at her feet, a young man after those two old husbands, a great charmer like herself — and the heir apparent. But she was a thoroughly good woman and a good Catholic: nothing could come of it. George wept; he got ill; he struck attitudes; he rolled on the floor. In the end, desperate, he staged a mock suicide with a good deal of blood, and she was persuaded to visit his sickbed, with the young Duchess of Devonshire as moral support. Moved, she gave him some kind of promise and accepted a ring, probably the Duchess's. Next day, Maria thought she had been fooled, and left in haste for the continent, accompanied by a mutual friend, Lady Anne Lindsay, author of *Auld Robin Gray*, another charmer, who was running a lively salon with her older sister. The sisters were poor, the salon run on a shoestring, Lady Anne may have loved her friend, but her practical help went to the Prince. She kept him posted so that he was able to pursue Mrs Fitzherbert with so many importunate letters that the French Government suspected a plot and arrested three of his messengers. He tried to follow her abroad, but his father forbade it. In the end, after a year of wandering between Paris, Aix-la-Chapelle and Switzerland, she received a forty-two page proposal of marriage, full of impossible promises, and returned home, tacitly yielding.

When she got back to England in the winter of 1785, the Prince's friend and political adviser Charles James Fox sent him a warning letter, tactfully spelling out the appalling consequences of a marriage not only in contravention of the Royal Marriage Act but to a Catholic, thus also contravening the Act of Succession. George wrote Fox a grateful, lying letter saying he had no intention of marrying, and set about finding a clergyman who could be bribed to do it. They were married at her house on December 15th, 1785, with her uncle and brother present to make it entirely respectable. Maria had solemnly promised the Prince that she would keep the marriage secret, and she kept her word. They continued to live apparently separate lives, but he let it be known that where he was invited, she must also go, and that all rules of precedence must be waived, so that she could sit with him at table. In effect, she was to be treated as Princess of Wales.

Society shuddered. The Duchess of Devonshire wrote anxiously asking advice from her straitlaced mother, the dowager Lady Spencer, who replied that she must not join Mrs Fitzherbert in the box she had taken at the opera, but in the end the Duchess did. Everybody did. As usual the cartoonists were savage, and at Windsor the King and Queen must have wrung their hands, but at least the Prince was behaving better. He had been making himself ill with drink, now he was happy to spend his time at Brighton with his beloved and his plans for a gorgeous pavilion by the sea. He was rebuilding Carlton House too and it all cost a great deal. Not one of George III's sons seems to have grown up with the slightest idea of how money worked. They were not alone in this; the Duchess of Devonshire and her sister Henrietta Bessborough were just the same. Money was fairy gold to them. Of course they knew nothing about a day's work for a day's pay, but the idea of living within one's means was also totally alien to them. They doubtless sympathized with the Prince in his trouble with King and Parliament, but the public at large did not.

Trouble was inevitable. He had become a married man, with a married man's expenses, but without the additional funds that marriage to a suitable princess would have secured for him. And, since they had to have separate establishments, the expenses were actually greater. He bought Mrs Fitzherbert a house in St James's Square and gave her a lavish allowance. And the huge expense of Carlton House and his Pavilion at Brighton continued. He got deeper and deeper into debt. By 1787 it was so bad that the Prince got a Whig friend to put forward a motion in Parliament about his financial affairs. The House of Commons behaved impeccably. The name of Mrs Fitzherbert was never mentioned, but just the same they let it be understood that his marital status had a bearing on any increase in funding. Charles James Fox, his friend and adviser and the bright hope of the Whig party stood up and categorically denied that there had been a marriage. He thought he had the Prince's authority for this.

The Prince got his money but Mrs Fitzherbert was furious at the implication that she was his mistress. The Prince tried to persuade the Duchess of Devonshire's friend Charles Grey to clear Mrs Fitzherbert's name in the House. This was no easy task, and cautious Grey refused. In the end another friend, clever Richard Sheridan got up and made a vague statement about a lady whose honour had been unjustifiably attacked in the House. Mrs Fitzherbert was satisfied, Fox did not speak to the Prince for a year, and society, interestingly enough, stood by Mrs Fitzherbert. It was all very odd, said the Archbishop of Canterbury, she was more received than ever! 'I do not know what rules ladies govern themselves by,' he remarked. He might well have been baffled. The idyll continued. Lady Hester Stanhope told Dr Meryon: 'There are some people who are sweet by nature and who, even if they are not washed for a fortnight, are free from odour. Mrs Fitzherbert had a great deal of tact in concealing the Prince's faults. She would say: "Don't send your letter" . . . Or when he was talking of foolish things . . . "You are drunk tonight, do hold your tongue."'

Mrs Fitzherbert loved her Prince and bore with him. When he was drunk, George would bring equally drunken friends home to her London house and hunt her out, hidden under the sofa perhaps. One of the three dissolute Barrymore brothers, his good friends, once rode his horse up to her attic, where he left it, to be coaxed down next day by someone else. It was a mixed blessing, being almost Princess of Wales, but she made a good job of it.

Her hopes must have risen when the King went mad in the autumn of 1788. Suppose her 'husband' should become Regent, how different everything would be. Once again there was one of those tactful, civilized debates in the House of Commons in which her name was not mentioned but it was made clear that the Prince was not a man to be given unlimited powers. And just when a bill for at least a limited Regency went through, in the spring of 1789, the King recovered. It must have been a bitter blow. The Prince began drinking more. In Wales, Lady Eleanor Butler noted in June 1789 that 'the Prince was drunk at the Birthday. He would not behave decently . . . because Mrs Fitzherbert was not invited.' She would never be invited to any Royal occasion, and he knew it. His practical jokes got more savage, but he could be kind too. With the outbreak of the French Revolution in 1789 a stream of exiled Catholics landed in Brighton and he helped Mrs Fitzherbert in being good to them. But it all cost money.

He had nothing to do but spend money. His brothers served in the Army or Navy, whereas George was allowed only courtesy rank in the Army by his cautious father. When war with France broke out in 1793 he had to watch his brothers go off for active service while he designed expensive uniforms for his tame regiment, the Tenth Light Dragoons, at home. He and Mrs Fitzherbert had been together for eight years now, the strain of her half life was beginning to tell, and he was grumbling about her temper. She had probably not expected him to be totally faithful to her, few husbands were, but his liaison with Lady Jersey was too public for comfort. Frances, Countess of Jersey, was forty-one with grown up children, but she was still handsome with a sharp and witty tongue, and she was ambitious. Mild Maria Fitzherbert had small chance against her. But Lady Jersey was only the beginning of her troubles. The Prince's debts were now so bad that his only hope lay in a dynastic marriage. By the summer of 1794 he had decided that 'One damned German *frau* is as good as another', and his father was looking about for a suitable princess for him. Queen Charlotte's niece, beautiful Louisa of Mecklenburg Strelitz, had just been snapped up by Prussia, where she was to be much loved; they settled instead for George III's niece, Caroline of Brunswick. When the news broke, Mrs Fitzherbert behaved with dignity, saying nothing. If the Prince had hoped to keep up some kind of relationship with her, she soon let him see his mistake. He did at least arrange for her to keep her allowance of £3,000 a year, and she went quietly into a widow's retirement at Richmond, summering at Margate instead of Brighton. She said later that the whole royal family had been wonderfully good to her at this time, her friend the Duke of York acting as channel of communication.

Princess Caroline, the Prince's chosen wife, was still unmarried at twenty-six, a noisy, untidy girl who did not wash enough. Landing in England, she was met not by her future husband, but by Lady Jersey, who had been named her Lady of the Bedchamber. Caroline knew all about Lady Jersey. It was not an auspicious beginning. When he saw her, three days before the wedding, the Prince turned pale and asked for brandy. They were married on April 8th, 1795 and their daughter Princess Charlotte was born on January 7th, 1796, whereupon the Prince wrote to tell his wife that the marriage was finished. Even if disaster should befall the child he promised not to come near her again.

Having disposed of his new wife, who was later to say that she had never committed adultery except with him, the Prince of Wales hoped to get his old one back, and was soon wooing her all over again. He made and sent her a passionate will in her favour; he wrote her adoring letters; he threatened illness and death, and enlisted his family in the appeal. Lord Glenbervie later said in his *Journal* that even the Queen joined in. In the end Mrs Fitzherbert got her confessor to apply to the Pope himself for permission to resume the relationship and early in 1800 she actually received it. That June she invited her friends to a grand breakfast at her house in Tilney Street: 'To Meet his Royal Highness.' It was her wedding breakfast at last. Lady Jersey was there, hoping, but the Prince took no notice of her. It was the beginning of seven more happy, domestic years, during which Maria made friends with Mrs Creevey, wife of the great Whig gossip and diarist, and 'was confidential to a degree that almost frightens me,' wrote Mrs Creevey to her husband. It must have been a strange life. Mrs Creevey told her husband that Mrs Fitzherbert was always the Prince's best friend, doing what she could to prevent him from drinking too much.

They were both very fat now, devoted to each other and to a child Maria had adopted, little Mary Seymour, always known as Minny, the daughter of Lady Horatia, wife of the Prince's close friend Lord Hugh Seymour. Little Minny was born in 1798, but there was trouble between her parents, and her mother went abroad for her health soon after the birth, leaving the baby with her friend Mrs Fitzherbert. Returning in 1800, Lady Seymour let the child stay with her friend. She and her husband died soon afterwards and his family, the Hertfords, guardians of the other children, sued for the return of little Minny. Mrs Fitzherbert fought and finally won the custody suit with the Prince's backing. He was always devoted to Minny, who sat on his knee and christened him 'Prinny'. He gave parties for her, and promised her a dowry of £10,000 when she married. Mrs Fitzherbert was a remarkable woman. It is impossible to believe that if she had secretly had children of her own by the Prince she would not have contrived, somehow, to adopt them too and bring them up herself.

In the course of the long battle over Minny's custody, which finally went up to the House of Lords, the Prince had been thrown into company with the Marchioness of Hertford, wife of an immensely rich Tory peer, mother-in-law of Maria Fagniani. Here was another charming, ambitious grandmother like Lady Jersey, but one who cared about her reputation. She would be happy to be the Prince's friend, though probably not his mistress, so long as Mrs Fitzherbert acted as chaperone. Mrs Fitzherbert would not. When the Prince celebrated his birthday in Brighton in August 1807 little Minny was there, but Mrs Fitzherbert was indisposed. It was the beginning of the end. She loved him, and she suffered. She bore it all for a while, more easily in London than in Brighton where her house in the Steyne was awkwardly close to his Pavilion and his autocratic demands on her time. He was still trying to have it both ways, but she would have none of it. In 1809 she wrote to 'explain why I could not possibly accept the honour of your invitation to the Pavilion . . . The very great incivilities I have received these two years just because I obeyed your orders in going there was too visible to everyone present and too poignantly felt by me to admit of my putting myself in a situation of again being treated with such indignity . . . I have a claim upon you for protection. I feel I owe it to myself not to be insulted under your roof with impunity.' The Prince did not like being made to feel the cad he was and things merely got worse between them. And inevitably there were financial problems too, as she gently but firmly withdrew her life from his.

In the end, he was glad to let her go. His father's health had been visibly breaking up for some time and the golden prospect of a Regency was tantalizing him again. He wanted to enter on his kingdom with a free hand, not encumbered by a Roman Catholic lady with Whig connections. When he got his wish and became Regent in 1811 he celebrated with a summer fête at Carlton House. Maria was invited but told that she would not be sitting in her usual place at the royal table. She did not go, and it was probably small comfort to her that the Princess of Wales was not even invited. After that, when they met in public they ignored each other.

Mrs Fitzherbert refused to give up Brighton, where she was much loved, but lived quietly in London, bringing up Minny with high hopes of a great marriage for her. A young FitzClarence, son of the Duke of Clarence and his long-time mistress Mrs Jordan, fell in love with her, but neither Mrs Fitzherbert nor the Prince thought him good enough. There were other wooers, but Minny refused them all. In 1819 she met a gallant young officer called George Dawson who had had two horses killed under him at Waterloo. It seems to have been love at first sight and Mrs Fitzherbert was appalled. She fought it for five years and only gave way when Dawson's rich aunt Lady Caroline Damer made him her heir on the understanding that he change his plebeian name for hers. They married at last that summer, seem to have lived happily ever after, and were a great comfort to Mrs Fitzherbert in her declining years.

She lived until 1837, always a problem to the royal family. Many of them were very fond of her but the sticklers among them found her difficult to deal with. Was she the widow of the late King George IV or was she not? Tactful to the last, she died in March 1837 two months before her brother-in-law, William IV, thus removing the problem of precedence before the coronation of Queen Victoria. She was buried quietly but with great solemnity in Brighton where she had died. Her statue in St John the Baptist's Church there shows her wearing three wedding rings, one for each husband. And George IV was buried wearing her miniature as he had stipulated in that passionate, superceded will of his. He probably loved her more than he ever managed to love anyone, except himself, but if he had not sacrificed her for money, he would most certainly have done so for the throne.

* * *

Like Mrs Fitzherbert, Dorothy Jordan had money of her own when she met the Prince of Wales's younger brother, William Duke of Clarence, but she had earned it. In her case, there could be no question of a marriage, since she was an actress, still a career closely associated with prostitution. In fact, the status of actors in England had improved a little by the late eighteenth century, thanks to the influence of men like David Garrick in London and Tate Wilkinson in the provinces. The audience might not actually sit on the stage now, to pinch the actresses as they passed, but actors were still technically vagrants and actresses assumed to be prostitutes. Dorothy, who called herself Dora, was born into the profession in 1761. Her mother, Grace Phillips, was a Welsh clergyman's daughter who had gone on the stage, one of the few ways a talented woman could earn an independence outside domestic service or governessing. Clergymen's daughters were a civilizing influence in the seventeenth and eighteenth centuries: there were too many of them to find husbands on their own social level, so they often married down, taking their education with them. Grace Phillips went on the stage instead and met an equally stage-struck young Irish gentleman called Francis Bland. They probably went through some form of marriage, whereupon his family cut him off and they earned a precarious livelihood in the Dublin theatre. After the birth of at least two girls and two boys, his family persuaded him to have the marriage annulled, or admit it was no marriage, and make a 'respectable' one. He died four years later in 1778, leaving his first family nothing. His daughter Dora worked for a Dublin milliner for a while, then made her first stage appearance at the Crow Street Theatre, Dublin, at about eighteen, though she pretended to be younger. She was soon supporting her family. Richard Brinsley Sheridan's lively sister Betsy saw her in Dublin at this time and wrote a sealed prophecy: 'That little girl, if she lives, will be some time or other the first comic actress in England or Ireland.'

In 1781, Dora moved to the Smock Alley Theatre in Dublin where the manager, Richard Daly, was notorious for his fighting of duels and exertion of director's rights over his young actresses. She was soon pregnant by him and fled to England with her mother, breaking her contract. They arrived penniless, but Grace Phillips had worked with the actor manager Tate Wilkinson in the past and knew that he was now making a success of the northern circuit in England. Dubious at first, he agreed to give Dora a chance. She made her first appearance at Leeds in July 1782 as Calista in *The Fair Penitent* by Nicholas Rowe and her mother suggested she be allowed to come back and sing a ballad after dying tragically as Calista. 'I was not only charmed but the public also,' wrote Wilkinson. 'Managers do not always meet with jewels.' He offered his jewel fifteen shillings a week and she was grateful. It compared favourably with the £20 a year she might have earned as a governess.

By the time the company moved to York for race week Dora's pregnancy was beginning to show and Wilkinson coined the name Mrs Jordan to suit it. She repeated a Dublin success as Priscilla Tomboy in *The Romp*, a comic ballad opera in the vein of *The Beggar's Opera*, and added two new 'breeches' parts to her repertoire, Rutland in *The Earl of Essex* and Arionelli in *The Son-in-Law*. The public loved these parts because they gave it a rare chance to see the legs of its favourite actresses. A talent scout from Drury Lane saw her at this time and Wilkinson was glad he had signed her up for a three-year contract. All went well until Daly discovered where she was and threatened to sue for breach of contract if she did not come back and work out her engagement with him. Dora owed him about £250. Her career might have ended there and then in a debtors' prison had not a rich admirer stepped forward to pay the debt for her.

She took time off between performances on November 2nd and December 26th to bear a daughter, Frances, and spent the next three years practising her trade on the northern circuit. It was a hand-to-mouth life. If they did well in one town, they took the coach to the next one; if they did badly, they walked. If they had done really badly, they went hungry. Her success exposed her to furious jealousy from the company's other leading lady, but she learned to deal with this, as well as with that dangerous animal, the audience. She got boos as well as cheers, but soon discovered that comedy was her forte, her laugh infectious, and that the most recalcitrant houses could usually be won with a song and a wink. She was not strictly speaking beautiful and her voice was untrained, but she had stage magic and the gift of laughter.

In 1785 Dora's three years with Wilkinson were up and she moved to Drury Lane, at a salary of £4 a week. Tragedy was all the rage: Mrs Siddons had been queening it since her first triumph in 1773 and Dora was actually engaged as a second-string tragic actress for Siddons' nights off. She was originally announced as making her first appearance in a tragic role, but there was a tradition that an actress had the right to choose her first play. She asked for *The Country Girl*, a rewrite by Garrick of Wycherley's *Country Wife*, which had a perfect comic part for her in Peggy, another romp, who went into breeches in the last act. She chose well. London was beginning to tire of Mrs Siddons' tragic frenzy and grand respectability. Dora was unknown, the first night's was a small audience, but it loved her. Word got around. Her second appearance as the country girl was a crowded triumph, and at her third the Prince of Wales appeared in a box. She was launched. From then on her life was London in the winter and tours, mainly on Tate Wilkinson's northern circuit, in the summer. Her salary increased, but so did her expenses. She had tried to get a brother launched in the Drury Lane Theatre, but he did not have her talent. She was the wage earner for the whole family, and not surprisingly got a name for driving a hard bargain.

Soon she had other commitments. Richard Ford was the son of one of the three owners of the Drury Lane Theatre. He was a charming young barrister with his way still to make in the world and when he and Dora fell in love he gave her a solemn promise of marriage – later. For the moment, he was entirely dependent on his father, who had other plans for him. He was to go into Parliament. Dora was twenty-five now, supporting herself and her family. She was an actress, which was bad enough, and had an unexplained child, which was worse. She had seen enough of the world to know what a handicap an actress wife with an illegitimate child would be to Ford's political hopes. Why did she believe him? Was she too much in love to care, or was her longing for respectability so strong that she grasped even at its shadow?

She set up house with Ford in Bloomsbury, and had a daughter, Dorothea Maria, in August 1787 during the Edinburgh season. A son died at birth in 1788 and another daughter, Lucy Hester, was born in 1789. Dora called herself Mrs Ford in private life now, and her 'husband' introduced her as his wife to some but not all of his friends. The newspapers enjoyed it immensely, punning on her two names, Ford and Jordan. And she went on earning her own and her growing family's living. She was an immense success by now, rival queen of the stage to Mrs Siddons, but the two of them never got on. Mrs Siddons gave readings to the royal children at Windsor, though she was never allowed to sit down to do so. Mrs Siddons, supporting idle Mr Siddons and their children, made great capital of her respectable married state, which may have helped push Dora into becoming 'Mrs Ford' in the first place.

In comedy, Dora reigned supreme. She had a tremendous success in 1790 as Little Pickle in a farce called *The Spoil'd Child*, which she and Ford may have written together. The part of the horrible little prankster was perfect for her and at one point she came on as a sailor boy and brought the house down with a sentimental ballad, 'What girl but loves the merry tar?' When the King's third son, the Duke of Clarence, semi-retired from the Navy, appeared in a box she doubtless sang it for him.

William Duke of Clarence was twenty-five in 1790. He had always had an eye for a pretty girl and his early career in the Navy had been punctuated by occasions when he fell in love with an available young lady and his royal father had to move him quickly on. There had been a great many other women, too. Like his friend Nelson, he went for 'dollies' in every port, and he suffered bouts of the pox from Hanover tarts when his father sent him there for a miserable couple of years. His anomalous position probably made it impossible for him ever to succeed in the Navy, but he was a muddle-headed fellow, without the gifts that made Nelson great, and by 1790 he had totally lost the confidence of his superiors by flagrant disobedience of orders. Back in England in disgrace, he had compounded the offence by siding with his brothers over the regency crisis, and had more or less blackmailed the King into giving him his dukedom by proposing to stand for the House of Commons. He was a bluff, ignorant, hard-swearing sailor, and he had learned to dislike foreigners in Hanover, so the kind of dynastic marriage his father might have had in mind for him was out of the question.

William had a country house at Richmond, where he shocked the neighbours by installing a prostitute called Polly Finch. The Fords had a house there too in the summer, convenient for her appearances at the Richmond Theatre, and William doubtless saw her perform there as well as in London, but when she first crossed his path he was pursuing Sheridan's wife who had been Elizabeth Linley, a brilliant young singer. The Sheridans' had been a love match, but now her successful husband was pursuing Henrietta Duncannon and Elizabeth thought seriously about the young Duke's proposition. She told a friend that she would probably have run away with him if he had not been so much younger, and then 'have hung myself a week afterwards'.

She very sensibly turned the young Duke down and he switched his attention instantly to 'Little Pickle'. She entranced him, as she did everyone. There was something so likeable about her comedy, it comes out in everybody's comments on her. Of course he could not marry her, but by the spring of 1791 he was offering everything else in the form of a legal settlement. If Dora hoped that this would bring Ford to the point of an honourable proposal, she was disappointed. The stress of it all made her ill and she was glad to accept an invitation from her old friend Tate Wilkinson for a summer season at York. But country morals were stricter than those in town, and the gossip columns were fuller than ever of jokes about Jordan and Clarence and Ford. As usual, Ford had accompanied her on the tour, and the ladies of York made no bones about referring to her as his mistress. Worse still, they thought *The Country Girl* 'rude and vulgar'. There was only a moderate house for it and her listless appearance in *As You Like It* did not improve matters. Ford was not much support, there was a muddle about her engagement at Edinburgh, she lost her head and behaved badly, the tour was a disaster.

Back on the London stage in her favourite part of Little Pickle, she read the jokes about private fords and the open sea and thought about the future. She had three illegitimate daughters to support now and Ford had proved himself a broken reed. She stopped calling herself Mrs Ford and listened to the Duke of Clarence's proposals. He was younger than her, which was flattering, and he was prepared to be good to her children, which was always the main point with her. She moved into his Richmond house that autumn and was soon busy decorating his apartments in St James's Palace in a flamboyant style that suited her. King George summed up their arrangements: 'Hey, hey; — what's this, what's this, what's this?' He was famous for repeating himself. 'You keep an actress . . . How much do you give her, eh? A thousand? A thousand? Too much, too much! Five hundred quite enough, quite enough.' George III was always frugal.

Dora did her best to make firm financial arrangements for herself and her family. Accepting an allowance from the Duke, she made generous settlements on her three daughters, who were to live with her sister Hester, supported, of course, by Dora. She also kept up her London house. When she moved in with William, the newspaper comments were so savage that they made her ill. She missed a performance as a result and was then reduced to writing to *The Times* to defend herself against accusations of malingering and being mean to her children. She was booed when she returned to the stage but bravely went forward to speak to the house. She told them that she had never missed a performance unless it was due to ill-health and therefore felt herself entitled to public protection. It worked. The stage gossip James Boaden said it was the high point of the evening.

That crisis passed, Dora and her William settled down to twenty happy, domestic years. He was not faithful to her, of course, but nor was he flagrantly unfaithful like his eldest brother. And her status as star actress probably made her position as royal mistress easier. Anyway they were both domestic creatures who liked their home comforts and raising their ten children. She went right on working, in London in the winter and with provincial tours in the summer, and wrote him loving family letters when she was away, enclosing her earnings as they came in. Their finances got inextricably mixed up and the columnists remarked that it was hard to tell 'if he keeps her or she keeps him.' She was a comfort and support to him through the doldrums of his professional career, when he had to watch his old friend Nelson go from glory to glory while he remained on shore, with only token promotion. His father gave him a pleasant consolation prize when he made him Ranger of Bushy Park in 1797 and they moved their growing family from Richmond to the elegant comforts of Bushy House.

Dora's first brood of children were growing up by now. The oldest, Fanny, daughter of the unreliable Richard Daly, was twenty-one in 1803 and Dora established her and her two Ford sisters in a house in

Golden Square. The Ford girls had some support from their father until he died young in 1806, but Fanny was entirely on Dora's hands and when she married a young civil servant called Thomas Alsop in 1807 they became a new drain on her resources. But her stage success continued; her earnings were immense; if she worried she must have shrugged it off. Her eldest son George FitzClarence joined the army as a boy and was sent on active service to Spain, at sixteen, in 1808. He arrived just in time for Moore's bloody retreat on Corunna and distinguished himself. Dora had written him some good advice about not referring to his father as 'papa' but as 'my father' or maybe better still 'The Duke'. On leave in Brighton, under the wing of his approving uncle the Prince of Wales, he made friends with Mrs Fitzherbert and fell in love with her Minny.

Dora's last child, Amelia, was born in 1807, and about then the Duke asked her to stop acting in London, though she went on with her exhausting provincial tours, as far afield as Dublin, mainly to provide for her three oldest daughters. The older Ford girl, Dodee, had married a friend of Fanny's husband. Frederick March was another young man on the make, the illegitimate son of Lord Henry Fitzgerald. This marriage was going to be expensive for Dora too. She wrote to a friend from Bath one summer to say that she hoped to net eight or nine hundred pounds between there and Bristol, and went on to describe a painful little incident in a fashionable library where she had gone to read the papers: 'I . . . was entertained by some ladies with a most *pathetic* description of the parting between me and the Duke. My very dress was described, and the *whole conversation accurately repeated*! Unfortunately for the *party*, a lady came in, who immediately addressed me by *name*, which threw them into the most ridiculous and . . . unpleasant embarrassment imaginable.'

Dora was fifty in 1811 and getting stout, but she still put on her breeches for Little Pickle and the audiences still loved her, though she was getting reproving letters from the expanding sect of Methodists. She wrote to the Duke from Manchester about a letter telling her that, 'God *had allowed* me to make use of magic for a certain time, and . . . was only *watching* for a good *opportunity* to send me to the *gulph* of Hell. What an idea . . . of the mercy and justice of a great Being!' In another letter she wrote that, 'I feel the fatigue and absence from you all more every time and if I can get myself out of debt the next excursion, I will give it up, and the only regret I shall feel will be at the idea of being . . . an additional burden to you – for it is a melancholy truth that, notwithstanding your liberal allowance, I shall be poorer on the day I quit my profession than the day on which I entered it.' She had given dowries of £10,000 each to her three eldest daughters, but this poverty after such a long and brilliant career is still a surprise. Association with the sons of George III was expensive.

Was she wise to write to him so frankly? She was fifty, he was in his robust late forties, and he was beginning to think ambitious thoughts. His career had foundered; he was in debt; his brother was Prince Regent now; the Royal Marriage Act might no longer be inviolable. And there was something else. He was George III's third son, but the Duke of York was married and childless. The Regent's daughter Princess Charlotte would no doubt marry and produce an heir to the British throne, but as a woman she could not succeed in Hanover. William was determined to outlive his two older brothers. He meant to be King of Hanover; and he would need a legitimate heir.

With these ideas in mind he went, in June 1811, to Carlton House for the Prince Regent's fête in honour of the exiled Bourbon princes. Mrs Fitzherbert had refused to come, Mrs Jordan had not been invited. Here the Duke met a delightful young lady called Catherine Tylney-Long who was said to be worth £40,000 a year. She charmed him, and he was sure he had charmed her, splendid as he was in his Admiral's uniform with decorations. He said nothing about the meeting to Dora, who went off on a tour of the north and wrote him the usual cheerful letters. She told him about meeting the great singer, Catalini, and promised to make no engagements for the autumn without consulting him first.

She wrote to him again from Cheltenham where the tour ended: '*Money, money, cruel money*; since my first setting out in the world . . . I have spun *fairly and honestly* out of my own brains above £100,000, and still this cruel *pelf* robs me of even comfort and happiness . . . We have nothing to do with our *own fate*. I may fairly say what a strange one mine has been and *is likely to be*!'

She was a true prophet. This letter crossed with one from the Duke asking her to meet him at Maidenhead to discuss the terms of a separation. It was the brutal end to their affair. She was in hysterics all that day but, professional as always, went on in *The Devil to Pay* that night. At one point she was supposed to burst into uncontrollable laughter, fell into helpless tears instead. But she met him at Maidenhead and behaved, he said, like an angel. He had said the same thing about her during the months before they began living together.

There was not much else she could do. Her position was hopeless, and recriminations might alienate the Duke from her beloved children, of whom the eldest was now seventeen and the youngest four. She did one very wise thing. She refused to budge from Bushy House until a settlement had been agreed. He was away, busy courting Miss Tylney-Long, so she had the house and her troubles to herself, and with not much support. Working mistresses have little time for making friends. The papers attacked the Duke savagely when they got wind of the separation but she would not say a word against him. At first she tried to spare her children the facts of the case, with the result that fourteen year old Henry first heard about it when he was shown a newspaper report by friends at the Royal Military College. He sat down and wrote a furious letter to his older brother George: 'If this be true I will never more go home except once to see my Dear Mother whom I consider as a Most Injured Woman . . . I am nearly mad I think I shall run away home.' George saved this letter, and the writer Claire Tomalin was much later to find it among his papers. Dora's oldest daughter Sophy on the other hand took her father's side. She was sixteen and already going into society with him, encouraged by her mother who urged the Duke to let Sophy act as hostess at his dinner parties at which she herself, fallen woman and actress, could not appear. While Dora fought it out at Bushy, Sophy was at Margate with her father, watching him court Miss Tylney-Long.

The settlement his men of business finally came up with seemed generous enough. Dora was to have a total of £4,400 a year from the Duke, but some of this was for the maintenance of the four youngest children, who were to live with her until they were thirteen, though the boys, of course, would go away to school. A monstrous proviso stipulated that she would lose custody of the children (and therefore their maintenance) if she returned to the stage. And the agreement took no account of the burden of debt, built up while she was living with the Duke, that she had still not managed to clear. Not surprisingly, no money came through for a long time. The Duke was fathoms deep in debt. Dora needed to find a house, but had nothing to buy it with. She even appealed to the Duke's brothers for help, but they took no notice. In the end she managed to find a house in Cadogan Place and settled there with the children early in 1812.

There were other problems to plague her. Her daughter Fanny's marriage had broken down and she and her husband were disastrously in debt. Dora pulled strings to arrange a job for him in India and the

Duke actually helped get his passage there. But in the course of that sad autumn she must have realized that she had lost William as friend as well as lover. She still wrote to him because she had to, but the tone of her letters changed. She called him 'Your Royal Highness' now, and 'Sir'. Was he too stupid to notice, or too callous to care? Very likely he simply did not read the letters, leaving her in the ruthless hands of his men of business, who thought only of protecting the royal name.

Meanwhile the press continued to hound her. The children missed the country delights and comfortable living of Bushy. And Dora, granted the way the Duke had treated her, must have worried increasingly that out of sight might well prove out of mind in their case too, so far as their volatile father was concerned. She had always known that all their hopes for the future lay with him. Better an acknowledged royal bastard than one cast off. At the same time she was plagued with the expense of her two older daughters' unlucky marriages. By the summer of 1812 she had decided that the only way out was to let the children return to their father and go back on the stage herself. It meant losing part of her allowance, but that was nothing compared to losing the children. She did it undoubtedly because she thought it best for them and in this at least their futures proved her right.

Dora managed to do this without affronting the Duke. He had been turned down by Miss Tylney-Long and was now in hot pursuit of other heiresses, and made no objection to her seeing and writing to her children, even though she planned to return to the stage. Young George was invited to Windsor for the first time that August for the celebration of the Duke's birthday which he had always celebrated with Dora. 'I give you joy of this day,' she wrote to George. 'I hope your being at Windsor will be the means of introducing you to your *amiable grand mama* . . . She can scarcely leave you out on this day.' Apparently Queen Charlotte could. Dora's next letter begins: 'The old b——h conduct was just what I expected.' She had started talking straight to George and it must have done her good, though it may have been a strain for him.

Dora was fifty-one in 1812, returning to the stage after a traumatic year of absence. Her heart must have been heavy as she turned down an unsatisfactory offer from the new management at Drury Lane and decided on an autumn tour instead. She was no longer young, she was stout, and off-stage she was sad, but she could still entrance an audience. A young actor, William Macready, saw her at Leicester that autumn and wrote: 'With a spirit of fun that would have outlaughed Puck himself, there was a discrimination, an identity with her character, an artistic arrangement of the scene, that made all appear spontaneous and accidental, though elaborated with the greatest care . . . Who that heard that laugh could ever forget it? . . . So rich, so apparently irrepressible, so deliciously self-enjoying, as to be at all times irresistible.' It is the tribute of one professional to another, and it is also a consoling reminder that while she was at work, at least, Dora was happily absorbed.

But there were warning signs. Managers began to suggest she play older characters, but she refused. So long as the audience wanted her as Little Pickle, Little Pickle she would remain, stout or not. When she opened at Covent Garden in February 1813 it was to a packed and enthusiastic house. But next day her old enemy *The Times* printed a vicious attack on her. Speaking of 'this degraded woman' it referred to 'those who should never abandon her to poverty' and to her children 'strangely allowed to move among the honourable people of England.' The evangelical shadows were beginning to fall, but *The Times* had misjudged its market, she got an ovation from her public next day. She was safely back at the work she loved. Leigh Hunt called her 'the first living actress in comedy' and Byron praised her Miss Hoyden. Refusing to dwindle into Juliet's nurse, she appeared generously in benefits for other actresses, and began to hope that she would be able to retire, solvent, in the spring of 1815. Her sons George and Henry had distinguished themselves in the fighting that led up to the fall of France in 1814 and Sophy was being squired by the young Duke of Devonshire. But Fanny, left behind when her husband went to India, was running up debts and writing unpleasant and threatening letters to the Duke, who was himself in such dire financial straits that he threatened to sell up Bushy and retire to be a public problem at St James's. He was also, amazingly, collecting pictures of Mrs Jordan. It makes one a little sick.

Dora did retire in 1815, but the circumstances were not at all as she had planned. Her voracious family had made it impossible for her to save as she hoped. Money was tight, and, much worse, George and Henry had fallen foul of the military establishment and been shipped off to India in unjustified disgrace. Fanny was in financial difficulties again and Dora realized that by the time she had dealt with this she would have to go abroad to economize. Her favourite son-in-law Frederick March was handling this business for her. In fact, she had given him too much authority and he was running up debts in her name. She came back from her final engagement at Margate in August 1815 to learn that he had plunged her into disaster. All her life she had been haunted by fear of the debtors' prison. She panicked and consulted the Duke's man of business, who encouraged her to go abroad, letting her think he would sort things out for her. She went, expecting to be summoned back in a week or so. It was a terrible mistake. The Duke's man cared only about the Duke's reputation. This time, out of sight was indeed out of mind. Dora waited in vain for the letter he had promised, telling her that her affairs had been settled and it was safe to return. Living frugally, first in Boulogne, then outside Paris, she was cheered for a while by visits from her son Frederick, there with the army of occupation, and wrote to her fourteen-year-old Adolphus that 'dear Frederick is all kindness and attention to me.' Later in this letter she wrote: 'As for money, my dear Boy, what ever I can spare you can have . . .' Her family were still battening on her, apparently unaware of her wretched circumstances. She was living in hiding, calling herself Mrs James and literally worrying herself to death, waiting for the letter that never came. She died on July 5th, 1816. Her belongings were sold to pay the funeral expenses and she left an estate of £300. But eight of her children by the Duke made marriages that would have delighted her. Did she recognize that vanishing from their lives was the kindest thing she could do for them?

The Duke became King William IV in 1830. His marriage to Adelaide of Saxe-Meiningen was successful in everything but children, but she was a kind step-mother to the young FitzClarences. As for the new King, one of the first things he did was to commission the fashionable sculptor Francis Chantrey to make him a full-size sculpture of a young Dora Jordan with two of her children. It was to be a problem to his niece Victoria.

7
Love for Sale

MRS FITZHERBERT married money, Mrs Jordan earned it. For thousands of women there was little alternative to selling themselves. Cities seethed with available girls, their prices ranging from a penny for a quick toss against a wall to half a crown for a 'flying leap' or five shillings for a night's lodging with a bottle of wine on the side. At the other end of the scale were the Cyprians, the lucky few who made a name for themselves and lived in ostentatious luxury, spending maybe £3,000 a year on their clothes, their carriages, and their snug little Mayfair houses. They formed their own society with their own balls and their own boxes in the theatre, where they shared the attention of the gentlemen with the ladies of quality in the boxes around them. It was splendid while it lasted, but old age and pregnancy were twin threats. Sensibly distrusting the men's easily available 'armour', condoms made of sheep gut or even less reliable linen, knowledgeable women used sponges as protection. This useful if not infallible device seems to have been unknown among upper-class ladies. As for old age, only early death can save one from that. A few careful managers contrived to save some of their earnings and start businesses, often brothels. A few made lucky marriages, the majority sank without trace.

Martha Ray seemed lucky. Plucked out of the gutter in her teens and educated to be his mistress by the much older Earl of Sandwich, she had nine children by him, three of whom lived. Her beautiful soprano voice was the centrepiece of his musical evenings, but the guests knew better than to speak to her. He kept her in luxury but made no financial settlement on her or her children, so that she was entirely dependent on him. Covent Garden Opera House once offered her £3,000 and a benefit performance if she would do a season with them, but she did not dare tell Lord Sandwich. After fifteen years of this curious life, Sandwich brought home a charming young officer called James Hackman and she fell in love with him. They may have meant to behave, but he was snowed up on a visit to Sandwich's country house, Hinchingbrook, and the result was inevitable. He wanted her to marry him; she was afraid for her children's future. In the end, maddened by jealousy, he shot her as she came out of the Opera House one evening, then tried to kill himself. He failed and was hanged for her murder. Desolate, and publicly mocked, Sandwich brought up Martha's children as she would have wished.

It was not always such a hazardous profession; poverty rather than murder was the main risk. Harriette Wilson was an outstanding courtesan, flourishing in the early years of the nineteenth century, of whom we know a great deal because when she fell on hard times later in life, she had the ingenious idea of writing her *Memoirs*. She was helped and encouraged in this by the disreputable publisher, John Joseph Stockdale, who published her scandalous reminiscences by instalments, letting it be known that gentlemen who wished to be left out could pay £200 upwards for the privilege. It was the mid eighteen-twenties by now and the moral climate had changed. Young men who had adored Harriette in the riotous early years of the century were middle aged, with families and careers to consider. Many of her victims paid up and were duly passed over; others paid the price. 'Publish and be damned,' the Duke of Wellington is supposed to have said, and it sounds like him. He certainly refused to pay. Harriette painted a vivid picture of him, back on a brief visit from the Peninsular War, standing under her window in the pouring rain, while her current keeper the Marquess of Lorne pretended to be her house-keeper and shouted down at him to go away. It made a good story, but Elizabeth Longford points out that Wellington never did come back on a brief visit from the Peninsula. He told his friend Mrs Arbuthnot that the story was untrue, while admitting that he had associated with Harriette Wilson earlier in his life, and sent her money when she needed it.

Her treatment of Wellington illustrates the basic problem about Harriette Wilson's immensely entertaining *Memoirs*. She wrote them in haste, for money, years after the events described, and for serial publication, with all the pressures that implies. Stockdale and her sinister husband William Henry Rochford very likely helped her. Either she had total recall, or they between them had a remarkable gift for dialogue. The *Memoirs* have the gripping immediacy of a play by Sheridan, and there is an unmistakable sharp flavour to them. That it is Harriette's own voice we are hearing is confirmed by letters she wrote to Byron, which are witty and entertaining in just the same vein. 'Throw away your pen, my love, and take a little calomel,' she wrote to him about *Don Juan*. And the fact that she remained on good terms with Byron and corresponded with the novelist Bulwer Lytton later in life tells us a good deal about her intelligence too. One cannot help liking Harriette, but one must not necessarily believe every word she says. She said herself that she scorned dates, and she did not care much about titles either, calling Wellington and Argyll dukes long before they achieved that rank.

But the basic facts of her story were confirmed as a result of one of her mistakes. In the *Memoirs* she gave a vivid description of the death of her friend and rival Julia Johnstone, and Julia, still very much alive, came out of retirement with a volume of *True Confessions*, which confirms the main lines of Harriette's story, while quarrelling with the details. Written in haste, it did not achieve anything like the success of Harriette's *Memoirs*.

Harriette was not Wilson at all. She was born in 1786, daughter of a Swiss shopkeeper called Dubochet who lived precariously with his handsome, promiscuous wife and their fifteen children in a tiny house in Mayfair. Lord Craven was a neighbour. Harriette begins her *Memoirs* with spirit: 'I shall not say why and how I became, at the age of fifteen, the mistress of the Earl of Craven.' She does not say that he was her first keeper; he was most certainly not to be her last. He took her to Brighton and bored her with descriptions of his campaigns, but she resisted the advances of charming young Frederick Lamb at first, because he had no money. 'What the Devil can you possibly have to say against my son Fred?' asked Lord Melbourne (who was probably not Fred's father), buttonholing her on the Steyne. But Craven heard about Fred, refused (perhaps rightly) to believe she was innocent and turned her away. She joined Fred, who was with his regiment in Hull, was received rapturously, but soon decided he was a cold-blooded, selfish fellow, spending much more on himself than on her.

She had already written to proposition the Prince of Wales, but been dissatisfied with his answer, and failed to pursue the matter. Now she wrote to the Marquis of Lorne, suggesting a meeting: 'I will not say in what particular year of his life the Duke of Argyll [then Marquis of Lorne] succeeded with me. Ladies scorn dates!' A lively-minded woman, she educated herself through her lovers. Fred might have bored her with his meanness, but he taught her to love Shakespeare. She had made friends with Julia Johnstone by now and she and Julia, with Harriette's sister Fanny, shared an opera box and were known as the Three Graces. Two of Harriette's sisters, May and Sophia, were also professionals, but Sophia retired on marrying Lord Berwick while still in her teens. Sir Walter Scott said that Harriette used to amuse herself by spitting on her respectable sister's head from the box above her at the opera. This was a splendid hunting ground, though Harriette did not enjoy watching her own current protector in another lady's box. She met Beau Brummell there. They became good friends and it is she who quotes him as advising, 'No perfumes, but very fine linen, plenty of it, and country washing.'

Harriette tells us that the great love of her life was John Eric Ponsonby, who became Lord Ponsonby on the death of his father soon after they became lovers. She refers to him as Lord Ponsonby throughout and he is not to be confused with William Ponsonby, Henrietta Bessborough's son, who is savagely mocked in her *Memoirs* as her sister Fanny's boorish wooer. Harriette paints a romantic picture of how she fell in love with John Ponsonby's handsome dark-haired figure before she knew who he was. Characteristically she soon managed to find out and catch his attention. A passionate three-year affair followed, though she speaks of qualms about his young wife, Frances, one of Lady Jersey's daughters. Very much younger than her husband, Frances was beautiful but very deaf after nearly dying of scarlet fever; no companion for a man, he told Harriette, as husbands will. But in the end he gave Harriette up, suddenly, overnight, saying he had promised his wife he would do so. He kept his promise and presumably also refused to pay up when the *Memoirs* were being touted. Later, according to Charles Greville's *Memoirs*, she tried to blackmail Ponsonby over some letters of Lady Conyngham's that she had got hold of when they were lovers. By then, Lady Conyngham was the powerful mistress of George IV, and, says Greville, Ponsonby was hurriedly packed off as Ambassador to Buenos Aires, the start of a successful diplomatic career.

At the time, Harriette refused to believe he really meant to give her up. She had hysterics, got ill, wrote him a desperate letter and received a curt answer. She haunted his house at night, caught scarlet fever and nearly died. She lost her looks for a while and paints, for her, an unusually sympathetic picture of Wellington worrying about her and offering her money: '"Good God! how thin you are grown! . . . There is no humbug about you; and, when you cry, you are sorry, I believe. I have thought of you very often in Spain . . .".' She says he wrote her a cheque then and there. Argyll, too, was kind to her at this low point of her career; she was outraged when she discovered that he was also keeping her sister Amy. This seems to have stimulated her into recovery, and she was soon enjoying her sister Sophia's adventures, and flirting with a lover of Julia's. They seem to have had a very good time together, these women, sharing a remarkable solidarity most of the time.

Frederick Lamb was in the diplomatic service now, and when he came back from a posting in Sicily he wanted to take up their old affair. Harriette resisted and he tried force, but she pulled his hair so hard that he let her go. He sensibly forestalled her by telling this story against himself next day. Amy was now pregnant by Argyll and full of hopes of bearing him a legitimate heir, a possibility under Scottish law, but Argyll eluded her, hastily marrying someone else.

Harriette reports making one of her approaches to Lord Granville Leveson Gower at the time when he was breaking hearts in London, suggesting that he meet her in Marylebone Fields on Sunday morning, but when he appeared, she found his looks disappointing. 'This must be Leinster's Apollo,' she thought, as he 'spoke, and smiled, and blushed, and bowed.' It was a hot day; she walked him briskly to the top of Primrose Hill and back to her house, by which time he was wiping sweat from his brow and begging to be let in if only to sit down. She dismissed him summarily and retired to her room to read Lady Mary Wortley Montague. It makes a satisfactory story, and one can only hope there is some truth in it, for the sake of all those 'fair Scavonians' whose hearts he had broken. Presumably he too refused to pay Stockdale later on. One gets the impression that all the Devonshire House set were equally firm. Harriette is habitually savage about Hartington, the young, deaf Duke of Devonshire.

The Duke of Leinster (husband of Sarah Napier's aunt Emily) was keeping Harriette at this time, but she was perhaps beginning to think about the future. When young Lord Worcester, son of Granville Leveson Gower's older sister Lady Beaufort, fell passionately in love with her, she played him expertly and he was soon talking of a runaway match at Gretna Green. They had a halcyon time in Brighton together before his anxious parents packed him off to serve in Spain as aide-de-camp to Wellington. They parted swearing eternal love, and Lady Bessborough reports in a letter to Granville

Leveson Gower of September 24th, 1813, that Harriette is 'living at Ryde . . . she passes for the most Virtuous Woman . . . She is waiting for Lord W's coming of age when he is to return and marry her. She shew'd some of his letters, all ending yr affen Husband.'

But the Isle of Wight was dull. Harriette was soon back in London, being pursued by a rich sugar baker called Meyler, who had previously been one of Lady Beaufort's own train, which may have added to his charm for Harriette. Besides, she heard that Worcester had a lady in Spain. She hoped for an annuity from his family, but in the end got only a sum of £1,200 for handing over his letters promising marriage. The clouds were gathering. Meyler was not an easy man; Prince Esterhazy asked her to act as procuress for him; her sister Fanny died in tragic circumstances. Quarrelling more and more, she and Meyler went to Paris, either in 1814 or after Waterloo, and at about this time a chance pickup brought William Henry Rochford into her life. He reminded her, she says, of Ponsonby, and from now on she kept him, not he her.

She had had a good time, while it lasted. Her *Memoirs* are full of the gusto that must have entranced her lovers. Sir Walter Scott says that she was not beautiful but 'a smart, saucy girl with manners like a wild schoolboy.' She liked to outride and out-talk her men, black curls tossing in the wind. Perhaps she outsexed them too. 'I have the *diable au corps*,' she confessed, explaining her affair with Meyler. She had tried her hand at a play, which was turned down probably unread by John Murray; she wrote three novels after the success of the *Memoirs*, but they did not take. The publisher Stockdale was bankrupted by libel actions, Harriette just vanished.

* * *

Another woman who capitalized on her relations with the great was Mary Anne Clarke. Born some time in the 1770s in a slum off Chancery Lane, she married a stonemason and worked her way up to become mistress of Frederick, Duke of York. The King's second son had secured himself an income of £40,000 a year by marrying Princess Frederica of Prussia in 1791, but she had failed to produce a child and they had soon gone their separate ways. She settled contentedly as an English country lady, with good works and dogs at their country house Oatlands Park near Weybridge, and was loved and called Lady Bountiful by the neighbours. He stayed in London with a succession of mistresses and a career in the army. Despite leading two unsuccessful campaigns in the Netherlands he was Commander-in-Chief when he met Mary Anne in the early 1800s. She was brilliant, witty and bold like Harriette Wilson, and more beautiful. The Duke was enthralled and set her up in a house in Gloucester Place, and also one at Weybridge so that he could visit her when weekending with his wife. He gave her only £1,000 a year to support all this. George III would have thought it twice too much, but it was not nearly enough for the style of living she expected. She supplemented it by accepting bribes from people anxious to obtain advancement in the army for themselves or their relations. Worse still, when the Duke tired of her and moved on to a Mrs Cary in Fulham, Mary Anne sold her story to the Opposition Whigs. A question was asked in Parliament in 1809 and a public enquiry followed. It was a field day for the press and hideously embarrassing for the royal family. Mary Anne enjoyed the limelight despite being caught in lie after lie, but the Duke's doting letters to her were read aloud and children in the streets were tossing 'Duke or Darling' instead of 'Heads or Tails'. In the end, the Duke was cleared by a majority of eighty-two in the House, but felt compelled to resign his military post. In fact he had been doing a good job for the army; he was reappointed two years later and publicly thanked by the Duke of Wellington in 1814. Mary Anne tried to make more capital out of the affair by publishing a book called *The Rival Princes* in which she claimed that the accusations against the Duke of York had been backed by his younger brother the Duke of Kent, who wanted to be Commander-in-Chief himself. There may have been some truth in this but the book had nothing like the success of Harriette Wilson's later *Memoirs*.

* * *

Amy Lyon was to be much more successful than either Harriette Wilson or Mary Anne Clarke. She was born of peasant stock, probably in 1765, in Cheshire, and there are all kinds of stories about the vicissitudes by which the ravishingly beautiful country girl turned into Emma Lyon, mistress of Sir Harry Fetherstonehaugh of Uppark in Sussex. Tradition says that she danced naked on his dining table for the entertainment of his friends, presumably after his mother had gone to bed. It did not last. She had recognized her power over men, but not its limits. When she became pregnant at sixteen, Fetherstonehaugh was not convinced that the child was his. He gave her her fare home and abandoned her. It could have been the end of her story, but she was lucky, she had a grandmother in Wales to go home to and a friend in London to advise her. She had little Emma in the country while negotiating her future with the friend, who may already have been her lover.

He was the Honourable Charles Greville, impecunious younger son of the Earl of Warwick, older cousin of the diarist. His father had left him a mere £100 and he lived on £500 a year left him by his mother. A Member of Parliament, he had hopes of office under the Whigs, which vanished when they went into the wilderness in 1784. He was much more interested in his collection of artistic rarities, a passion he shared with a rich uncle, his mother's brother Sir William Hamilton, British Ambassador in Naples. Greville lived a comfortable bachelor life in London, hoping for a rich wife, but not working at it very hard, and acting as agent for his uncle.

Luckily for her, Emma could write, though her spelling was erratic. 'I am almost distracktid,' she wrote Greville. 'I have never hard from Sir H and he is not at Lechster now . . . What shall I dow, good God what shall I dow . . . Oh G . . . that I was in your posesion, as I was in Sir H what a hapy girl I would have been . . . O dear Grevell write to me. Write to me G.' She signed this letter Emily Hart and enclosed her certificate of baptism; they were getting down to business.

He added her to his collection, making his careful terms clear. He would pay for little Emma to be fostered in Wales, and set Emma herself up in a house in Edgware Row, off Paddington Green, with her own mother as housekeeper and chaperone. Emma must curb her wilful temper, live frugally on £20 a year, keep accounts and improve herself. She did all this, and Greville's friend George Romney painted her over and over again. She was his ideal of beauty, with a classic profile and abundant chestnut curls. It was safety for her, safe sex for Greville and an idyll while it lasted.

But Greville was a poor man, with expensive tastes. He had hopes of being his uncle's heir. Sir William had married Catherine Barlow for her £8,000 a year and they had had twenty years of happy marriage when she died childless in 1782. Sir William brought the embalmed body home from Naples for burial next year and took an instant fancy to Emma, commissioning his old friend Sir Joshua Reynolds to paint her portrait. He never could resist a pretty girl, as his wife had known to her cost. When Hamilton appeared at court, the King asked if he meant to marry again, which made Greville anxious. A new wife might well produce an heir. Brooding about a rich

1. The marriage of George III and Charlotte of Mecklenburg Strelitz, by Reynolds.
She was not on the first shortlist of possible brides

2. The Duke and Duchess of Devonshire on parade.
They did not often appear together in public

3. Queen Charlotte and her family by West. The girls had to stay at home while the boys got away

4. The Duchess of Devonshire with her daughter Georgiana, by Etty.
The Prince of Wales caused a crisis by kissing the Duchess when she was pregnant

5. Princess Augusta by Beechey. She fell in love with a soldier and considered herself married to him

6. Princess Sophia by Beechey. 'A little trifle will slur a young woman's character for ever'

7. Henrietta Duncannon with William and Frederick by Hoppner. She had six children, two of them illegitimate, and managed to keep the friendship of both husband and lover

8. Lady Elizabeth Foster by Reynolds. The Duke of Devonshire could not manage without her

9. Lady Harriet Cavendish by Mrs Surtees. A plain, formidable child, she was called Harryo to distinguish her from the aunt whose lover she loved, married and continued to adore

10. Lord Granville Leveson Gower. 'Adored Granville who would make a barren desert smile'

11. Lady Sarah Bunbury sacrificing to the Graces, by Reynolds. Unfortunately her first husband preferred horses

12. Gillray's view of Dora Jordan and the Duke of Clarence. The cartoonists liked to play on her name

22. Elizabeth Inchbald.
She preferred independence
in an attic

23. Mary Wollstonecraft by Williamson.
She lived as vigorously as she wrote,
but her life harmed her work

24. Horatia Nelson by Holmes. She
looked like her father, but resolutely
refused to believe Emma Hamilton
was her mother

25. Princess Charlotte turns
on her German grandmother.
In fact, Queen Charlotte
favoured the marriage to
Prince Leopold (*seen in the
background*)

26. Princess Charlotte and
Leopold of Saxe-Coburg,
'the perfection of a lover'

marriage for himself, he conceived the ingenious idea of passing Emma on to Sir William, thus both providing for her and perhaps insulating him from husband-hunting ladies who were beginning to appear. At this point, in 1785, Emma was about twenty, Greville thirty-six and Sir William fifty-five. A successful diplomat, he had made Naples popular with English tourists by his urbane manner and entertaining conversation. He had also contrived to endear himself to the almost moronic King Ferdinand of Naples and his powerful Habsburg Queen Maria Carolina, daughter of Maria Theresa of Austria and sister of Marie Antoinette. He was a man to be reckoned with.

The two men corresponded at length about their interesting project. Greville, writing that 'a cleaner, sweeter bedfellow does not exist,' took it for granted that Sir William would establish Emma and her mother in convenient seclusion, but this was not Sir William's idea at all. They would live in the Embassy, he said. The next thing was to get her there. Greville, who had a new heiress in view, told Emma a lot of lies about his plans for the summer and suggested she write and invite herself and her mother to visit Sir William in Naples, since they had become such good friends while he was in London. As an inducement, he promised to come and fetch them back in the autumn. He would go on supporting little Emma in country seclusion. Emma, who had almost learned to spell, wrote a charming letter to Sir William. He duly responded, and Emma and her mother set out on the adventurous journey in March 1786, escorted by a fashionable painter called Gavin Hamilton. In Naples the Palazzo Sessa was luxurious comfort and Sir William a charming host. Emma enjoyed herself, and described her adventures in loving letters to Greville, but she must soon have begun to wonder just what was going on. They got to Naples at the end of March and by the end of April she was writing to Greville: 'He can never be my lover . . . I belong to you.'

But she went on enjoying herself, sailing with Sir William in his yacht and helping him entertain guests in his English garden. She had singing and Italian lessons, and her portrait painted over and over again, and all the time the facts of her position became more and more clear to her. When Sir William revealed that her lover had never meant to fetch her in October as he had promised, she wrote: 'I love you to that degree that at this time their [*sic*] is not a hardship upon earth, either of poverty, hunger . . . or even to walk barefooted to Scotland to see you, but what I would undergo . . .'. Greville did not answer. Still she held Sir William off, so that he began to feel slightly foolish. He was writing to Greville too, of course. Emma tried a new tack in her letters, describing her social success. The King of Naples adored her, made his musicians play for her, and 'made his bow and said it was a sin he could not speak English.' The King did adore pretty ladies, and practical Emma was learning Italian. The summer wore on and there was still no comfort from Greville. Emma finally wrote him a warning: 'You don't know the power I have hear [*sic*], only I will never be his mistress. If you affront me, I will make him marry me.'

Some time that autumn, Emma yielded to Sir William, and some time that winter she decided to be in love with him. Cold-blooded Greville's docile pupil had grown up and started to think for herself. Now when Sir William went off on a hunting trip with the King, whose favourite pastime it was, she wrote him the kind of emotional letters that she used to write to Greville, only with more sex in them. She and Sir William were having a very good time together. Greville had expected that his uncle would enjoy Emma for a while, then give her a well-earned endowment and send her back to England in the spring. Nothing of the kind happened. It made him anxious.

Even in broad-minded Naples, home of the cicisbeo, Emma could not appear at court, or accompany Sir William officially, but she did everything else with him, and she and her capable mother, now known as Mrs Cadogan, started making the living more comfortable both at the Palazzo Sessa and in the country villa at Caserta where they stayed when the King was on the great hunts he and Sir William both enjoyed. The two women were quietly making themselves indispensable to Sir William. 'What divine beauty: She's a Madonna,' the crowds cried as Emma passed. But she needed more than beauty to establish herself as a celebrity in her own right. She worked hard at her singing, but her real success was with the Attitudes Sir William worked out with her. Dressed in a becoming Greek tunic she posed for his friends, gliding from one mythological character to the next. It was soft porn of the most elegant kind. Did she remember dancing on the table for Sir Harry's friends? She entranced the visiting poet Goethe, and Horace Walpole called her Sir William's 'Gallery of Statues'. One way and another she was making a name for herself. And she wrote regularly to Greville, telling him all about it.

She was making progress with her Italian, and singing so well, she told him, that she received an offer from the Madrid Opera House:

'Sir William is in raptures with me.' Sir William however was more realistic, writing to Greville, 'I fear her views are beyond what I can bring myself to execute.' He meant to pension Emma off in the end on the £150 for herself and £50 for her mother he was now allowing them. Her temper, he explained, was erratic. But he was reckoning without his guest. Their position was becoming very fluid. When his kinswoman Elizabeth, Duchess of Argyll, came to Naples with her daughter, Sir William introduced Emma to them and to their companions Francis, Lord Elcho, and his wife, who wrote that she was sure Sir William and Emma were secretly married. Sir William had been planning a trip to England for some time, and had written to Greville about the problem Emma would present, but in the end they went together in 1791. Emma wrote to an anxious Greville that he need not worry: 'I wish to be an example of good conduct, and to show the world that a pretty woman is not always a fool.'

She was not at all a fool, and Greville was right to worry. A friend wrote him a warning: 'Her influence over him exceeds all belief; his attachment exceeds admiration, it is perfect dotage.' Later that summer, Sir William wrote to his friend Lady Spencer: 'I flatter myself I am not deceived in Emma's present character ... Not a day passes without her having testified her true repentance for the past.' But when the couple arrived in England, and Emma shared his lodgings in Bath, Lady Spencer bolted to Longleat to avoid a meeting. However, Emma did meet her daughter the Duchess of Devonshire, and Lady Elizabeth Foster, who were in Bath at a critical point in their own lives. Lady Elizabeth described Emma as 'a very handsome Woman, but coarse and vulgar,' but was impressed, like everyone else, by the Attitudes: 'It was a Helena, Cassandra or Andromache ... everything she did was just and beautiful.'

Sir William went to Windsor and seems to have got tacit approval from his old friend the King for his marriage. His niece's husband wrote to her that, 'The King joked him about Em at a distance and gave a hint that he thought he was not quite so religious as when he married the late Lady H.' They were married, quietly, on September 6th, 1791 and left two days later to go home to Naples by way of revolution-torn Paris. In Naples, everyone said how well Emma behaved. Queen Maria Carolina accepted the situation without any great enthusiasm at first, but more and more English visitors flocked to the lively Embassy Emma ran. Lady Webster found her vulgar, but Lady Webster had problems of her own with the gloomy husband she was soon to abandon. Prince Augustus, Duke of Sussex, came to Naples for his health and dined with them; Lady Malmesbury admired the Attitudes; they thought nothing of dining parties of fifty, whom Emma might or might not delight with her singing. 'I like Lady H too well not to wish that she had never learned to sing,' wrote Lady Palmerston.

In the spring of 1793 the Duchess of Devonshire's party came to Naples during her long exile from England after the birth of her daughter by Charles Grey, and Emma renewed her acquaintanceship with the three devoted women, Georgiana Devonshire, Henrietta Bessborough and Elizabeth Foster. Henrietta was ill and she and her mother Lady Spencer actually stayed with the Hamiltons at Caserta, where Emma won Lady Spencer over by her kindness to the invalid. It was at this time that Henrietta first met young Lord Granville Leveson Gower, and one does long to know what he and Emma Hamilton thought of each other, rival charmers that they were. Emma throve on success, but Sir William was finding all the entertaining and all the good food and drink too much. He suffered from severe bouts of bilious illness from now on, devotedly nursed by Emma, who must have been immensely frightened by them.

The Queen, who had held off at first, became more friendly as the political situation of the Kingdom of Naples and Sicily worsened. As long-term allies of Austria, they were inevitably involved in the war with France that broke out in 1793. England and her fleet became important and Emma and the Queen became better and better friends. Emma basked in royal favour. 'Against my will . . . I am got into politics,' she wrote to Greville, asking him to send her information for her 'beloved Queen'. And the Queen reciprocated by passing private papers to Emma for transmission to England. It was all very gratifying.

In September 1793 an unknown English captain called Horatio Nelson sailed into the Bay of Naples with despatches for Sir William. He had come from Lord Hood, the British admiral who was helping defend Toulon, where the citizens had rebelled against the bloodthirsty government in Paris. Nelson and Sir William took to each other at once and Sir William was helpful in getting Lord Hood's request for Neapolitan troops quickly approved. Nelson entertained Sir William and Emma on the *Agamemnon* and from then on the three of them corresponded. Unfortunately the defence of Toulon crumbled, partly due to a bright young French artillery officer called

Napoleon Bonaparte, and the Neapolitan troops disgraced themselves.

By 1795, Napoleon was conquering northern Italy and Sir William was anxious about the fate of his priceless collection of antiquities, in case of French victory and the inevitable looting. King Ferdinand then made a shabby secret peace with France and the English Navy had to retreat from the Mediterranean, since the Kingdom of Naples and Sicily had been their last ally there. But Sir Gilbert Elliot, in flight from Corsica, had time to enjoy the Attitudes and thought that Emma had taken wonderful pains to educate herself, though there were still 'inveterate remains of her origins'. And Lady Holland (who had mutated from Lady Webster through elopement, divorce and remarriage) noted Emma's strong provincial accent. 'Don't be afeard Sir Willum I'll not break your joug,' said the exquisite water nymph, posing with a priceless Greek vase.

By 1797 the French had taken Rome, Naples was full of refugees and also of secret Jacobins sympathetic to the cause of France and liberty. The King and his government were trying to please everyone, and Sir William was in steady correspondence with Nelson, now back in the Mediterranean with a new British fleet. Searching for the French who had got out of Toulon, Nelson had trouble getting supplies in Sicily, and Emma always maintained that only her direct intervention with the Queen secured them for him. He found and destroyed the French fleet at Aboukir Bay in August 1798 and when he reached Naples, a hero, Emma fell into his arm (he only had one by now), crying, 'Oh God, is it possible?'

Nelson's attempts to put some backbone into the Neapolitans proved disastrous. The King marched on Rome, took it, then fled in panic when the French counterattacked. He then packed his whole court secretly on to British ships and fled to Sicily. It was December. Storm-tossed on the way, the *Vanguard* with the royal party and the Hamiltons on board nearly sank. Everything was chaos; one of the little princes died of seasickness in Emma's arms. Life in Palermo was hideously uncomfortable, and housing was short. Nelson stayed with the Hamiltons. Sir William had not distinguished himself at sea, and was distraught at the loss of his precious antiquities, shipwrecked on their way to England. He was sixty-eight now and beginning to feel his age; Nelson was forty and tasting the glory he had always expected. The son of a Norfolk clergyman, he had had his own way to make in the world, and made it, but he was not entirely at ease there.

Aware of slights, he throve on adulation. Emma gave it to him in abundance, and so did the Neapolitan Court. He was enslaved. For the next year or so his actions were largely guided by the whims of Emma and her 'beloved Queen'. Nelson was a religious man and a married one; it meant nothing. As for Emma, after the shock of Greville's treachery, and the compromise with Sir William, she was probably still capable of passion, but not of love for anyone but herself. She liked glory, too, and comfort.

Sir William also liked comfort, and Emma and her mother gave it to him. He had always been afraid that Emma might be unfaithful to him, but he was getting old. Now that it had happened, and it was with his good friend Nelson, perhaps he was relieved. He played the com-plaisant husband to perfection, sitting up till all hours with his two dear friends, and joining in the gambling card games which were an old passion for Emma and a new one for Nelson. They called them-selves the tria juncta in uno, the three-in-one, and meant it.

Back in England, the tide of gossip rose. The result was inevitable. By the summer of 1800 both men had been recalled to England. And Emma was pregnant by Nelson, something she had never achieved with Sir William, nor Nelson with his Fanny Nisbet, though she had been a widow with a son of her own when they married. Her son Josiah was with Nelson in Sicily, making a failure of a naval career and scenes over Nelson's behaviour. Fanny, living with Nelson's old father in England, cannot have lacked information about what was going on.

Recalled ostensibly on grounds of ill health, Nelson wanted to take the Hamiltons home to England with him, but Admiral Lord Keith, now in command, would not spare a ship. Instead Nelson joined the Hamiltons and Queen Maria Carolina in an extraordinarily risky journey to Vienna overland from Leghorn via Ancona and Trieste. The French had won the battle of Marengo and were loose in Italy. It was more by good luck than good management that the odd little party avoided capture.

In Vienna a hero's welcome awaited Nelson. The news was so bad that the Austrians needed something to rejoice over, and found it in him. Fêted everywhere, the party visited Prince Esterhazy at Eisenstadt where Haydn was delighted with Emma's singing of Handel, then, loaded with expensive presents from the grateful Queen, they set off on the journey home. There were illuminations for them at their hotel in Prague, but they found the price added to their bill. In Dresden, an unfriendly witness, Mrs Melesina St George Trench, described Emma's figure as colossal but well shaped: 'Sir William is old, infirm, all admiration of his wife . . . never spoke . . . but to applaud her . . . She puffs the incense into his [Nelson's] face, he . . . snuffs it up very cordially.'

The dilettante Elector of Saxony refused to receive Emma. Nelson was furious that Sir William went to court without her, but Emma consoled herself on being told that the frugal Elector never gave dinners or suppers. 'What . . . no guttling!' she cried. Mrs Trench described her as made up of 'vanity, avarice, and love for the pleasures of the table.' And their host, Hugh Elliot, summed up the couple as 'Antony and *Moll* Cleopatra.' It was not a happy omen for England, though Elliot gloomily thought that the odd couple probably would be received at court. Emma had brought a letter of recommendation from Queen Maria Carolina to Queen Charlotte.

He was wrong. They reached London on November 9th and at last the devoted trio had to separate. The Hamiltons were lent a house by their millionaire friend William Beckford, who had a fairly odd reputation of his own, and Nelson found his wife coolly installed with his father at St Nerot's hotel. The two couples dined together on the first night, but the occasion was not a success. Fanny tried to behave as if nothing had happened, but the situation was impossible, and Emma was getting desperate. It was no wonder she had been described as colossal on the journey, she was, in fact, carrying twins. She must have built immense hopes on Nelson's overwhelming delight at her pregnancy. Surely he and Sir William, and even perhaps useful Charles Greville, would put their heads together and work out some way by which she could have Nelson's child (she did not of course know there were two of them) respectably. She was deluding herself. Under the law of the time, there was no way it could be done, however expensively. Sir William might have managed to divorce Emma, naming Nelson, but as the law then stood there was no way Nelson could then get rid of faithful Fanny.

So while Nelson was snubbed by the King at court, and fumed because Emma was not received, Emma and her mother laid their plans, undoubtedly with Sir William's tacit collaboration. Her babies were born in the London house at the end of January, and, remarkably, nobody knew. Confronted with two girls, Emma must have taken an instant decision. One was sent off at once to the Foundling Hospital, oddly enough identified as Emma Hamilton, and vanished from the story. The other she took herself, a few days later, to a reliable nurse called Mrs Gibson. This baby was given the more important name, Horatia. Nelson, at sea, was told one twin had died. He was almost mad with joy, writing Emma a series of hysterical letters, ostensibly about the birth of a child to a protégée of Emma's, Mrs Thompson. He had left his wife by now, and made a generous settlement, but Emma's triumph was far from being complete. She was beginning to realize how much their future relationship was going to be altered by the fact of little Horatia. But for the moment she had got away with it.

Nelson destroyed her letters to him at this time, and told her to do likewise. If she had done so, the truth of Horatia's birth might have remained a secret for ever, though Nelson's own behaviour was to make it a fairly open one. Ordered to the Baltic, he wrote Emma a letter by safe hand: 'Now, my own dear wife, for such you are in my eyes and in the face of heaven . . . There is nothing in this world I would not do for us to live together, and to have our dear little child with us . . . This campaign will give us peace, and then we will sett [*sic*] off for Brontë [the estate he had been given by the King of Sicily] . . . I love, I never did love anyone else. I never had a dear pledge of love till you gave me one, and you, thank my God, never gave one to anybody else.' He knew about eighteen-year-old Emma Carew, now living with a family near Manchester, but thought her merely Emma's protégée.

Emma herself was busy making friends with Nelson's family and attempting, successfully, to turn them against his wife. Life in London was not turning out as she had hoped. The longed-for summons to court never came, and Sir William was having trouble securing the pension to which he was entitled as a retired Ambassador of thirty years good service. In the end he got less than he had hoped for, without reversion to Emma, and she had to sell her diamonds to furnish the house they rented in Piccadilly, while he sold what remained of his collection. But they were soon entertaining old friends like Prince Augustus, while a proposed visit from the Prince of Wales threw Nelson into paroxysms of jealousy. Victory at Copenhagen in April 1801 reinforced Nelson's position as national hero and he spent all his time on shore with Emma and Sir William. He had recognized that the idea of fleeing with Emma to Brontë was not practical, and had now decided to buy a country house just outside London, and establish the curious *ménage à trois* there, adding little

Horatia to it, under the guise of adopted child. It is a measure of Nelson's heroic status, that the threesome were socially accepted to the extent that they were. Interestingly enough, Elizabeth Foster, member of another unusual trio, had become a good friend of Emma's.

Emma found a house in Merton; Nelson bought it sight unseen and she and Sir William moved in and set about putting it in order, installing modern water closets and extra bathrooms and building verandahs for ladies to sun themselves. Arriving tired out in October, Nelson was delighted with 'Paradise Merton'. He was a Viscount now, and Vice-Admiral of the Blue, and the negotiation of the Peace of Amiens in the spring of 1802 freed him for domestic life at Merton. Emma acted as hostess and filled the house with his nephews and nieces for Christmas to give a gloss of respectability to the unusual situation. Sir William made no objection, so why should anyone else? But he was seventy-one, tired out by the incessant entertaining and beginning to worry about money. He was paying the rent for the Piccadilly house that was the trio's London base, as well as a third of the cost of Emma's extravagant hospitality at Merton. It was more than his diminished means could bear and he remonstrated with Emma, but in vain. She had the bit between her teeth now, dreaming of the day when two deaths would make her Viscountess Nelson. And the curious household had been accepted at Merton, parish and parish priest delighted with their famous – and generous – local hero.

Lady Nelson lost her best friend in the family when old Mr Nelson died at Bath in the spring of 1802. Nelson did not even attend his father's funeral, busy with his happy life at Merton, and the rest of his family gravitated more and more to the luxury there, though little Horatia was still with reliable Mrs Gibson in London. Sir William was now talking about the possibility of 'a wise and well concerted separation' and had been shocked by discovering that Emma was overdrawn at Coutts' bank. He paid off her £700 overdraft, wore himself out helping her give a grand concert in London in February 1803, got ill and died, devotedly nursed, of course, by Emma and her mother.

Emma was probably surprised at what a shock her husband's death was, and his will was a shock too. Charles Greville was the heir, at last. Emma got an annuity of £800, her known debts paid, and a lump sum of £800, all of it paid meanly and slowly by Greville. Nelson had moved out of the Piccadilly house the night Sir William died; now

Emma had to surrender it to Greville and move into a smaller though still luxurious one in Clarges Street. Her friends all thought the provision inadequate, and she began a long, unsuccessful battle to get a government pension for her own services at Naples.

Worst of all, war broke out again in April 1803 and Nelson was ordered back to sea. The idyll was over, and Emma was left to face her curious double widowhood alone. She drifted between Clarges Street and Merton (Nelson allowed her £100 a month for expenses there), taking with her Nelson's niece Charlotte, the first of the little girls she took under her wing, perhaps as future cover for her own daughter Horatia, still with Mrs Gibson. She made ruthlessly sure that Nelson never learned the truth about her other daughter, Emma Carew, left to her own devices in the Midlands. Emma herself missed having a man about the place, and ate and drank, for comfort, more than ever. And she spent too much, lavishing presents she could ill afford on Nelson's family.

Nelson came back only once, briefly, in September 1805, and Horatia was actually installed at Merton, as Horatia Nelson Thompson, for the occasion. Then he went back to sea: to death and glory at Trafalgar. Emma was crushed. Her friend Lady Elizabeth Foster called to condole and found her in bed. 'What shall I do?' she said, as she had once before asked Greville. Now there was no one to answer.

Nelson had left her Merton and the income from the Bronte estate, which was to prove illusory. A codicil left £4,000 to his 'adopted daughter' Horatia Nelson Thompson, stipulating that she change her name to Nelson and be brought up by his 'dearest friend' Lady Hamilton. A second codicil, written just before the battle, left 'Emma, Lady Hamilton, a legacy to my King and Country, that they will give her an ample provision to maintain her rank in life. I also leave to the beneficence of my country my adopted daughter, Horatia Nelson Thompson . . .'. Emma had high hopes of this optimistic gesture, but the government, lavishing money and titles on Nelson's family, would have nothing to do with Emma and Horatia.

She had grown used to her daughter, now a lively and intelligent four year old, and from now on they were inseparable. She took her to stay with her Nelson relations, where she was an instant success. They knew her, of course, for Nelson's child, never dreamed that she was Emma's. Emma used to lose her temper with Horatia, as she had with Sir William, and wrote her savage letters about her conduct as she grew older.

Emma's mother had been worried about her debts before Nelson died, and now they could only get worse. Neither Greville nor Sir William had succeeded in teaching her economy, and Nelson had barely tried. His family thought her amply provided for, as well they might, relict of two successful men. Charles Greville died in 1809, which meant still more confusion about the payment of her annuity. Worst of all, her capable mother died in 1810. Living increasingly from hand to mouth, Emma still had her gift for people and made new friends to borrow from, but by 1813 she had been arrested for debt and was living within the Rules of the Court, Horatia with her. Once again her friends made vain attempts to get her government money, but government was busy with the war Nelson had helped it to fight. Desperate for money, Emma sold Nelson's letters to a disreputable publisher, and their publication in 1814 did her great harm. Queen Maria Carolina did not answer her appeals, but Nelson's brother the new Earl helped her. So too did Sir Henry Fetherstonehaugh, snug at Uppark with a housekeeper, and Alderman Joshua John Smith, a new London friend. At last enough of her debts had been paid so she could escape from the Rules of the Court and flee to France, open again since Napoleon's defeat in the spring of 1814. She was only about fifty, but worn out with drink and hard living. Reaching Calais, she took to her bed at once, nursed by thirteen-year-old Horatia, who was reduced to pawning her mother's jewels and her Indian shawl, and applying for help to the Nelsons. Horatia was to say later that the illness arose from 'being bled while labouring under an attack of jaundice . . . The baneful habit she had of taking spirits and wine to a fearful degree, brought on water on the chest.' Horatia begged the sick woman to tell her the truth about her birth, but Emma refused to do so, and died on January 15th, 1815, just before Horatia's fourteenth birthday.

Emma died penniless and the English Consul and his wife helped Horatia with the funeral. Then the Nelson family swooped down and took the orphan over. She spent the remainder of her girlhood in the English countryside, married a clergyman, had eight living children, and died a respectable Victorian widow in 1881, still furiously refusing to believe that Emma Hamilton was her mother.

* * *

Elizabeth Armistead's origins were as obscure as Amy Lyon's, her rise as surprising, and her ending much happier. There was more love and less ambition in her career. In later years she would never talk about her early life, referring to herself always as 'a foolish giddy girl'. Born Elizabeth Cane in 1750, by the time she was twenty she was Mrs Armistead (or Armitstead), one of London's leading Cyprians in the heyday of that profession. George, second Viscount Bolingbroke had met her in a brothel and liked her so well that he established her in lodgings and got her a chance on the stage at Covent Garden. Her looks, rather than her acting, made her a success, but she found prostitution a more profitable career. She was fashionably tall and well built, handsome rather than beautiful, and had learned her trade in the rigorous if often friendly school of the brothel. Adept already in the management of men, she went on to educate herself, studying both her men and their books, and moved deftly from one lover to the next as the whim took her.

She achieved 'settlements' from two unnamed patrons and by 1776 was able to take a house of her own in Bond Street. Later she moved to Clarges Street, where she entertained a widening circle. A rich nabob, General Richard Smith, had started her off financially, but most of her men were aristocratic Whigs. Elizabeth seems to have had the gift of sliding from love to friendship, and back again. Lord George Cavendish, the Duke of Devonshire's younger brother, was one of her faithful; the Earl of Derby and the Duke of Dorset both had their turns, and by the late 1770s her Clarges Street drawing room was a gathering ground for bright young Whigs like John Townshend, George St John and Richard Fitzpatrick, Charles James Fox's friend. But Elizabeth herself was nearing thirty now and beginning to look to the future. She needed an establishment, and she aimed high. When the gossip columns that specialized in the doings of the Cyprians reported a cooling in the Prince of Wales's affair with the actress Mrs Mary Robinson, Elizabeth set her cap at the volatile Prince, and got him. Unfortunately he turned out to be a bad payer. Cooler headed than either Mrs Fitzherbert or Mrs Jordan, she ended the affair by escaping to Paris. She must have been prospering, despite his meanness. Before she left, in 1781, she leased a country house, St Anne's Hill, near Chertsey, which was to be her real home for the rest of her life.

From Paris she went on to fashionable Spa, where she collected Lords George Cholmondeley and William Coleraine, and ended up touring Italy with Coleraine. But they all hurried home in the spring of 1782, on hearing that the Whigs were actually back in office.

Charles James Fox wrote to his friend Kirkpatrick that 'Mrs Armitstead arrived yesterday from Paris and seems to be quite well, tho' she certainly looks (one cannot conceal it) a little old.' But the Prince of Wales always liked older women and was soon her slave again. 'The Armstead,' wrote the *Morning Herald*, 'with very subordinate personal attractions, has contrived to out-jockey the whole *stud* of first rate *impures*, by the superiority of her understanding ... she has not only ... outstripped them in the *race amorous* for a certain *Royal sweepstakes*, but has contrived to touch the *plate*, which none of the others could do.' Elizabeth had seen to it that the Prince paid up this time.

The Prince's friend Charles James Fox had meanwhile been helping him deal with Mary Robinson's demands for hush money. Fox was thirty-three and the young star of the Whig party when they got back into office in 1782. His father, who had married one of the beautiful Lennox sisters and become Lord Holland, had made, as some do, a very good financial thing out of his political career. He had also spoiled his brilliant younger son horribly, but almost everyone loved him. An unfortunate exception was the King, who had never forgiven Fox his characteristic and bold opposition to the Royal Marriage Act. He had spent a fortune by now, run deep into debt, and damaged his health by riotous living. He had never been handsome, now he was stout, but he had immense charm and was known as the most brilliant talker of the day. His name had been coupled with those of the Duchess of Devonshire and another great Whig hostess, Mrs Crewe, but in fact he had tended towards easy women from the streets, which cannot have been good for his health. Now his business dealings with Mary Robinson led to her bed, and a logical progression from there led to that of his old acquaintance, her rival Mrs Armistead. And something very odd happened to them there. They fell in love.

Fox's public life was traumatic at this time. He was briefly in office in 1782, and longed for a return to power that would enable him to put through the liberal reforms he planned. To achieve this, he threw in his lot with an old enemy, Lord North, and they attained precarious office under the Duke of Portland in 1783. It was an unpopular coalition and hated by the King, but Fox plunged passionately into his work as Secretary of State for Foreign Affairs. Among other things he meant to reform the East India Company, about which he made one of his famous speeches: 'What is the end of government? ...

Certainly the happiness of the governed.' But the King was working all out against him. The East India Bill was defeated in the Lords, the government fell in December, and young William Pitt became Prime Minister at twenty-four.

While all this was going on, Fox and Elizabeth had quietly become monogamous. They were passionate lovers and dear friends, and she saw to it that he ate his meals and went to bed at a reasonable hour and had all his buttons sewed on. Clarges Street had always been convenient for the House, now he became a regular guest at St Anne's Hill too. He was beginning to take it for granted that he was a permanency. By the autumn of 1783, when he was back in office, Elizabeth was beginning to get frightened. She had had no paying customers for about a year; she was running into debt; it was time to call a halt. When Fox went off for his autumn round of visits to Newmarket races and shooting parties she wrote to tell him she was going to leave him and settle in Europe. She received a passionate answer. Wherever she went, he would go too: 'I could change my name and live with you in the remotest part of Europe in poverty and obscurity. I could bear that very well, to be parted I can not bear . . . I can not live without you.' She relented, and was there for him at St Anne's Hill throughout the political crises of that winter. It culminated with the 1784 spring election in which the Duchess of Devonshire and her friends saved Fox's Westminster seat for him, but his party went into the wilderness for years. During most of that time Fox was in effect leader of the opposition.

Personally, they were years of deep happiness for both of them. He and his Liz, as he called her, filled a deep need in each other and built up a contented pattern of living, within the limits society imposed on them. More than ever, their London house was a gathering place for Whig men. No ladies, of course. The men also visited St Anne's Hill, where some of the neighbours, too, gradually and cautiously let curiosity conquer convention. You met the most interesting men at St Anne's Hill, and it was difficult not to like Liz Armistead, though impossible, of course, to approve of her. Fox already had two illegitimate children being brought up by their mothers, and Liz took an interest in them. She herself was probably barren, a useful attribute in a Cyprian, but a cause of sadness to them now. Instead, she and Fox created a beloved garden at St Anne's Hill, and entertained Fox's bright little nephew Henry, who had become Lord Holland in infancy when Charles's older brother died young.

Liz had always liked reading and her education continued. They read aloud to each other, Herodotus, Ariosto, the *Iliad*, Chaucer, and she was learning Italian to understand Ariosto better. She preferred not to go to London while Parliament was in session, the social problem must have been much more obvious there, but she always went if he particularly wished it. Her presence meant a more healthy way of life for him in those hard drinking days. If she was there, he came to bed. When he left for the usual autumn round of visits, on which she could not accompany him, she took herself off to Cheltenham for the sake of her worsening rheumatism. They were settling down, but they were also, inevitably, plunging further and further into debt. Mrs Armistead had sold her settlements during one of his crises, now she was entirely dependent on his erratic finances. His immense debts had been paid once, when his father died in 1774, now they were once more threatening to engulf him. A bankrupt cannot be a Member of Parliament. It is a measure of how much Fox was loved that in 1793 a committee was formed, without his knowledge, to take up a subscription for him. Small and great alike contributed and enough money was collected to pay off his debts and give him an income for life. 'I think it is the most honourable thing that has ever happened to anyone,' he wrote to his nephew young Lord Holland, now touring abroad in pursuit of Lady Webster.

Everyone knew about Fox and Mrs Armistead, but in the eyes of the world he was still a brilliant and highly eligible young man, obviously in need of a rich wife. In 1787 he had had a curious letter from Thomas Coutts, the banker. Coutts had offered him financial help, and then gone on to talk about his three daughters, all then unmarried. Quite ignoring the talk of the Misses Coutts, Fox had gratefully accepted the offer of finance and introduced Coutts to his friend the Duchess of Devonshire, the start of a relationship useful to both. Fox became a regular caller at the Coutts' comfortable house in the Strand, but when Mrs Coutts asked for a lock of his hair for their still unmarried daughter Fanny in 1795, it alerted Liz. She wrote Fox a firm letter. The time had come for them to part, she told him: this was his chance, Fanny Coutts could give him children as well as money. Fox replied with as much fervour as he had to her earlier suggestion that they part: 'I love you more than life itself indeed I do.' It satisfied her, there was no more talk of separating. But it had made him think. It was time they married. Oddly, they did so in secret, that September, which hardly solved their problem in society and meant that he could not make a settlement on her.

When Lord Egremont decided to marry his long-time mistress, mother of his many children, it was the beginning of the end of the affair. It was not so with the Foxes, whose happiness was merely solidified. He had more time at home too in the last years of the century since he was increasingly isolated and powerless in Parliament. Unlike most of his Whig friends, who had been sickened by the bloodshed of the Terror, he still spoke up for revolutionary France, and was also a lonely voice in opposing the government's increasingly repressive measures against the rising tide in favour of reform. But political isolation meant more time with his 'dearest Liz' and happy Christmases at St Anne's Hill with all the children they could gather around them. His illegitimate son and daughter were a bitter disappointment, Harry stone deaf, and Harriet a compulsively silly talker. Perhaps it was just as well that Elizabeth did not have children.

Fox was writing the life of James II, partly as an occupation, partly for money, and when the precarious Peace of Amiens was signed in March 1802 he and Liz decided to go to France, combining research with pleasure. Perhaps remembering previous holidays they had taken in Europe, when friends had contrived to greet him while cutting her, Fox decided that the time had come to announce their marriage. The surprise news was not well received. The fact of it was shocking enough, but the fact that it had taken place in secret seven years earlier was outrageous. Society had been wrong-footed and disliked it.

It must have been particularly pleasant to get to France and find himself received as a hero, and Elizabeth without question as his wife. In Paris, she was in good company. Madame Bonaparte and Madame Talleyrand both had interesting pasts too. But her friendly reception did not please the aristocratic English ladies who were also flocking to Paris. In order to avoid being presented to Madame Bonaparte on the same day as Lady Holland, the wife of Fox's beloved nephew Henry, Elizabeth pretended her dress was not ready. Lady Holland took umbrage just the same. Relations between the two women were never good. Having merely committed adultery herself and borne her husband a child before marriage, Elizabeth Holland resented being put in the same category as the reformed prostitute. The rest of Fox's family were much more friendly towards Elizabeth, perhaps finding they liked her the better of the two women. Fox's cousin Lady Sarah

Napier had her own history, and his mother's sister Emily, Duchess of Leinster, had surprised society by marrying her children's much younger, plebeian tutor soon after her husband's death. Leinster himself, of course, had been one of Harriette Wilson's patrons.

In London, some doors would always stay closed to Liz, and the Palace naturally remained hostile. In the spring of 1804 there was talk of a coalition government including Fox, but the King, recovering from a fit of madness, refused even to consider the idea. It gave the married couple the leisure to visit his widespread family in rural England. 'A *train* of Foxes and Lennoxes' as Lady Sarah Napier described it. And back at home their guest list at St Anne's Hill included the Bessboroughs and their old friend the Prince of Wales. Everything changed when Pitt died in January 1806, worn out by the crushing military defeats that had destroyed the new alliance against Napoleon in the autumn of 1805. Napoleon had made himself Emperor by now and even Fox had lost his illusions about the way France was going. In the chaos that followed Pitt's death it became obvious that no one could form a government without Fox. George III gave in, and the Ministry of All the Talents was formed under William, Lord Grenville, with Fox as Secretary of State for Foreign Affairs.

It was the end of the easy life. Fox threw himself into the business of office, returning every day late and exhausted to the house their friend the Duke of Bedford had lent them in Stable Yard. Adaptable Liz turned herself into a political hostess. They managed a few days now and then at St Anne's Hill, but politics meant a return to late nights and heavy drinking. Fox's health, already damaged by those early riotous years, could not stand it. By Easter his legs were so swollen that at St Anne's Hill he had to play ball with their child visitors from a wheelchair. Elizabeth watched and protected him as best she could, but it could not have been easy. The war with France was infinitely more important to Fox than his health.

In May 1806, she boldly gave a ball and supper in her capacity as diplomatic wife, borrowing Bedford House from her friend the Whig Duke. Lady Elizabeth Foster was afraid this was too bold a move and would prove a disaster, but everyone came, and Fox was not too tired, Liz said. He got his longed-for Bill laying the foundations for the Abolition of the Slave Trade through the Lords in June, but by now his friends were worried about his health and he was urged to accept a peerage and the comparative tranquillity of the Lords. He refused. He was hoping to achieve a negotiated peace with France, something he felt only he could do. By August he was too ill even to get to St Anne's Hill and their friend the Duke of Devonshire lent them his country house at Chiswick. He died there on September 13th. His last words were, 'It don't signify my dearest dearest Liz.' He wanted to share a grave with her, but she had to agree to his being buried alone in Westminster Abbey.

She survived him for almost thirty-six years, living on at St Anne's Hill supported by their friends and his relations, with one notable exception. The Prince of Wales did not call, and cut her when they met in society. She minded it very much, and it is good to know that many years later, in 1823, she met him, now King George IV, at the Pavilion in Brighton and he spoke to her with all the old warmth, and presently gave her a very welcome £500 a year from the Privy Purse. Like everyone else, she was running into debt, partly because of her extensive gifts to charity. After the death of her beloved free-thinking Charles, she became a regular churchgoer, and when she died at last just before her ninety-second birthday, a crowd of Foxes and friends and loving neighbours buried her in her local graveyard.

8
Literary Women & Love

LOVE AND LITERATURE are never an easy mix, particularly from the female point of view. It is a rare husband or lover who is prepared to take second place to a book, and children present their problems too, even in a world with servants. One solution, of course, is to stay single and throw one's heart into one's work instead, as Maria Edgeworth and Jane Austen did, by default, and Elizabeth Inchbald too, after a short, uncomfortable marriage. I propose to consider them in a separate chapter.

Literature may be a charming pet, but is more likely to be a hard master. The bluestocking ladies of the second half of the eighteenth century treated it successfully as a pet. They were upper-class married women, in their middle years, who wished to distance themselves from what they thought the social and sexual excesses of the younger generation, but suffered like them from the tedium of a society geared towards such masculine pastimes as hunting, shooting and drinking. Bored with the card games that filled their evenings and drained their purses, they tried a new form of entertainment, an evening of conversation in the mode of the French salons. Their husbands were rich, so the logistics of the business were simple enough. Servants did the work.

It was a success. This was not at all a feminist affair; they aimed at equal numbers of men and women, mixing aristocrats with writers and artists, most of these, naturally, men. And the interesting men came, or at least enough of them did. The central ladies were Mrs Boscawen, Mrs Montagu and Mrs Vesey, according to Hannah More, who was happy to be patronized by them and wrote a poem about them called 'Bas Bleu'. The refreshments were supposed to be simple, but they were good, and so was the talk, within limits. These were comfortable straitlaced women who took their position in life for granted; there would be no radical talk, whether political or sexual, in their elegant rooms. 'The generality of women who have excelled in wit have failed in chastity,' Mrs Montagu summed up her own attitude. She found Fanny Burney's *Evelina* vulgar, which was one of the reasons why Dr Johnson did not really like her, though he and his friend David Garrick formed part of her circle. Johnson found her pretentious, which she probably was, and would not flatter her the way Hannah More did, but he was a snob in his own way, so he went, when invited.

One interesting thing about the bluestockings is how little they have left behind them, aside from the name, which was probably coined by Mrs Boscawen's admiral husband. Their own writings were largely occasional, or dull, or both. Hannah More was an outstanding protégée of theirs. One of the schoolmistress daughters of a country schoolmaster, she was only able to make writing her life because a rich older man called Turner had jilted her and insisted on giving her an annuity to make up for it. Thus liberated, she plunged into an extremely successful career as a propagandist for the evangelical movement with a series of topical works such as *Thoughts on the Importance of the Manners of the Great in Society* (1788), *Strictures on Female Education* (1799) and *Hints towards forming the Character of a Young Princess*, published in 1805, when Princess Charlotte was nine. In the turbulent early 1790s, she and her sisters produced a spate of *Cheap Repository Tracts*, moral tales in opposition to the revolutionary theories of Tom Paine, and she also wrote successful plays and a popular novel, *Coelebs in Search of a Wife*. She did a great deal of good, particularly in education, insisting that the poor would behave better if taught to read, and promoting schools for their children, to the outrage of country gentry, who preferred their workers illiterate. She throve well into the nineteenth century, her country house, Cowslip Cottage, a place of tourist pilgrimage. The bluestocking ladies were doubtless proud of her but I doubt if anyone reads her for pleasure today.

'Vulgar' *Evelina* on the other hand will last as long as the novel does. But then Fanny Burney was a very different creature. Hannah More made the most of famous spinsterhood, Fanny was a young lady with marriage in mind, but her standards were high. She did not mean to make a mere marriage of 'prudence and convenience'. Her problem was that like Hannah More she was of no particular background. Her father, Charles Burney, was one of the bluestocking ladies' delicately patronized guests. A gifted musician, he had his own way to make in the world, and had started out under the patronage of a dilettante kinsman of Charles Greville. Unlike Charles, Fulke Greville was rich and could indulge his musical leanings by taking talented young Charles Burney under his wing, showing him the great world and introducing him to his friends. When Greville eloped with an heiress in 1747, Charles Burney gave the bride away, but a couple of years later he too fell in love and married and their paths diverged, though Greville always felt he had rights in the Burneys. It was his behaviour on a cold night in the Burney house that called forth a celebrated snub of Dr Johnson's: 'If it were not for depriving the ladies of the fire, I should like to stand upon the hearth myself.'

Charles Burney and his increasing family lived the hand-to-mouth life of the self-employed. His first wife died in 1761, when Fanny was nine, leaving him with six children of whom Fanny was the second. He made another love match in 1767 with an old friend, Mrs Allen, a handsome widow with bluestocking tendencies, two daughters of her own, and a short temper. She must have run a comfortable house, because everyone came to call, but to Fanny she was a stepmother just the same. And Fanny was plain, short-sighted, backward (she did not read until she was eight) and almost pathologically shy. While her brothers started on careers and her sisters were sent to school in Paris nobody bothered about educating Fanny, she just slid into the position of secretary to her increasingly successful father, who was then planning an ambitious *History of Music*.

Fanny was always there, sitting in the parlour, listening to the guests, more noticing than noticed, getting used to the very best in conversation. Johnson and Garrick came, poor mad Christopher Smart, the poet, and Arthur Young, the agricultural journalist. Fanny listened, and wrote letters to her sisters, which developed into a diary, sent in instalments. It was a sociable life. The Burneys went to the theatre and to the opera, which she liked even better, and when Fanny was seventeen she and her older sister Hester went to a masquerade and met a young man called Tomkin, who invited them to the Chelsea Assembly. Their father said they must return the tickets: 'He must be a very bold young man or a young man who knows nothing of the world.'

Fanny's journal was meant partly for her favourite sister Susan, but also for a much older friend, Samuel Crisp, another rich dilettante who lived an idle, civilized, luxurious life at Chessington in Surrey.

Charles Burney had met him in the old Greville days and the friend-ship had lasted. Now Crisp was Fanny's beloved 'Daddy Crisp', a strong influence on the whole family. He was consulted when a young man called Seton became too attentive towards Fanny and her older sister Hester and they were made to cut the connection. Hester settled for marriage to her cousin Charles Burney, but Fanny was never going to compromise. At twenty-three, now the oldest daughter at home, she met a handsome young man called Barlow at Hester's house. Very worthy, he was not at all agreeable and she was horrified when he took advantage of some general family embracing to kiss her. A few days later he wrote her a wonderfully comic letter. His 'ardorous Pen' had difficulty, he said, in conveying his 'softer emo-tions'. She wanted to write and put him in his place at once, and was shocked when her family opposed this. Her maiden aunts warned her against sharing their fate, and even her father thought she should give the young man more time. But a fool was always a fool to Fanny Burney. Her father failed to post the firm letter she wrote her suitor and she had to refuse him in person. She 'wept like an infant' after-wards, as if, she thought, already married. An interesting comment by a twenty-three year old on the married state. She was in disgrace even with Daddy Crisp for a while, but her father kissed his useful daugh-ter and told her he had no wish to get rid of her.

The pattern of her spinster life seemed set. But while her step-mother ran the house Fanny wrote a novel based on a childish romance she had burned one dramatic day when she was fifteen. She showed it to no one, though her brother Charles and sister Susan knew about it. When it was finished she transcribed it very carefully in a feigned hand. It must be published anonymously. The lending libraries were full of trashy sentimental stuff, and a young lady looking for marriage must not be associated with that kind of thing. But she did mean to be published. She wrote to Dodsley, one of Dr Johnson's publishers, but he did not want to deal with an anonymous author. Thomas Lowndes then offered her twenty guineas, which she took, though not happily. Later, he was to give her another £10 for it. *Evelina* came out in January 1778 and Fanny suffered a great deal, as authors will. Her journal gives breathless details of the gradual stages by which she learned that it was a success. It was in all the circulating libraries. It was the talk of the town. She had 'great difficulty in refraining from laughing' and saying 'thank you' when she heard it praised, but she managed. Her cousin Richard Burney loved the book and actually knelt at her feet when she revealed that she was the author. Then her father got hold of it and liked it vastly but promised to keep the secret because, 'Poor Fan's such a prude'. He read it aloud to his wife in bed in the mornings and Fanny heard them roaring with laughter. It must have been one of the happiest moments of her young life.

The secret did not stay a secret for long. Daddy Crisp must be told, and Dr Burney told someone else. He had met the prosperous Thrales through teaching their daughter Queeney and had become an *habitué* of the unusual household where Dr Johnson lived as a permanent and cherished guest. The great man enjoyed *Evelina* and told Mrs Thrale that elegant Mrs Cholmondely meant to have it on her table all summer, and everyone longed to know the author. This was too much for Dr Burney, who told all. Mrs Thrale saw the chance of having a tame lioness of her own and took up her music master's shy daughter. They became immense friends, writing each other the passionate letters of the day, but with some private reservations. Fanny adored Mrs Thrale, but wondered if it was all a little too good to be true, and Mrs Thrale, lavishing gifts on Fanny, noticed her tiresome shyness and her tendency to become ill in moments of crisis. They both kept journals, of course. Mrs Thrale was something of a bluestocking herself. Of better family than her rich brewer husband, she had been persuaded into a marriage of not much convenience. One of the bonds between Thrale and his friend Johnson was a shared tendency to hypochondria, and Mrs Thrale, busy producing child after child, without a living male to show for it, had to bear with both of them and watch her habitually unfaithful husband court her best friend.

She had probably taken on Dr Johnson reluctantly at first, but he had made their house fashionable. Did she now produce Fanny as her protégée in competition? If so, it worked to a marvel. Dr Johnson took one of his instant fancies to shy Fanny and enjoyed teasing her, and she kept a record of everything he said in her journal. But she was not a very satisfactory lioness, refusing to roar, and stammering into help-less silence if her book was so much as mentioned. Fashionable ladies called her 'toad' and 'little rogue' and she watched them all and wrote a play. *The Witlings* caused gales of laughter when it was read aloud at Chessington but cautious old Daddy Crisp thought its satire of the bluestockings went too close to the bone and advised Fanny to sup-press it. As so often, but not always, she took the advice of her elders. She turned to a new novel but it went slowly, her life having become too hectic for composition. She had three homes now, the Thrales' in Streatham, Crisp's in Chessington and her father's in St Martin's Street, but when she wanted to write she went to Chessington.

It all changed in 1781 when her sister Susan, with whom she had shared everything, got engaged to their brother James's friend Captain Molesworth Phillips. Mrs Thrale was delighted, planning to take Susan's place with Fanny, but nobody could do that. Mrs Thrale's own life changed still more drastically that year: her husband finally worked and ate himself to death. It was more of a shock to her, perhaps, than she had expected. She was basically a man's woman and had never got on very well with her daughters. Fanny was her confidante through the difficult years that followed. The gossips were sure she would marry Dr Johnson, so it was not surprising that she ran away to Brighton even before her husband's funeral, inevitably causing more comment. Worse still, her name was soon linked with Gabriel Mario Piozzi, a successful Italian singer then performing in London. Worst of all, from Fanny's point of view, was the fact that Hester Thrale, widowed mother of many daughters, was actually in love with Piozzi. It would not do. Fanny knew the rules. A woman, marrying, took her husband's rank, and singers had none. Besides, Piozzi was that dreadful thing in English eyes, a foreigner. There were family conferences, Mrs Thrale solemnly gave Piozzi up and he went back to Italy; she got so ill that the doctors feared madness or suicide. The family relented, she sent for him back. He came, rather slowly, and they married in 1784. For Johnson and, alas, for Fanny, she might as well have died. In fact, she went to Italy with Piozzi and lived there happily for a while before settling in Wales, where they made friends with the Ladies of Llangollen. After Piozzi's death, she moved to Bath and met widowed Fanny there, but still they did not speak.

Meanwhile Johnson, deprived of the comforts of the Thrale household, dwindled into old age and death, lovingly visited by Fanny, one of the few people he would see. She was writing *Cecilia*, which came out in 1782 and was an immediate success. This time her father had made the arrangements for her and was pleased with the £250 he got her, to which the publisher Payne & Cadell added another £50 and a pair of gloves on the book's success. 'She ought to have had a thousand,' said one of her sisters. This time Fanny had studied her market and taken advice, perhaps too much of it. But it was a book calculated to please her bluestocking patronesses, and it did. It also made Fanny some new friends. Through prim Mrs Chapone she met old Mrs Delany and through Mrs Delany she met the King and Queen.

Her life was running a little dry. There had been a rich Mr Crutcheley, perhaps Thrale's illegitimate son, but nothing had come of him, despite or because of some rather heavy-handed matchmaking by Mrs Thrale. Daddy Crisp had betrayed her by dying in 1783, Mrs Thrale by marrying in 1784, and in 1785 her youngest sister Charlotte married a young man who had come back from India with the express intention of marrying the author of *Evelina*. Charlotte was twenty-five, Fanny thirty-three. Sarah Harriet, Dr Burney's daughter by his second wife, was growing up, and her mother was letting Fanny see that she was old to be still at home. And then, in 1786, a delicate approach was made to Fanny by the court. One of the two German ladies Queen Charlotte had brought with her to England twenty-five years before was retiring as Second Keeper of the Royal Robes. Would Fanny consider taking the job? On the surface, Fanny's reaction was a predictable flight into negative bashfulness. It was impossible. It was unthinkable. But she thought about it. A letter to her sister shows her considering the chances of a pension for life if she took the job, a serious consideration to a single lady without means. She was afraid that she might have written herself out, and she may indeed have been right. Did it ever occur to her that she was putting so much of herself into her journal that there was not enough left over for fiction? At some point she certainly began to think in terms of eventual publication of the journal.

She said she could not possibly take the position, but she let her ambitious father push her into it. He was convinced that great things would happen to the family as a result. 'I am *married*!' Fanny wrote to Susan, collected her trousseau and plunged into the extraordinary, regimented court life of George III and his Queen. It was full of shocks to Fanny's delicate sensibilities. She was summoned by a vulgar bell to the Queen's presence, and she was subject to the tyranny of the Queen's remaining German attendant, rude, jealous old Mrs Schwellenberg. The job had worn out her predecessor in the end and it is easy to see why. It began at about half past seven in the morning, when Fanny was summoned to help dress the Queen, and it went on till midnight when she undressed her for bed. And in what spare time she had, she must see to it that her own clothes, which had always bored her, were up to the demands of her position. The Queen had perhaps meant to use her as reader, but one trial of poor Fanny stammering over the *Spectator* changed her mind about that. It had to be clothes.

Fanny stuck it out for five eventful years and left a fascinating record of her experiences. She was certainly writing with an eye to publication now, and not a word of criticism of her adored Royals escapes her. The Queen is kindness itself; the Princesses everything that is lovely; she even manages to give a vivid description of the King's first serious bout of madness without a harsh word about the Prince of Wales. During the tense time of the King's madness, Fanny had a tantalising glimpse of romance. The gentlemen about the court took their tea with the ladies of the bedchamber, and one of them, Colonel the Honourable Stephen Digby, had recently lost his wife and turned sentimentally to Fanny for comfort. He actually managed to get careful Fanny talked about, and she was not the only one who was surprised when he suddenly announced his engagement to Charlotte Margaret Gunning, a beautiful maid of honour. Fanny edited this bit of her diary later in life, but it still comes over as an intensely painful episode, with everyone watching, and the Queen behaving very kindly to her.

Digby married Miss Gunning in 1790 and at about the same time Fanny broke it to her shocked father that she was miserable at court; it was making her ill; she must retire. The Queen tried hard to keep her and she did not get away until 1791, when the Queen gave her the hoped-for pension of £100 a year. By then she was so ill and exhausted that she went to Bath with a friend to recover. There she met Lady Spencer with her two daughters, the Duchess of Devonshire and Lady Duncannon, not to mention Lady Elizabeth Foster. Then it was time to settle down once more with her father and stepmother. They had rooms in Chelsea College now, where Dr Burney was organist, thanks to his friend Edmund Burke. The family had gained nothing from Fanny's association with the court, except of course Fanny's well-earned pension. She was forty in 1792 and it must have been uncomfortable, however much of a relief, to be a daughter at home again, subject to her stepmother's sharp tongue. She was tidying up the three tragedies that were all she had written (except the journal) while she was at court, but not much good was to come of them.

She made some new friends that autumn. Her sister Susan and her husband were living near Norbury, under the auspices of the talented Locke family who had become dear friends of the Burneys. It was the year of the bloody September massacres that altered so many people's views of the French Revolution. A group of French refugees had settled nearby, at a house called Juniper Hall, and soon Susan was writing enthusiastically about them. Staying with Susan, Fanny met this remarkable group of people which included Madame de Staël and Talleyrand, out of favour for once. Fanny made great friends with Madame de Staël, but her father pointed out her shocking liaison with Monsieur de Narbonne and compelled Fanny to cut the connection. 'Is a woman a school-girl for life in this country?' asked Madame de Staël, amused.

Then Fanny met another of the refugees, General d'Arblay, and this time nothing would make her give him up. Alexandre Jean-Baptiste d'Arblay was a career soldier who had been Chief of Staff to General Lafayette and had gone into exile with him when he was accused of royalist sympathies. About forty, d'Arblay was one of the aristocrats who had at first believed in the Revolution. He was charming, handsome, conversable, and he seems to have fallen in love with Fanny at first sight. Soon they were exchanging French and English lessons and writing each other essays loaded with feeling. He was penniless, of course, but Fanny had her pension and £20 a year from the investment of the proceeds of *Cecilia*. They met in January when the French colony were in deep mourning for the execution of Louis XVI. Clothes-conscious for once, Fanny wrote to her half-sister: 'Oh what a tragedy!' and asked her to send 'my round black Gown and my new black Linnen, and some black ribbon.' Having made sure that the pension would continue, they married in July. Cautious Dr Burney was against the match and refused to be present, but his daughter summed it up years later: 'Never, never was union more blessed and felicitous.' She had held out for the real thing, and got it.

They took a little house at Great Bookham, two miles from Norbury, and Fanny capably bore a son there, at forty-two, in 1794, Alexander Charles Louis Piochard d'Arblay. The same year Kemble and Sheridan insisted on putting on one of the tragedies she had written at Windsor. But *Edwy and Elgiva* was a disaster, even with Kemble and Mrs Siddons in the leading parts. Fanny withdrew it next day and Mrs Siddons said she was wise. Instead she went to work on *Camilla*, which was 'to be a little portion to our Bambino'. This time, meaning to make the most of her book, she published by the old-fashioned method of subscription in which the author took the risk and kept the profits. She made over £2,000, enough to build them modest Camilla Cottage.

They lived there contentedly until the Peace of Amiens in 1802, when d'Arblay felt he must go back to France. After that, Fanny's own story, faithfully told in the journal, turns into high romance, with hazardous sea voyages, partings and battles (Waterloo) off stage. She survived a hideously painful mastectomy without anaesthetic, made many friends in Paris and published *The Wanderer, or Female Difficulties* in 1813. Visibly influenced by contemporary feminist writing, its description of the plight of a young refugee lady who cannot for some reason give her true name could have been fascinating if it had not been told at such sententious length. It pleased nobody, but she got at least £1,500 from it, which she put towards sending Alexander to Cambridge. He was a brilliant, idle boy, however, and dwindled into an unsuccessful clergyman, despite or because of all his mother's urgings. D'Arblay retired on a pension after Waterloo, worn out by his return to active service in the royalist cause. Fanny was Countess d'Arblay now, but they did not feel they could afford the title, and never used it, living quietly within their slender means at Bath until his death in 1818. His last thought, he whispered to Fanny, was '*notre réunion*'. She moved to London to be near her family, outliving her son as well as her husband. But she was the author of *Evelina* and had been greeted as 'Madame la Comtesse' by Louis XVIII. I wonder which pleased her more in her declining years.

* * *

Fanny Burney was a conformist who managed to find both literary and personal fulfilment within the constraints of her time. Mary Wollstonecraft challenged them, both in her life and in her work. Born in Spitalfields in 1759, she was the granddaughter of a rich, self-made manufacturer, but the daughter of a waster and his battered wife. She learned at six that the world is not a fair place, when her grandfather died leaving a fortune to her older brother, not even mentioning Mary and her sisters. Spoiled Ned was always the favourite. Their father moved his family from place to place, failing everywhere, getting poorer and poorer, drinking away his troubles and then assaulting his helpless wife. Mary had to listen to her mother's screams, sometimes interfered and was not loved for it. She grew up bright, passionate, at odds with the world, but got some schooling when they were living at Beverley, and found friends there to advise her about her omniverous reading. Through them she formed at sixteen a passionate friendship with a slightly older girl, Fanny Blood, also living on the margins of society, the oldest daughter and prop of another impoverished, hard-drinking father.

At nineteen, Mary struck out for independence, going as companion to a rich, difficult old lady in Bath. Arriving at the height of the season, she got a drudge's-eye-view of society at play and did not much like what she saw. It may have been a relief to be summoned to her mother's sickbed, but her dying was a wretched business, with her husband worse than useless. After it, exhausted, Mary went to live with the Bloods for a while and helped the women of the family eke out desperate poverty by long sweated hours of needlework, with Blood often drinking away the proceeds. After two years of this, she was summoned by her brother-in-law to help her sister Eliza through the birth of her first child. Eliza suffered from what sounds like an extreme form of post-natal depression after her daughter was born, and duly handed her over to a wet nurse. She convinced both herself and Mary – or did Mary convince her? – that her only chance of sanity was to leave her husband. The sisters ran away together, leaving the baby behind. When Eliza began to miss the baby (who died before she was a year old), and showed signs of weakening, Mary made her stand firm. She intended that she and her sisters and Fanny Blood should set up an all-woman enterprise together.

Borrowing where they could, they thought of a shop but decided on a school. They none of them had either training or experience and their first venture, at Islington, failed. Moving to Newington Green, they found a lively society of intelligent dissenters grouped round the radical Unitarian minister, Dr Richard Price. At twenty-five, Mary had found people she could talk to at last, but the amateur-run school did badly and they had to take lodgers as well. Worse still, for Mary, Fanny's brother George, a good friend of hers, was accused of getting a local servant girl pregnant and fled to Ireland, and Fanny received a firm proposal at last from a long-time wooer and went to Lisbon to marry him. She had consumption and hoped for a cure, but pregnancy made her worse, and Mary, arriving to nurse her, was just in time for her death and her baby's.

Back in London, after a stormy crossing, in 1786, Mary found that the school had run into debt in her absence. Desperate for money, she applied through one of her new friends to Joseph Johnson the radical publisher and he gave her a £10 advance on a book called *Thoughts on the Education of Daughters* which she wrote at great speed. It contained her first tentative statement of the wrongs of women: 'Few are the

modes of earning a subsistence [for women], and those very humili-
ating.' Companion, schoolteacher or governess were the best of
them, she said.

Mary was next to try her hand at being a governess herself. Friends
got her a position with Viscount and Lady Kingsborough, one of the
richest young couples in Ireland. Cousins, and both heirs to fortunes,
they had made an arranged marriage in their teens and settled down
to breed twelve children and live a life of luxurious idleness. They
were in their early thirties when Mary went to work for them; her
oldest pupil, their daughter Margaret King, was fourteen and she
herself was twenty-seven. As in Bath she was shocked by the frivolous society around her and more shocked still by the contrasting
savage poverty of the Irish peasants. She had grown handsome in a
rather formidable way and become a brilliant talker. At Dublin
parties, people were horrified to find they had actually been talking to
the governess, and Lady Kingsborough may not have liked seeing
both her husband and her current admirer listening engrossed to the
young woman who was in her drawing-room on sufferance. Mary had
not expected to be happy, and she was not, but the children loved her.
In fact they loved her too well and their parents, unsure where they
were with their brilliant employee, decided her influence was getting
too strong. She only stayed with them a year but made a lasting mark
on Margaret, whose parents' marriage broke up soon after she left.

Offered a loan by a friend, Mary decided to chance her luck as a
self-employed writer in London, a bold act. Again she turned for help
to Joseph Johnson, and in 1788 he made her a remarkable proposition.
He would publish her semi-autobiographical novel *Mary*, an
amalgam of her experiences and the Kingsboroughs', and set her up
in rented lodgings. In return she would act as editorial assistant in his
thriving publishing house and work on the *Analytical Review*, a
monthly magazine he had just founded. It was her chance, and she
took it. Johnson was much older, a confirmed bachelor, and she was
soon a central figure in the casual, agreeable literary and radical gath-
erings at his house. She wrote to George Blood: 'I succeed beyond my
most sanguine hopes and really believe I shall clear above two
hundred pounds this year . . . I daily earn more money with less
trouble.'

Her two sisters descended on her, assuming that her success was
theirs. She helped them, but she would not have them to live with her
again. She was busy with her own life. She acted as publisher's reader

for Johnson, she translated, she edited, and she went on with her own writing. If there was gossip about her and Johnson, it cannot have bothered her. There had been various unproductive episodes with young men over the years, but in Johnson she had found a friend.

When Burke's *Reflections on the Revolution in France* came out in 1790 its reactionary tone infuriated Mary and she sat down to write *A Vindication of the Rights of Men*. Some of it could be a text for today: 'Man preys on man and you mourn for the . . . empty pageant of a name when slavery flaps her wing and the sick heart retires to die in lonely wilds . . . the sick wretch who can no longer earn the sour bread of unremitting labour steals to a ditch to bid the world a long good night – or neglected in some ostentatious hospital breathes his last amidst the laughs of mercenary attendants.' Published anonymously, it sold well and was reprinted with her name in December that year.

She followed it two years later with her most important book, *A Vindication of the Rights of Woman*, which she wrote, as usual, at high speed, with the printer's devil waiting at the door. She was not satisfied with it and meant to add a second volume, but never did. It is a powerful if disorganized plea for much of what we now take for granted as basic women's rights, and a good deal that we are still fighting for. For a just society, she argues, women must be educated to be the equals of men and be treated as such. Tyranny debases the tyrant. Women 'may be convenient slaves, but slavery will have its constant effect, degrading the master and the abject dependant.' The book was an instant best-seller, arousing furious passions. Horace Walpole called her a 'hyena in petticoats' and a 'philosophizing serpent' and Hannah More refused to read it simply because of its title. Widely translated, and published in America, it was the high point of her career.

Unluckily for her and for us, Mary was writing at a time when the radical tide had just turned as a result of the drastic developments in France. Her powerful arguments were drowned in the ebb. And her personal life did not help with her audience. She was at the heart of radical society now, meeting men like William Godwin (who thought she monopolized the conversation), William Blake and Henry Fuseli. Instead of writing the second part of her book, she fell in love with Fuseli. He was eighteen years older than her and already well launched in his career as artist of the romantic grotesque. Unluckily for Mary, he had married one of his models a few years before, but she convinced herself that this was no impediment in a free-thinking world. Passion was its own justification. She started to pay unwonted attention to her appearance and wrote him a series of emotional letters. When she proposed a *ménage à trois* his wife forbade her the house and Fuseli backed away.

Humiliated, Mary decided on a dramatic gesture. She would go to Paris. Radical society had been divided by the news of the bloody September massacres that autumn of 1792, but she was still hopeful: 'Children of any growth will do mischief when they meddle with edged tools.' She was thirty-three and beginning to make wry jokes about being 'a spinster on the wing'. Believing as she did that passion nourishes the spirit, she deeply felt the lack of it in her life. As always, there were friends to help her in her new venture, but it was disconcerting to arrive at the Paris lodgings that had been arranged for her and find that her hosts had discreetly retired to the country. The King was on trial, Paris was a city in turmoil, nobody was safe, but Mary stayed on, gradually making her way into the kind of society that suited her. Tom Paine was there, in flight from England after the publication of his *Rights of Man*, and she made friends with him as well as with Madame Roland and the English author Helen Maria Williams.

She lived through the King's execution and the other savage events of that winter, her skirts spattered with blood from the guillotine, and when in the spring war broke out with England she found herself trapped in Paris. She probably did not care. She had met an American called Gilbert Imlay and fallen in love again. He was handsome, intelligent, radical, half businessman half adventurer, and she completely misread him. It was an early case of the classic Anglo-American emotional misunderstanding. For her, it was a grand passion; for him it was an affair. For a while she bloomed and he was carried away on the tide of her emotion. She moved to the comparative safety of Neuilly for an idyllic summer. They did not marry but he registered her as his wife to give her the protection of neutral American citizenship. When she found herself pregnant in August things began gradually to change. She did not much like his business friends. 'The house smells of commerce,' she said once, but he must make money, he countered, so as to take her and the expected child to safe America. That winter he went off on business to Le Havre, leaving her to live through the Terror, pregnant and alone. She comforted herself by writing a *Historical and Moral View of the French Revolution*, a bold act considering that friends like Madame Roland were going to the guillotine, and she was eventually to smuggle it successfully out of France for Johnson to publish. She joined Imlay in Le Havre in February and her daughter Fanny was born, with no trouble, in May 1794. Imlay found the baby entrancing, there was a short spell of happiness and then he left for London on business. Only for two months, he said. Again she followed him with loving, importunate letters: 'Will you not be a good boy and come quickly to play with your girls?'

Beginning to lose hope, she went back to Paris and spent another lonely winter there, writing to Imlay: 'Come to me my dearest friend, husband, father of my child! All these fond names glow at my heart at this moment and dim my eyes. With you an independence is desirable; and it is always within our reach, if affluence escapes us — without you the world again appears empty to me.' At last, in the spring of 1795, worn down, perhaps, by her pleading, he wrote suggesting that she join him in England. She had liked the freedom of life in Paris, where she could appear at parties with her baby in her maid's arms beside her, but of course she went, her American papers making the journey possible. Imlay failed to meet her at Brighton, she went to London, found him still aloof and made an abortive attempt at suicide with laudanum.

Shamed into action, he asked her to make a business trip to Scandinavia for him, half promising to meet her in Basle at the end of it. Always an intrepid traveller, she accepted and took the baby and her nurse along for the voyage from Hull to Sweden, where they were landed from a small boat on a desolate shore. She coped with everything, did a good job for Imlay, and described the adventurous journey in a series of vivid letters. But it became obvious that he did not intend to meet her at Basle and when Mary got back to England she found that he was living with a young actress. She wrote him a note, saying she was going to drown herself, gave it to a servant for delivery, and walked to Battersea Bridge. The tide was low; she hired a boat and rowed herself through the rain to Putney Bridge. She had learned to row in Sweden. At Putney Bridge she moored the boat, paid her toll, climbed over the rail and jumped in. Held up by her petticoats, she endured all the agony of drowning before being pulled out by some watermen.

Recovering, she once again suggested a *ménage à trois*, this time with Imlay and his new mistress. When he refused, she pulled herself together, went back to Johnson and set doggedly to work to turn her Scandinavian letters into a book. She was now using Imlay's name, but would take no money from him. The travel book was a great success. William Godwin wrote, 'If ever there was a book calculated to make a man in love with its author this appears to me to be the book.' He too had had a great success with *Political Justice* in 1793 and *Caleb Williams* in 1794 and was surrounded by notable women like Mary Hays, Amelia Alderson and Elizabeth Inchbald. In 1796 Amelia Alderson wrote to a friend: 'Mrs Inchbald says, the report of the world is that Mr Holcroft is in love with her, *she* with Mr Godwin, and Mr Godwin with *me*, and I am in love with Mr Holcroft!' But Godwin was on record as not believing in marriage. Mary joined their circle in the spring of 1796, calling uninvited on Godwin in his lodgings. It was another of her bold acts, and it worked, she was welcomed. Godwin was beginning to think about settling; he proposed something, probably marriage, to Amelia Alderson in Norfolk that summer and was turned down. Returning to London he found that Mary had moved into lodgings close to his and they became lovers. '*Chez moi*,' he wrote in his diary.

Writing about their relationship after Mary's death Godwin said: 'One sex did not take the priority which long established custom has awarded it, nor the other overstep that delicacy which is so severely imposed. I am not conscious that either party can assume to have been the agent or the patient, the toil spreader or the prey, in the affair.' Which does make one wonder if Mary had not decided to have him. Had she found London stifling after liberated Paris?

The relationship was not an instant success. Next day Godwin wrote a note of apology, asking if she would take him: 'As it shall happen, full of gaiety and life, or a puny valetudinarian?' She answered: 'Full of your own feelings, little as I comprehend them, you forgot mine . . . It is my turn to have a fever today – I am not well – I am hurt – But I mean not to hurt you. Consider what has passed as a fever of the imagination; one of the slight moral shakes to which you are liable – and I – will become again a *Solitary Walker*.' It got her an admirable answer, delicately warning her against egotism: 'You have the feelings of nature . . . do not let them tyrannise over you.' But, 'I will be your friend, the friend of your mind, the admirer of your excellencies . . . Do you not see, while I exhort you to be a philosopher, how painfully acute are my own feelings?'

It was to be a complex relationship, with Mary supplying the passion and Godwin the philosophy, but they did become the loving friends he wanted them to be, though they quarrelled too. It is idle to speculate as to whether it would have lasted. Mary felt his continuing relationship with Mrs Inchbald a threat, and when she found herself pregnant in December it added a new stress. At thirty-seven she had probably assumed she was past child-bearing, now she found herself faced with a second bastard. She made a great scene, told him she wished they had never met, and still he did not propose marriage. It is always awkward to climb down from a publicly held position, but in the end he did so. They were married quietly in March 1797. Most of their friends took it well, but Mrs Inchbald made an unpleasant scene at the theatre and by the summer Mary was forbidding one of Godwin's female admirers the house, as Sophia Fuseli had once forbidden her. But she throve on domesticity and looked forward to another easy birth like the last, when she had been up and about after a week, most unusual in those days. She did not want a doctor, preferring to rely on an experienced midwife, but it proved a difficult birth, the placenta did not come away and a doctor had to be hurriedly summoned for the agonizing extraction, without anaesthetic. At first all seemed well, she had a few days of apparent recovery, then septicaemia set in and she died ten days later on September 10th, 1797, after a desperate fight for life.

Left desolate, with a new-born baby and three-year-old Fanny Imlay (now known as Godwin) on his hands, Godwin turned for comfort to Mrs Inchbald and was ruthlessly snubbed. He occupied himself by writing a remarkably frank *Memoir* of Mary which he published in 1798. Unfortunately, the story of her unorthodox life proved a weapon for the reactionaries attacking her feminist thinking. Her unfinished novel, *Maria, or the Wrongs of Woman*, published at the same time, did not help. Less a novel than a chilling collection of case histories of man's inhumanity to woman, it shows all her virtues of passion and all her faults of disorganization. The fact that she could get no further from her own name than Maria suggests to me at least that Godwin was right about her egotism. Like many other leading feminists, then and now, she never achieved the detachment that carries conviction. But then, she died at thirty-eight.

Her daughter, another Mary, grew up in Godwin's free-thinking impecunious household in the care of their small-minded neighbour, Mrs Clairmont, whom her father married after finding none of his circle of literary ladies prepared to take on his problems. He was only forty-one, but his best days were passed. The spirit of reform was in abeyance, and he turned, with his new wife, to publishing little books for children, a recently discovered market. Mary was a frail child, but she adored her father, competing for his attention with her new step-sister, Claire Clairmont, six months younger than herself. Sent to Scotland for her health, Mary came back to Godwin's house at seventeen, in 1814, and met a disciple of his, a twenty-two year old radical poet called Percy Bysshe Shelley and his even younger wife Harriet.

Shelley had thought the revered author of *Political Justice* dead, been delighted to learn he was alive. He was of good Whig family, though his grandfather had been born in New Jersey, returning to England to make his fortune by marrying two heiresses in succession and finally achieving his baronetcy in 1806. The newness of the title probably added to the two older Shelleys' outrage when the heir was sent down from Oxford for publishing a pamphlet advocating atheism. Shelley had then compounded the offence by making a runaway match with Harriet Westbrook, a respectable bourgeois schoolfriend of his sisters. His grandfather kept a mistress in Lambeth, his father would gladly have paid the upkeep of any bastards, but this marriage to a young nobody enraged them. Shelley's allowance was stopped, and he and Harriet lived a vagrant life pursued by creditors and relying on expensive loans from money lenders, based on Shelley's expectations as heir to his grandfather's fortune. The Oxford débâcle had closed the professions to him, any other form of earning for a young aristocrat was unthinkable. He probably never did think of it: he was going to be a poet and change the world.

He and Godwin shared a belief that wealth should be equally distributed, which meant, in practice, that Shelley was financing Godwin out of the loans he got on his expectations. He and Harriet were constant and welcome visitors at Godwin's house when Mary came home to it. Nineteen-year-old Harriet already had a daughter, Ianthe, and was pregnant again. Shelley liked his partner's attention to be centred entirely on himself and his relationship with Harriet had suffered. Besides, Harriet was an agreeable young woman, Mary was spirited, intelligent and the daughter of two famous liberals. They met in May, declared their love over Mary Wollstonecraft's grave in June, and eloped in July. They had been surprised when Godwin proved conservative and objected (though he went on taking Shelley's money) but Shelley convinced both himself and Mary that Harriet had been unfaithful to him. It seems a curious failure of logic considering that Shelley, who said he believed in free love, had earlier wanted to share Harriet with his friend Thomas Jefferson Hogg.

It was now Mary's turn to share Shelley's vagrant, wilful, unpredictable poet's life and she made a better job of it than Harriet had, but they made the mistake of letting her step-sister Claire Clairmont join the elopement, perhaps on Shelley's invitation. Claire was to prove as much complication as support, competing for Shelley's attention as she had for Godwin's. Her mother pursued them to Calais to urge Claire, not Mary, to return, but she failed and Claire stayed with them for a rambling, uncomfortable journey through France to Switzerland. They were short of money, the country had been ravaged both by French and allied armies during Napoleon's retreat on Paris that spring of 1814. Mary got ill, Shelley sprained his ankle, but he wrote and invited Harriet to join the party, with Mary's agreement. Luckily for everyone she did not come.

Through all the discomforts, Shelley and Mary were ecstatically engaged in exploring each other's minds. Switzerland was a relief after filthy France and they took a house, then ran short of money again and hurried back to England, by river this time, in one of Shelley's panic moves. Mary started a book called *Hate*, but never finished it. Arriving penniless in London, they found Godwin's door closed against them and actually borrowed money from Harriet, who was now far advanced in pregnancy. Her son Charles was born in November, heir to the baronetcy. Mary was pregnant too. Liable to depression like her mother, she was unwell during the pregnancy and resented both Shelley's delight in Harriet's son and the cheerful way he went about with Claire while she was ill at home. That winter she wrote a curious series of love letters to his friend Hogg. Shelley must have told her about offering to share Harriet with Hogg.

Old Sir Bysshe died in January 1815 and after some painful negotiations Shelley's father agreed to give him an allowance of £1,000 a year, of which he at once made £200 a year over to Harriet. Mary's baby was born prematurely in February. Ten days later they moved lodgings and the infant died, an early case of cot death, four days afterwards. Mary was desolate and Hogg paid for a country holiday for them. Shelley wrote to him: 'I shall be very happy to see you again and give you your share of our common treasure of which you have been cheated for several days.' But Mary seems to have felt that writing love letters to Hogg was going quite far enough. She and Shelley spent a happy summer in a house on the fringes of Windsor

Great Park, and Shelley wrote *Alastor*. An odd poem in the circumstances, it tells the story of a poet who dreams of an ideal love and wakes to find she does not exist. John Murray turned it down but Shelley had it printed himself and got some hostile reviews with phrases such as 'sublime obscurity' or, more simply, 'nonsense'.

Mary's son William was born early in 1816, and she was happily absorbed in her thriving baby. Shelley still believed in free love; Mary was busy and Claire was there. It does seem probable that when Claire forced herself on the attention of the now notorious poet Lord Byron in the spring of 1816 she was already pregnant by Shelley. She and Mary were not in fact blood kin, but they were step-sisters, and the law still forbade a relationship with a deceased wife's sister. Even Shelley might have felt that this would be a scandal too far. As for Byron, he was in the throes of his painful, public separation from his wife: 'I was fain to take a little love (if pressed particularly) by way of Novelty,' he wrote to his own half-sister, Augusta Leigh.

When Byron retreated to Switzerland, Claire urged Shelley and Mary to go there too, perhaps hoping that Mary and Byron would pair off, leaving Shelley to her. He was ill that spring. The doctors spoke gloomily of both consumption and abscesses on the lungs and urged healthy air abroad. Shelley was teetotal and vegetarian and suffered from nightmares and hallucinations. Mary did not pretend to housekeeping; they very likely never had quite enough to eat. Hogg complained of hunger in their house and Byron was later to refuse Claire custody of the child Allegra, saying he did not want her to 'perish of starvation and green fruit'.

In the end, Shelley and Mary yielded to Claire's persuasion and went to Switzerland where they took a small house not far from Byron's more ostentatious Villa Diodati. The two poets became great friends and spent a happy summer talking, writing and boating on the lake. One evening Byron suggested they all write ghost stories and Mary began *Frankenstein*. But at home the gossips who had said Godwin had sold his daughters to Shelley for eight and seven hundred pounds respectively now said Byron and Shelley were sharing their mistresses. Godwin was asking for money as usual; they had what Mary called an 'alarming letter' from her half-sister Fanny, and Byron had lost all interest in Claire whose pregnancy was now visible. They went home in September and settled in lodgings in Bath to keep Claire's secret as long as possible. In October, Fanny committed suicide with laudanum at Swansea, and in December Harriet Shelley drowned herself in the Serpentine. Fanny may have been in love with Shelley, or even pregnant by him; Harriet had led a chequered emotional life since parting from him. Shelley hoped to take charge of her two children and Mary agreed enthusiastically to the idea. To make this easier, they married very quietly in December. The Godwins were there, and Godwin was soon boasting about his aristocratic son-in-law.

Harriet's domineering sister Eliza would not part with the children and her father sued Shelley successfully for their custody. 'No words can express the anguish he felt when his elder children were torn from him,' Mary wrote later. She loved children too. Claire's daughter Allegra was born in January and Shelley wrote to Byron about her. He got no answer. Naturally, they looked after Claire and the baby, and naturally the gossips talked. But by March *Frankenstein* was finished and Shelley correcting it. It was a real partnership, they wrote their journal together and read each other's works as they were being written. Shelley was writing *The Revolt of Islam* that summer, but they were dangerously in debt again, partly due to Shelley's incorrigible generosity. Not for the first time, they had to part while he hid from his creditors, fearing the debtors' prison. Mary had a second baby, Clara, that September, and Shelley was ill again.

The Revolt of Islam and *Frankenstein* both came out early in 1818 and their reception may have put a strain on their relationship. Shelley's poem was a failure, Mary's novel, published anonymously, caught the contemporary public taste for the scientific macabre, as it has the modern one, and was an instant success. They had decided to go south again for Shelley's health and spent an exciting few weeks in London before they left, seeing the newly displayed Elgin Marbles and paying five delighted visits to Mozart's *Don Giovanni*, a current success at the Haymarket Theatre.

They went to Italy, taking Claire and her baby with them, and Shelley's health improved at once. Byron was in Venice, refusing to answer Claire's letters, so it was through Shelley that an agreement was reached by which she gave Allegra up to Byron, hoping he would establish her in life. It was a traumatic business, with Claire desperately unhappy and Shelley doing his best to comfort her and whipping the party off to Pisa as a diversion. That summer he took Claire to Venice to persuade Byron to let her see little Allegra, now established with the British Consul, Belgrave Hoppner and his Swiss wife. Byron asked him to stay and he sent for Mary to join him with the children, but the journey was too much for one-year-old Clara, who died in the hall of a Venice inn.

They were soon travelling again, visiting Rome and then Naples where, in February 1819, Shelley registered the birth of Elena Adelaide Shelley on the twenty-seventh of December. He named himself and Mary as the parents, but, unusually, Mary was not present at the registration, a midwife taking her place, and the baby was handed over at once to foster parents. Mary was a devoted mother; the child has to have been Claire's. They left for Rome, and Mary's diary speaks of a 'tremendous fuss' on the way. They meant to return to Naples, when Shelley and Claire presumably hoped to retrieve little Elena, but in Rome three-year-old William died of malaria, the third of Mary's children to succumb to the hazards of their father's restless wanderings. It was all too much. Mary fell into a deep depression: 'After my William's death this world seemed only quicksand, sinking beneath my feet.' In the end, Shelley got impatient: 'My dearest Mary, wherefore hast thou gone, And left me in this dreary world alone?' And all Godwin did was write and ask for money.

They went to Leghorn, both writing about incest. Shelley's *The Cenci* was published, but not staged, next year. Mary said that writing her *Matilda* 'helped to quell my wretchedness temporarily,' but she did not publish it. Shelley also wrote his formidable *Mask of Anarchy* that autumn of 1819 on hearing of the Peterloo massacre, when troops opened fire on a peaceful protest meeting at Manchester and killed nine people. He sent it to his friend Leigh Hunt for publication in the *Examiner*, but Hunt did not dare do so.

They moved to Florence for the birth of Mary's son Percy Florence in November. He must have been conceived about the time of the 'tremendous fuss'. 'Poor Mary begins (for the first time) to look a little consoled,' wrote Shelley, and she began a new novel, *Valperga*. It was a ferociously cold winter in Florence. Shelley had pains in his side and they moved again, to Pisa, where they made friends with a couple who called themselves Mason. In fact, Mrs Mason was Margaret King, Mary Wollstonecraft's favourite pupil, who had abandoned a titled husband and brood of children in Ireland to live happily with her 'husband' and their two daughters in Italy. She wrote books on child care, and that autumn she got Claire a job as governess in Florence, which must have taken a little pressure off the Shelleys.

It was just as well. That summer the scandal about the Naples baby broke, when their servant Paolo tried to blackmail Shelley about her.

To make it all the more painful, they learned that the baby had actually died in Naples. The Hoppners heard the story and passed it on to Byron who used it as a pretext to put little Allegra into a convent and keep Claire away from her. Mary wrote a firm letter to the Hoppners: 'The union between my husband and myself has ever been undisturbed. Love caused our first imprudence, love . . . a perfect trust one in the other, a confidence and affection, which . . . has increased daily, and knows no bounds.' All this was true, but it was not all the truth. She must indeed have loved Shelley very much.

Like other poets, he went on having his goddesses. There was Emilia Viviani, a beautiful Italian girl immured in a convent, for whom he wrote *Epipsychidion*, calling her, 'Seraph in Heaven! Too gentle to be human,' and speaking of Mary's coldness to him. And then there were Edward and Jane Williams, an unmarried couple with whom they made friends in the spring of 1821. Jane's conversation '*is nothing particular*', Mary wrote to Claire, but her voice was agreeable and Shelley bought her a guitar and wrote her some charming lyrics. Mary had a new friend too, a young Greek prince called Alexander Mavrocordato who taught her Greek and was soon to distinguish himself in the Greek War of Independence. Shelley found it hard to like Mavrocordato, and when Emilia finally married, Mary summed up that affair as 'Shelley's platonics.'

They all moved into Pisa for the winter of 1821, the Shelleys taking a flat in the same house as the Williams, while Byron lived opposite. 'Pisa, you see has become a little nest of singing birds,' wrote Mary. She did not much like Byron and saw little of him but visited his mistress Teresa Guiccioli regularly. She finished *Valperga*, studied Homer and began to go to church, Shelley making no objection. He had Jane Williams for a muse now.

A friend of the Williams, John Edward Trelawny joined the party early in 1822 and was amazed at Shelley: 'Was it possible this mild-looking beardless boy could be the veritable monster at war with all the world?' Mary liked Trelawny, he had 'the rare merit for interesting my imagination,' she said. She was pregnant again and anxious about Claire, who came to visit them but was away when the news arrived of little Allegra's death from typhus at her convent. In the general crisis that followed, the Shelleys and Williams moved into a house together. It did not suit anyone. 'Their servants and mine quarrel like cats and dogs,' wrote Mary. 'And besides, you may imagine how ill a large family agrees with my laziness, when accounts and domestic concerns come to be talked of.' It gives a gloomy picture of Mary's housekeeping, but also serves as a reminder that theirs was always poverty with servants. It is interesting to compare Dorothy Wordsworth. She had a poet on her hands too, but she had grown up in a more rugged north-country tradition and her *Journal* is full in equal parts of the raw material of poetry and the pies and bread she baked herself. It made for a healthier poet.

Shelley had a new boat, the *Ariel*, but Mary did not feel well enough to go out in it, so he took Jane Williams instead. Mary felt worse and worse. Sharing a house with Jane was not easy, even Shelley wrote: 'It is a pity that anyone so pretty should be so selfish.' But he also complained of Mary's 'hysterical affections'. A London publisher was being difficult about *Valperga*; Claire came to stay again; Mary had a miscarriage in June and quick-witted Shelley saved her life by sitting her in a bucket of ice. But he was suffering as he often did from dreams and hallucinations and used to come screaming into his sick wife's bedroom. His friend Leigh Hunt and his family arrived on a long-planned and rather unpromising visit to Byron and Shelley and Williams sailed up to Leghorn to meet them. As Shelley had feared, Byron was not very welcoming to the Hunts, and Mary, still unwell and in low spirits, was afraid he would bring them back with him. It was so stormy on the day the two men were to sail back that she and Jane Williams were sure that they would not have started. On the voyage up, the captain of the boat had been with them; returning they had only the boy. They were not experienced seamen, but Shelley had always been an impulsive taker of risks, even suicidal ones. Mary and Jane were not even anxious for a couple of days; it was nine more before the two bodies were washed ashore.

At the time, the two women clung together for comfort, but Jane soon went back to England and started telling people about Shelley's love for her, and the relationship cooled. Staying with the Hunts, Mary was shocked at how coldly Leigh Hunt treated her and horrified to learn that Shelley had grumbled to his friend during their last meeting about her low spirits and withdrawal from him. She felt guilty about this for a long time. She was in financial straits too. Byron promised financial help at first, but failed to produce it. Sir Timothy Shelley offered to bring up his grandson if Mary would part with him entirely. Refusing, she decided to be a poet's widow, perhaps easier than being his wife, live by her pen, and bring up her son on her own.

Returning to London in 1823 she found that *Frankenstein* was being staged. She published an edition of Shelley's poems in 1824 but this enraged Sir Timothy, who threatened to stop the small allowance he was giving her for young Percy unless she suppressed the volume and promised not to publish a life of Shelley. She had to agree. Later, when she published her next novel, *The Last Man*, Sir Timothy again threatened to withdraw the allowance but was persuaded not to do so. His other grandson, Harriet's Charles, died in 1826, leaving Percy the sole heir, which strengthened Mary's position and improved her finances. An American actor and dramatist, John Howard Payne, asked her to marry him in 1825, but she refused him, saying she was Shelley's widow, nothing else. He then decided she ought to marry his friend Washington Irving and even suggested this to Irving, but nothing came of it. Becoming more conservative, Mary was disappointed to find her unorthodox past still held against her by society, though she established herself as a figure in the literary world, publishing novels, stories and articles and editing Shelley's prose. His poems were reissued in 1839 and she began at last to get some income from his work.

She meant to bring up her son to be the genius his father had been, but Percy surprised her by growing up to be a pleasant, uninteresting young man. He became a baronet when Sir Timothy finally died in 1844 and married an equally pleasant young widow a few years later. Mary loved his wife Jane and the two of them sheltered her through an outbreak of blackmail that followed her belated inheritance of Shelley's estate. She spent the last years of her life comfortably in their shadow and died, at Bournemouth, in 1851. In 1889 Shelley's heart, which she kept in her desk wrapped in a copy of *Adonais*, was buried there with her. She had truly loved and deeply borne with him, but she had also managed without him for almost thirty years.

9
Love of One's Art

STRONG-MINDED Fanny Burney held out for love, and got it in the end, but many women settled for compromise marriages. If even Lady Hester Stanhope, with her aristocratic connection and government pension found spinsterhood an uneasy lot, what hope was there for the dowerless daughters of the middle classes? Jane Austen brilliantly analyses their plight in *Pride and Prejudice*. Jane and Elizabeth Bennet hold out for marriages of two minds, against the odds, and actually achieve them; realist Charlotte Lucas settles for what she can get and makes the best of her Mr Collins. All three of them know that marriage is their only hope of respectable independence, if such it can be called. Jane Austen herself came close to a compromise marriage and then cried off, but she had her writing to absorb, and her sister to support her.

Maria Edgeworth also had family and authorship to keep her going through a solitary life. Like Fanny Burney, she had a devoted father. Born in 1767, she was the second child and oldest daughter of the first of Richard Lovell Edgeworth's four marriages. She was tiny (under four foot seven), plain, and hideously shy, but her father, a successful man of letters, recognized her good mind and trained her to be his right hand, both on his Irish estate and in his literary work, until she gradually developed a line of her own. His wives, in succession, bore his children and looked after the domestic side of things. There was almost a hitch in the happy arrangement when Maria's second stepmother died and Edgeworth swiftly married a woman younger than Maria, whom she did not like, but they weathered it, and Maria was soon calling the new Mrs Edgeworth 'mother'.

By this time she was achieving a status of her own. Her father had encouraged her successful venture into the growing market for moral children's stories, but while he was occupied with his fourth wife, Maria launched into something he disapproved of, a novel. *Castle*

Rackrent was based on her first-hand experience of Irish life and was an instant success when it was published in 1800, and *Belinda*, a novel of fashionable life, did still better when it came out next year. Mr Edgeworth stopped objecting to the novel. Maria was fêted by the bluestockings but, like Fanny Burney, she disappointed them as a lion by refusing to roar. Deeply aware of her unprepossessing appearance, she still hoped for marriage, writing to her younger half-brother Lovell that, 'I have no doubt that my happiness would be much increased by a union with a man suited to me in character, temper, and understanding, *and firmly attached to me* – but deduct any of these circumstances and I think I should lose infinitely more than I should gain.'

She had her one chance of marriage on a family visit to Paris in 1802, made possible by the Peace of Amiens, when she was thirty-five. *Belinda* had been translated into French; she was a celebrity and met everyone. A Swiss professor, Marc-Auguste Pictet described her at this time: 'A small figure, eyes nearly always lowered, a profoundly modest and reserved air . . . But when she spoke which was too rarely . . . nothing could have been better thought, and nothing better said, though always timidly expressed.' A Swedish diplomat saw all this and proposed to her: 'Monsieur Edelcrantz, a Swedish gentleman . . . of superior understanding and mild manners . . . came to offer me his hand and heart!!' Edelcrantz was a bachelor of forty-six with an old mother at home and only his salary to support them. It would mean a formidably different life for Maria. She thought about it for a few days, then refused him and never heard from him again. Her father thought she loved Edelcrantz but was right to refuse him. He was charged with embezzlement later in life, so she may have been wise, but she never forgot him.

She went on with her successful career as a novelist, though her father's moralizing influence lies a little heavy on some of the later books. When he died in 1817, she and her 'mother' clung together for comfort, and then Maria gradually found herself the man of the family. Her brother Lovell, the heir, had been caught up in Napoleon's drastic swoop on English travellers in 1803 and had spent the next eleven years in captivity. It had damaged him, and he dwindled over the years into a remittance man in Liverpool while Maria capably ran things at Edgeworthstown. She was known now as a brilliant talker and her fame gave her a kind of titular rank as a married lady so that she could chaperone her younger sisters, which increased her self-confidence, though her interference in their affairs was not always happy. Welcomed in the great Whig houses, and friends with Sir Walter Scott, she published her last novel, *Helen*, when she was sixty-seven and died at eighty-two, at Edgeworthstown, with her beloved 'mother' at her side. If she had married Edelcrantz, she would very likely have died in childbirth like Mary Wollstonecraft.

* * *

Jane Austen too had family to support her in a life of more literature than love, but the Austens lived very much more modestly than the Edgeworths, and the constraints were inevitably greater. Jane was born in 1775, the second daughter and seventh child of a Hampshire clergyman called George Austen. He was a surgeon's son who had got a scholarship to Oxford, taken orders and married well-connected Cassandra Leigh. She made a good job of being a parson's wife on limited means, stretched as they were by eight children of whom one, a boy, was retarded. He was put into care and never spoken of. The other five boys were a healthy, intelligent, upstanding lot. Cassandra, the other girl, was born two years before Jane, and the last boy, Charles, four years after that, so Cassandra got to look after Jane.

It was a happy childhood with a few years at boarding school, always together. 'If Cassandra was going to have her head cut off,' said their mother, 'Jane would insist in sharing her fate.' Their father supplemented the family's modest income by taking pupils whom he taught with his own sons, so it was probably easier to send the girls away to school. Returning home as the boys began to launch out into the world, they joined a lively society. James was running his own monthly at Oxford; Henry contributed to it; Jane may have too. She was later to tell a niece that she wished that she had '*read* more and written *less*' in her teens, but she had the family in stitches when she read aloud her comic *History of England* and her lighthearted parodies of contemporary novels.

The brothers throve. James went into the church, Charles and Francis into the navy, Henry had several careers, while lucky Edward was richly adopted by relations and sent on the Grand Tour. The only career for the girls was marriage. Mrs Austen was too capable a mother not to have seen to it that they were trained in the essential accomplishments: Cassandra could draw, Jane played the piano, though she did not enjoy listening to music, they both sewed beautifully and wrote fine, clear hands. They were used to the company of

men, and when they first started to go to balls there were still brothers about to go too. They lived comfortably, if frugally, in the world
of country gentlefolk, whose fine shades Jane was to describe so well.
They paid long visits to relatives and friends, meeting young men at
balls in their houses and at the monthly winter assemblies at
Basingstoke. Much later, Mrs Mitford was to quote reports of Jane as
a 'pretty, silly, affected husband-hunting butterfly'. They were certainly attractive girls, if not beauties, and well educated by the standards of the day. Like their mother, they would have made admirable
clergymen's wives, but while she had brought her husband a small
income there was not much chance of dowries for them. The money
that did exist, tantalisingly, in the family was never to come their way.
'Legacies are a very wholesome diet,' Jane once wryly wrote to
Cassandra about someone else.

Jane's first surviving letter to Cassandra, written in January 1796,
when she was twenty-one, sums up their situation as it then was.
Cassandra had got engaged the year before to a young clergyman,
Thomas Fowle, an old pupil of Mr Austen's, which must have affected
her relationship with her sister. She was spending her twenty-third
birthday with Tom's family at his father's vicarage at Kintbury. Jane
begins her letter with good wishes and goes straight on to mention
another birthday, that of Tom Lefroy, who was staying with his aunt,
their friend and neighbour Mrs Lefroy, wife of yet another clergyman. Tom was being laughed at about Jane, she tells Cassandra, and
with cause. They had been to a ball at a neighbour's house: 'Imagine
to yourself everything most profligate and shocking in the way of
dancing and sitting down together.' Tom was about to return to
Ireland to read for the bar, but there was to be one more ball, at the
Lefroys' house, first. 'I rather expect to receive an offer from my
friend in the course of the evening,' writes Jane in her next letter. 'I
shall refuse him, however, unless he promises to give away his white
coat.' How serious was she? And did he propose? He did go back to
Ireland, where he married a few years later and ultimately became
Lord Chief Justice.

Jane and Cassandra took it in turns to visit their rich, adopted
brother Edward Knight, now married and settled in Kent. When they
were apart they corresponded regularly, but only Jane's letters
survive, heavily edited by Cassandra after her death. There were
visits to London too, but always problems of transport, since unlike
Mary Wollstonecraft, they never travelled alone. 'Tomorrow I shall

be just like Camilla [Fanny Burney's heroine] in Mr Dubster's summer house; for my Lionel will have taken away the ladder . . . and here I must stay till his return.' Unlike Mary Wollstonecraft, Jane Austen laughed about her constraints, but they were there: 'My Father will be so good as to fetch home his prodigal daughter from Town, I hope, unless he wishes me to walk the Hospitals, enter at the Temple, or mount Guard at St James'.'

Next year, tragedy struck. Disappointed in his hopes of a living, Cassandra's fiancé went to the West Indies as companion to his patron, Harriette Wilson's Lord Craven, described by Jane Austen as 'very pleasing' aside from 'the little flaw of having a mistress now living with him.' Tom Fowle caught fever and died in the West Indies and Lord Craven made matters more painful by saying he would never have taken him if he had known of the engagement. After her sister's death, Cassandra burned all Jane's letters for this sad year, so we do not know how they consoled each other but it must have strengthened the bond between them. Jane was only twenty-two and Cassandra twenty-four but they began to look like two daughters at home, and their hard-working mother reacted by sliding gently into invalidity. Cassandra took over the housekeeping, with Jane as her capable stand-in when she went on family visits: 'I am very grand indeed; I had the dignity of dropping out my mother's laudanum last night. I carry about the keys of the wine and closet, and twice since I began this letter have had orders to give in the kitchen.' And in another letter to Cassandra: 'I am very fond of experimental house-keeping, such as having an ox-cheek now and then; I shall have one next week, and I mean to have some little dumplings put into it, that I may fancy myself at Godmersham,' their rich brother Edward's house in Kent.

Jane met a Mr Blackall that year, again through Mrs Lefroy, to whom he wrote a curious letter after his visit: 'I am very sorry to hear of Mrs Austen's illness. It would give me particular pleasure to have an opportunity of improving my acquaintance with that family – with a hope of creating to myself a nearer interest. But at present I cannot indulge any expectation of it.' 'This is rational enough,' comments Jane, 'there is less love and more sense in it than sometimes appeared before and I am very well satisfied.'

From now on there was to be more sense than love in their lives. Their father had handed over his second living, at Deane near Steventon, to his eldest son when James married in 1792, with a serious loss in income of £50 a year. The war with France meant rising prices, and they felt it like the rest of the middle class: 'People get so horridly poor and economical in this part of the World that I have no patience with them,' wrote Jane. 'Kent is the only place for happiness. Everybody is rich there.' By 1798 the Austens had given up their carriage and the girls were dependent on friends for transport to their balls. They went on going, but less often. Their first nieces had been born in 1793 and when James's wife died in 1795 her little girl Anna came to Steventon to be looked after by her aunts. James soon remarried, and when his new wife, their old friend Mary Lloyd, had her first baby, Jane wrote to Cassandra: 'Mary does not manage matters in such a way as to make me want to lay in myself.' Elizabeth, Edward's wife, managed things better and, 'Was really a pretty object with her nice clean cap put on so tidily and her dress so uniformly white and orderly.' But then Elizabeth was rich. Jane was always aware of the usefulness of money.

When did she start thinking of her writing as a possible source of income? By 1797 she had written two full-length books, *Elinor and Marianne* and *First Impressions* (later *Sense and Sensibility* and *Pride and Prejudice*). Four-year-old Anna was to recall gales of laughter coming from the upstairs room where Jane was reading *First Impressions* aloud to Cassandra. That November Mr Austen wrote to Thomas Cadell, the successful publisher of, among other things, Gibbon's *Decline and Fall of the Roman Empire*, to offer him 'a three volume novel about the length of Miss Burney's *Evelina*.' The offer was declined by return of post. *Evelina* had been out nearly twenty years and there was not much appeal in a country clergyman writing from Steventon, Hampshire. They did not try again, but about this time Jane carefully copied out a short novel called *Lady Susan*. It was a new departure for her, a novel in letters like *Evelina*, and the central character is a brilliantly drawn and totally unscrupulous woman. Were it not in letters it might be a resounding success today, but Jane obviously meant to suppress it, since her next heroine was also called Susan.

One day in November 1800 Jane came back to Steventon with her friend Martha Lloyd. At twenty-five, they had actually travelled alone together: 'Our plan is to . . . throw ourselves into a postchaise, one upon the other, our heads hanging out at one door, and our feet at the opposite.' Arriving after this cheerful journey, they were met by a bald announcement from Mrs Austen: 'Well, girls, it is all settled. We have decided to leave Steventon and go to live at Bath.' Jane fainted.

George Austen was sixty-nine. He planned to hand the living to his son James and go to Bath for a comfortable retirement near to his wife's rich relatives, the Leigh-Perrots. Jane had never much enjoyed the family visits to Bath, now it looked as if she must spend the rest of her life there. If she and Cassandra felt this was a last attempt by their parents to get them married off at all costs it may have added to their dislike of the plan.

Two years later, in 1802, Jane accepted an offer of marriage. She and Cassandra had been staying with James and Mary back at Steventon and gone on to visit their friends Catherine and Alethea Bigg at their comfortable house, Manydown. Their brother Harris, an old friend, but six years younger than Jane, asked her to marry him and she said yes, then slept on it, changed her mind and refused him in the morning. Parting from their friends in floods of tears, she and Cassandra made their brother James miss his Sunday duties in order to take them home to Bath. Harris was heir to Manydown. It was Jane's chance of an establishment and she could not bring herself to take it. Harris married two years later.

Around this time Jane began a book called *The Watsons* about four sisters with no money, and their marriage problems, but she abandoned it after a while. Her nephew thought this was because it was set on too low a social level, with its vulgar details of knife boxes and the great wash, but it may well have been that the subject came too near the bone for her and Cassandra, facing life as spinsters in the 'white glare' of Bath. Jane was twenty-seven in 1802 and Cassandra twenty-nine. The long war had taken its toll, young men were in the army or navy, girls danced together at balls, older girls did not dance at all. Emma, the heroine of *The Watsons*, sums up what must have been the Austen sisters' attitude: 'To be so bent on marriage – to pursue a man merely for the sake of situation – is a sort of thing that shocks me; I cannot understand it. Poverty is a great evil, but to a woman of education and feeling it ought not, it cannot be the greatest – I would rather be a teacher at a school (and I can think of nothing worse) than marry a man I did not like.' Was this Jane and Cassandra's view of teaching? On another occasion, writing from Kent, Jane spoke with sympathy of the plight of the new governess of her brother's lively children. Like Mary Wollstonecraft, she and Cassandra were aware of women's alternatives, but they did not seriously consider them for themselves.

There was a family tradition of one other romance in Jane's life. They went on holiday in the west country one year and, the story goes,

Jane met a young man there and an attachment developed, only to end tragically with his disappearance or death. It has been suggested that the young man was Wordsworth's beloved younger brother John, an East India Company captain who went down with his ship in February 1805. It is a tempting theory. John Wordsworth was thirty-three in 1805. He was a man of deep feelings like all the Wordsworths, and was intending to make this his last voyage before settling down in England. He might well have been looking about for a wife, and Jane had three much-loved brothers in the navy, but it is only a theory.

Jane finished another book in the early years at Bath, and made another effort to get published. In 1803 Crosby and Co. actually gave her £10 for a book called *Susan* (our *Northanger Abbey*) but then failed to publish it. Ten pounds was a respectable sum to a young lady on an allowance of £20 a year, but the hope dashed must have added to the general gloom of those Bath years. Jane's writing seems to have slowed to a halt with the unfinished *Watsons*.

This was probably also due to the sudden death of Mr Austen early in 1804. His health had failed after his retirement, perhaps busy Bath suited him no better than it did his daughters. He had worked hard and saved nothing, and the income from Steventon died with him. His widow and daughters were left with £210 a year, part of which was Cassandra's interest on a legacy from her fiancé. It was the classic situation of the impoverished widow with sons deeply committed to lives and families of their own. Rich Edward promised his mother and sisters £100 a year, and Frank and Henry promised £50 each, though erratic Henry added a proviso, 'so long as my present precarious income remains.' The three bereaved women made the gallant best of things, moving into lodgings and away from expensive Bath. Martha Lloyd's mother died at about the same time as Mr Austen and she joined forces with her friends and their mother. For a while the foursome shared lodgings with Frank Austen and his wife at Southampton; he was a captain now, waiting for a ship, and just as hard up as the rest of them. Many years later, long after Jane's death, and by then a widowed admiral, he was to marry Martha Lloyd.

A passage in a letter to Cassandra suggests that in 1808 while staying in Kent, Jane refused a proposal from a clergyman called Edward Bridges, four years younger than herself. The news of his engagement to someone else very soon afterwards 'was *quite* news,' she wrote. That was the end of romance. From then on, she lived the life of a maiden aunt and put her heart into her work. We are the gainers.

Now that Martha was with them, Jane and Cassandra were free to go away together. They made themselves so useful as aunts and sisters that it is surprising that it was not until 1808, when they had supported him through his wife's death after childbirth, that rich Edward offered the four of them the choice of a cottage either near him in Kent or on his other estate in Hampshire. They chose Chawton Cottage, not too far from Steventon and their old friends. From now on life would be easier: 'Yes, yes, we *will* have a pianoforte, as good a one as can be got for thirty guineas, and I will practise country dances, that we may have some amusement for our nephews and nieces.' Jane had had to sell her piano when they moved to Bath, and had missed it. There were family jokes now about spinsters; the four of them had been tidily packaged into the old ladies at Chawton.

In 1809 Jane Austen tried to stir up Crosby about *Susan*, but he merely offered it back for the £10 he had paid for it, an impossible sum at that point. She went on making the breakfast, and playing the piano, and the maiden aunt, and behind the façade of 'dear Aunt Jane' she probably went through some kind of personal crisis in the next two years, for which no letters survive. In 1811 *Sense and Sensibility* was at the printers, and *Pride and Prejudice* was being revised. This time Jane Austen had decided to keep control. Her brother Henry found her a minor publisher called Thomas Egerton and advanced the money so that she could pay for publication of *Sense and Sensibility* and take the profits. It was published anonymously and achieved a modest success, netting her £140. 'I can no more forget it, than a mother can her sucking child,' she wrote while she was correcting proofs. She enjoyed hearing her niece Anna, unaware of its author, dismiss it as 'rubbish' in the local library. The older members of the family, who knew, were delighted, and the critics respectful. Lady Bessborough recommended the book to Granville Leveson Gower, though she said it ended stupidly.

Egerton was pleased with the book's success and offered £110 for the copyright of *Pride and Prejudice*. Jane accepted this and may have regretted it when it did much better than *Sense and Sensibility*. It was the only one of her books to go into a third edition, though Egerton may not have mentioned this to his author. 'I have got my own darling child from London,' she wrote, when it came out, again anonymously, in 1813, but her brother Henry was so delighted with its enthusiastic reception that he betrayed his sister's secret. She minded this very much, though she was characteristically nice about it, but she refused to be lionised, which may have contributed to her failure to achieve mass-market success.

Her next book, *Mansfield Park*, struck a more serious note and did less well. The first two had been revisions of lighthearted early work, this was new and more thoughtful, reflecting perhaps the moral crisis Jane had been through. Her own world and the world outside had changed enormously since those cheerful days at Steventon, and her letters reflect this. In 1809, writing about Hannah More's new novel, she had said, 'I do not like the Evangelicals.' By 1814 she was 'by no means convinced that we ought not all to be Evangelicals.' In 1813 she took the side of the Princess of Wales in her public conflict with her dissolute husband about the upbringing of their daughter Charlotte: 'Poor woman, I shall support her as long as I can, because she is a woman, and because I hate her husband . . . she would have been respectable, if the prince had behaved only tolerably to her at first.'

Egerton made a bad job of printing *Mansfield Park*, and she moved to John Murray with *Emma*, once again borrowing from Henry to pay for publication and take the profits, just over £220. Once again she refused personal publicity and never went to John Murray's literary lunches, where she would have met admirers like Scott and Byron. Granted her views on him, it must have been disconcerting to learn that the Prince Regent had copies of all her books in all his houses and had let it be known that she might dedicate the next one to him. She dutifully did so with *Emma*, but when it was further suggested that she dedicate the one after to Prince Leopold, fiancé of Princess Charlotte, and make it a 'romance about the august house of Saxe-Coburg' she drew a firm line. 'I could no more write a romance than an epic poem.' She must be able to 'Relax into laughing at myself or other people . . . keep my own style and go on my own way.' Instead of the Saxe-Coburg romance, she wrote *Persuasion*, many people's favourite of her novels. Annabella Milbanke, the future Lady Byron, had said that *Pride and Prejudice* was 'not a crying book'. *Persuasion* is.

Jane was not well when she was writing it, and had trouble with the ending, rewriting the last chapter. Then she started a new book, *Sanditon*, which would have been totally different and might have lost her some readers and gained new ones. The air is colder in Sanditon and the laughter more savage. It was never finished; and *Persuasion* was not published in her lifetime. She had Addison's Disease, curable now, fatal then, and declined into a 'very genteel portable sort of an invalid,' stretched out on three chairs so as to leave the sofa free for her mother. Her rich uncle Leigh-Perrot died, leaving his sister Mrs Austen nothing, and this made Jane worse, though she was ashamed, she said, to have to admit it. But she could still give good advice to a niece about her literary endeavours and write lovingly about Cassandra's devoted nursing. They moved to Winchester in May 1817, to be nearer the doctor, and she died there in July. She had made her own will and, remarkably, made Cassandra, not any of the brothers, her executor. She had earned, in her lifetime, a total of £671.16s. And she had changed the course of the English novel.

*   *   *

Elizabeth Inchbald tried a compromise marriage and, once widowed, decided she preferred the dangerous independence of the freelance author. Born Elizabeth Simpson in 1753, she wanted to be an actress, not a writer. She was a Suffolk farmer's daughter and never went to school, but they were a family who read a great deal, often plays, and visited their local theatres at Bury St Edmunds and Norwich. Elizabeth was charming, with a slight stammer, white skin and tawny hair. At sixteen she asked Richard Griffith, the actor manager of the Norwich Theatre, for work, and developed a girlish passion for him, despite being civilly rebuffed. 'Each dear letter of the name is harmony,' she wrote in her diary. Next year she visited her two married sisters in London, saw all the sights and met an actor called Joseph Inchbald, an older man with two illegitimate sons. He became her devoted wooer but she remained faithful to Griffith. Her diary for that winter remarks laconically: 'Jan 22. Saw Mr Griffith's picture. Jan 28. Stole it.' But a few days later she was disappointed at not receiving a letter from Inchbald.

And Griffith still would not give her a chance as an actress. Frustrated, she ran away to London at seventeen, leaving the traditional note of apology for her mother. In later years, she made a good story of her adventures as she looked unavailingly for work in the London theatre, the teenager's dream of being hailed as a star rapidly changing to the nightmare of pursuit and rape, which luckily for her, was only a dream too. After a few exciting days she found refuge with her married sisters, where Inchbald soon took up the pursuit, and her mother forgave her. The experience must have convinced her that she could not make her way as an actress on her own. She married Inchbald, also a Roman Catholic, that summer and appeared as Cordelia to his Lear in September. She soon discovered that her husband had poor health and was madly jealous: he used to go out drinking with a friend and make furious scenes when he came home. And he learned that she had a sharp tongue and a temper to match.

Like her he was a good actor but not a great one. Their life was mainly in the provinces, and it was in Liverpool that they met Sarah Siddons and her brother John Philip Kemble, who were just starting out on what was to be their brilliant stage career. The four of them became friends and Inchbald was soon jealous of handsome Kemble when Elizabeth appeared in a play of his and he took an interest in the novel she was writing.

Then, in 1779, Inchbald suddenly died. Kemble composed a Latin epitaph for Inchbald, but did not propose to his widow as she must have hoped. In her diary she wrote: 'Began this year a happy wife – finished it a wretched widow.' Her husband left only £380, but Tate Wilkinson, for whom they were working at the time, offered her another year with his company at an increased salary of a guinea and a half a week. Next year she made her London début in a breeches part at Covent Garden. She was kindly but not passionately received and it was soon obvious that she would never be a star, but must be content with the fluctuating two to three pounds a week received by middle-ranking actresses. She was twenty-seven and charming. Other propositions abounded, some of marriage, some not. She herself summed up the dubious position of an actress. An accident had happened in the dressing room of an actress of doubtful reputation, Elizabeth wrote: 'She ran in haste to the dressing room of Mrs Wells, to finish the business of her toilet. Mrs Wells, who was the mistress of the well-known Captain Topham, shocked at the intrusion of a reprobated woman, who had a worse character than herself, quitted her own room, and ran to Miss Farren's crying, "What would Captain Topham say, if I were to remain in such company?" But, Miss Farren flew out at the door, repeating, "What would Lord Derby say, if I should be seen in such company?"'

Elizabeth did not mean to be tarred with that brush. Sir Charles Bunbury, her local MP, long divorced from his wife Sarah, offered her protection, and a rich Mr Glover promised her a settlement of £500 a year if she would marry him. There were other offers too, but not from Kemble, and she refused them all. She had learned about husbands. She would make herself independent by writing, with her stage salary as security while she got started. Unfortunately her finished novel was rejected by Stockdale to whom a friend of hers took it. But she had another string to her bow. She was busy writing plays. Several were turned down, but when she appeared in her own farce, *A Mogul Tale*, in 1784 it was a resounding success, netting her a hundred guineas and a letter of praise from Kemble: 'Your regular and continent life gives you the promise of many healthful years; and your uncommon talents, having now forced themselves into notice, will crown you with growing reputation . . . There is no *woman* I more truly admire, nor any *man* whose abilities I more highly esteem.'

She did not appear in her own *I'll Tell You What*, which was a success in 1785, but it netted her £300, of which she invested £240 in government stock. She was always careful with money, a remarkable contrast to her rival Dora Jordan at Drury Lane. Dora in fact was soon acting in her plays. The next one, *Such Things Are*, mixed social realism with its comedy, setting a story about prison reform sensibly far afield in Sumatra. She got it just right: the King and Queen took the three oldest Princesses to it and were 'greatly delighted', and there were frustrated queues in Bow Street. It got her a publisher in successful George Robinson who cared about his authors and kept open house for them. Soon she had squirrelled away enough capital to give her an income of £58 a year. It was hardly riches, and she faced increasing demands from her family, but she was able gradually to give up acting and live by her pen.

She paid a debt to her hairdresser with her first earnings as a playwright and did not mean to be in debt again. She lived frugally, high up in a succession of lodging houses in the Soho area, carrying her own coals, making her own clothes and working hard, producing a play in ten days if necessary and paying for the overwork in bouts of ill health. She wrote over twenty plays, some of them translations, like *Lover's Vows* by the German dramatist Kotzebue, which was to cause a bit of trouble at Jane Austen's Mansfield Park. Comedy was always her forte, her one tragedy, *The Massacre*, a bloodstained story of the French Revolution, was never staged.

It is for her novel *A Simple Story* that she is remembered today. This was a reworking of the book that had previously been rejected, and Robinson, whom she described as the best friend she ever had, gave her £200 for it and published it in 1791. It went rapidly into several editions. Much of its fascination lies in the portrait of the hero, based on Kemble, who had married a widowed actress in 1787. Handsome, romantic, intelligent and emotionally crass, he wreaks havoc in the lives of his wife and daughter. I doubt if Kemble wrote her a letter of praise about this one.

She had moved from theatrical to literary society now, partly through Robinson, partly through her old friend Thomas Holcroft, another actor turned dramatist. His translation of Beaumarchais' *Mariage de Figaro* – memorized from frequent visits to the Paris theatre – had been a great success when it was put on as *The Follies of a Day* in 1784. William Godwin was also one of Robinson's authors, and there was a romantic passage of some kind between him and Elizabeth at this time, but nothing came of it and they continued good friends. He later told his daughter, Mary Shelley, that, 'When Mrs Inchbald came into a room and sat in a chair in the middle of it as was her wont, every man gathered round it and it was vain for any other woman to attempt to gain attention.' He also spoke, years later, of her admirable criticism of his radical novel *Caleb Williams*, which was published in 1794, a year of extreme social unrest. Their friend Holcroft was actually arrested for high treason but discharged without a trial after a public outcry.

While continuing to write successful plays, Elizabeth also wrote a progressive novel of her own at this time, *Nature and Art*, published in 1796. A brave book, ending with a judge condemning to death the woman he has reduced to prostitution, was not such a success as the more romantic *A Simple Story*. She told Godwin that *A Simple Story* had taken her ten months, made her ill, and earned her much less than she could get from a play that took her ten days. She was a practical woman and a professional. She did not write another novel.

Her relations with Godwin changed drastically when he suddenly married Mary Wollstonecraft in 1797. It came hard on all his devoted circle of women friends; Elizabeth Inchbald certainly took it very badly. Did she know that the new Mrs Godwin referred to her as 'Mrs Perfection' in her letters to him? The nearest Elizabeth got to apologizing for her rudeness to Mary was to write: 'If I have done wrong, when you next marry, I will act differently.' Not surprisingly, this did not mend matters. Mrs Inchbald, carefulness itself, knew all about the new Mrs Godwin's past. When Mary Godwin died six months after the wedding, her husband wrote to Elizabeth at once and got a savage answer: 'I did not know her. I never wished to know her; as I avoid every female acquaintance, who has no husband.' Amazingly, he still wanted to continue the correspondence, but she would have none of it. She must have decided that she did not want to take on a difficult widower with two small girls on his hands, but it was bad luck for the two small girls, who got Mrs Clairmont instead.

In the early years of the nineteenth century Elizabeth Inchbald moved gradually from play-writing to editing, producing several collections of plays with her own prefaces. Her friend and publisher Robinson died in 1801, whereupon his firm went bankrupt and was taken over by Longman in 1805. She was offered £1,000 for her *Memoirs*, and wrote them, but a friend advised her not to publish, and Longman did not like them. She left instructions that they were to be burned after her death. She moved gradually into a slightly less radical and literary and more social circle, letting faithful Sir Charles Bunbury take her to Carlton House, and meeting the Prince Regent at a masquerade. She visited Lord Abercorn at Stanmore and enjoyed being patronized by fashionable Lady Cork and Orrery, friend of Dr Johnson. She lived as frugally as ever on her careful investments in her tiny room: 'I have not far to *walk* to reach anything I want; for I can kindle my fire as I lie in bed; and put on my cap as I dine, for my looking glass is obliged to stand on the same table with my dinner.' But she liked to describe how she would hurry down from her attic to get into the coronetted coach waiting for her below.

She grew a little lonely as the siblings she had supported died off, and told a friend that she thought people were beginning to neglect her. She tried retiring to a sisterhood of Roman Catholic single ladies at Turnham Green, but found the constraints more than she could bear and soon moved back to lonely independence in London. She went on making friends, Maria Edgeworth and Madame de Staël and Godwin's daughter Mary Shelley, but Coleridge was frightened of her. He wrote to Godwin: 'Mrs Inchbald I do not like at all . . . thro' worlds of wilderness I would run away from that look, that heart-picking look.' Perhaps that was what had scared John Philip Kemble. She lived, always within her means, until 1821, when she left £5,000, largely to her surviving nephews and nieces. It had been a remarkable life for her extravagant times.

10

*Marriage out of
their Time*

SOME WOMEN MARRIED not so much for love of a man or for
establishment as in pursuit of an idea. They saw the lot of the
single woman as disempowered and decided to accept marriage
as a means to an end. It was a chancy thing to do, of course, the end
might so easily be lost amid the constraints of the means. Elizabeth
Gurney loved God first and man second, but she took a chance on
marriage and made it work. She refused Joseph Fry at first, and when
she finally accepted him, after a long day of dramatic vacillation, she
had made her terms. In their marriage, her duty to God must come
before anything else. Joseph promised, and he kept his word, but it
made for an unusual marriage.

Elizabeth had been born in 1780, the fourth of the twelve children of John and Elizabeth Gurney of the Norwich Quaker
banking family. Her parents lived comfortably in their Quaker faith,
using the Quaker 'thee' and 'thou' but not going to extremes of
dress and observance like the Plain Quakers. It was a happy, well
organized childhood divided between the Norwich house and the
country, but Betsy, as she was always called, grew up the odd, shy
one in a group of successful, outgoing siblings. Her beloved
mother's death when she was twelve left her miserable and more
than ever the odd one out, while her eldest sister Kitty took over the
running of the family.

Betsy developed a habit of nervous illness in her teens and kept a
journal describing the ups and downs of her depressive search for a
purpose in life. A brief, mysteriously terminated engagement to a rich
and suitable young Quaker, James Lloyd of the banking family, hurt
her badly. She was excited at meeting the King's nephew, the Duke of
Gloucester's son William Frederick, when this liberal-minded young
man came to dine at the family's country house, Earlham. But afterwards she wrote: 'It shows me the folly of the world.' William

Frederick was to marry his cousin Princess Mary in the end and prove less than liberal as a husband.

In 1798, when Betsy was eighteen, a young American Quaker called William Savery came to preach in Norwich. Betsy heard him and he changed her life. 'Today I felt there is a God,' she wrote. But she fought his influence for a while, persuading her father to take her to stay with Quaker cousins in London and sample its pleasures. She felt so ill on the journey there that her father had to dose her with laudanum and brandy. Once in London, she went to a double bill of *Hamlet* and *Bluebeard*, called on Mrs Siddons and saw the Prince of Wales at the opera. But she also went again to hear William Savery preach: 'I really did cry with a sort of ecstasy.' From now on, she wanted to become a Plain Quaker, wearing their sober dress and keeping their austere rules, which banned such pleasures as music or the theatre, and forbade attendance at other people's churches. Her cheerful, comfortable family were appalled at the change in her, but she was gradually working out a life of her own, moving away from them. She visited the local sick and began to read to their children on Sundays, discovering the power of her speaking voice, and the extent of rural poverty. She still broke down from time to time to enjoy a dance or a donkey race with her lively sisters, who thought nothing of holding hands across the road to stop the London coach in its tracks. But she was dressing more plainly and beginning to dream of speaking at a Quaker Meeting.

She met Joseph Fry that same year of 1798, and next year he proposed to her. He was another rich young Quaker, and a Plain one, but her sisters did not think him good enough for her. The tea-importing Frys lived in London on a less elegant scale than the banker Gurneys, though Joseph was better educated than them, with a taste for music and the theatre. Betsy duly refused him. She described herself as 'weak and nervous' later that summer and went on, 'It may be owing to laudanum.' The tincture of opium and alcohol was a widely prescribed medicine then, the aspirin of the day. Nobody knew it was addictive. The Gurneys were great believers in the virtue of porter (strong brown ale) and wine, so Betsy may already have been suffering from a mild double addiction. This may have helped to give her the courage to speak for the first time at the Norwich Quaker meeting that winter, though she was not happy with what she said. She was brooding about whether there was any way she could combine marriage with what she felt to be her religious calling: 'If I have any active duties to perform in the church . . . are they not rather incompatible with the duties of a wife and mother?' But when Joseph Fry wrote and proposed a visit she agreed to his coming, only to refuse him again in the end. He came back the following spring with an ultimatum: this was the last time. He would not return. After a day's hesitation, she accepted him. Despite his ultimatum, she seems to have decided that she was the stronger of the two and would be able to run their marriage as she wished. She was also in love with him, and he adored her. And she was growing in self-confidence. She could read aloud at Women's Meetings now, and the week before the wedding, in August 1800, she 'spoke very well in both Meetings.'

Joseph insisted on a proper honeymoon at his uncle's Norfolk shooting lodge, and they were passionately happy there. She was to bear him eleven children in twenty-one years, and neglect both them and him when religious duty called, and he would love and support her through it all. They began their married life with his parents at their pleasant country house Plashets in Essex, an easy commute from the City, where the Frys had their business. Betsy found the Fry family kind but dull and they were alarmed at her sophistication. It must have been a relief to everyone when Mildred's Court, the family's London house, was ready for the young couple. Here the counting house was on the ground floor, and the warehouse next door, so it was very much a case of living over the shop. In some ways, Betsy may have been glad. She had discovered that her Joseph was an idle fellow, loath to go to work. He was also extravagant, shocking her by going out and buying pictures and even sometimes sneaking off to concerts. They had little privacy since the Fry house was an established Quaker centre, always open to country visitors who took food and shelter for granted. It made for extravagant housekeeping and Betsy had little time for herself, but she discovered the appalling poverty of the City streets. She also met a young Quaker called Joseph Lancaster who was working out a new system of schooling for the poor, in which he taught them to teach each other.

Betsy's first child was born just a year after the marriage. It was a painful birth and she felt guilty about not bonding instantly with little Katharine. But she was soon worrying about both the child's health and her own: 'I sometimes think of leaving off malt liquor and wine.' She knew they made her languid but was equally sure they kept her well. She was soon pregnant again. Rachel was born nineteen months after Katharine, and Betsy suffered from post-natal depression, but she found comfort in ministering to the desperate beggar women who were making their way to her charitable door. Loving the poor was more interesting than loving her own children. Her next child, John, was born in 1804 and again she was depressed afterwards, afraid of becoming a 'careworn and oppressed mother.'

The solution to this problem was gradually presenting itself as she got better known among London Quakers. In 1805, at twenty-five, she was appointed Visitor to the Friends' School and Workhouse in Islington. Joseph agreed to this, but they were both disconcerted when a Friend from their Meeting called to make sure that their own children's religious education was not being neglected. By now Betsy had discovered how she could hold a group of people spellbound by her extempore prayer. There was to be no looking back. By 1808 they had a governess for the children and next year they moved out to the spacious comfort of Plashets on the death of Joseph's father. That same year Betsy's father also died and she was moved to speak at his funeral, shocking some of her own family but launching her on her career as a minister, then a possibility for Quaker women.

By next year, Joseph was staying at home with the children while Betsy travelled about the country speaking at Meetings. Her seventh child was born in February 1811. Next month she was formally acknowledged as a minister and that autumn she electrified a Norwich Bible Society Meeting when she was suddenly inspired to speak to them after dinner. But once again her own family were shocked and there was talk of her neglected, unruly children. Worse still, they were in financial trouble. Joseph had launched into banking like the successful Gurneys, but he had never been as industrious as they were and may have been distracted by home responsibilities. The long war had affected trade and there was a City panic in October 1812. His bank was threatened with bankruptcy, an appalling prospect for a Quaker. A Friend who failed his creditors tended to be expelled. But the Gurneys stood by them and the bank was saved. They moved back to Mildred's Court to cut their expenses and Betsy found worse poverty than ever in the London streets.

Stephen Grellet, a French émigré who had turned Quaker in America, came to her for help that winter. He had been allowed to visit the female prisoners in Newgate and been appalled at what he found. The desperate women had little clothing for themselves and none for their new-born babies. Betsy instantly got together a working-party of women Friends to make clothes for the babies, and next day she and her sister-in-law Anna Buxton took the clothes to Newgate and managed to persuade the reluctant Governor to let them take them in to the women. Deeply shocked at what they found, they went back several times, taking basic necessities like straw for the women's beds. When Betsy was moved to pray she reduced some of the hardened women to tears. But again her family disapproved.

When the long war with France ended in 1815, recession followed with unemployed soldiers begging in the streets and workers in the industrial north rioting and destroying the machines they felt had cost them their jobs. Joseph's bank was in trouble again in 1816, and again the Gurneys bailed him out. To help cut down their expenses, Betsy's married sisters took over the older children, which caused a good deal of critical comment but suited the children. Betsy missed them and wrote to her eldest daughters urging them to study hard: 'I look forward to your return with much comfort as useful and valuable helpers . . . I shall be glad to have the day come when I may introduce you into prisons and hospitals.' But they were growing away from her, and from the Quaker faith.

The public was becoming aware of the shocking state of the prisons, more overcrowded than ever in those difficult post-war years, when it was a question of steal or starve. Betsy's brothers-in-law Fowell Buxton and Samuel Hoare had helped found a Society for the Reformation of Prison Discipline in 1816. That Christmas Betsy went back to Newgate and found that things were as poor as ever, with ragged, neglected children exposed to every kind of bad influence. She spoke to the women themselves about this: 'Is there not something we can do for these innocent little children? Are they to learn to become thieves or worse?' When the women agreed enthusiastically to the idea of a school for their children, Betsy went to work to persuade the authorities to make it possible. It was not easy, but she had influence now, and great powers of persuasion. In the end she succeeded. At every stage she consulted the women themselves, leaving it to them to select one of their own number to teach the children, and encouraging them to organize the teaching on the self-help lines that she had learned from Joseph Lancaster.

Soon the women were begging to be taught too, and given work to do. This was more difficult. Betsy turned for help to her brothers-in-law and their new Society but they did not believe the women to be reformable and said that to provide materials for their education would be merely to waste them. Betsy turned to her own sex instead, forming a women's committee to further the enterprise. Her husband stood by her and hosted a meeting at Mildred's Court at which Betsy managed to persuade the Governor of Newgate to let her show him how eager the prisoners were to cooperate. Next week he attended a meeting at which a group of seventy well-conducted, tidily dressed women prisoners promised good behaviour. Won over, the Governor himself addressed the women, warning that any breach of the rules would mean the end of the experiment.

Before this vital meeting Betsy had written in her journal: 'I hope I am not undertaking too much, but it is a little like being in the whirl-wind.' Her committee of Quaker women worked like Trojans. Quaker merchants supplied materials free; the Governor had a room whitewashed and cleaned for them; they got the contract for supplying clothes to the prisoners deported to Botany Bay. Within a week the school was opened, and the women were stitching away at their first project, a patchwork quilt. Betsy spoke to them, introducing the matron whom her committee had found to superintend their labours, and getting the women to vote on a set of rules. This experiment in democracy worked. Two weeks later a male visitor was amazed at the prisoners' decorous behaviour. The Lord Mayor came to see the phe-nomenon and the authorities were so impressed that Betsy's set of rules were officially adopted.

The remarkable success of this undertaking made Betsy a public figure, but success brought criticism, and the painful charge that she neglected her own family. The fact that there was an element of truth in this perhaps made it harder to bear, but she soon had her oldest daughter running her house and helping in her correspondence. She was also fighting a spiritual battle of her own because she found it impossible not to enjoy the publicity, and was ashamed of herself for doing so. But it was hard not to be pleased when she was invited to give evidence to a House of Commons Committee on London Prisons, one of the first women to do so. Interestingly, she asked her brother Joseph, not her husband, to go with her. Perhaps he was at home with their nine children. Katharine, the eldest, was sixteen in 1817, little Betsy had died in 1815, to her mother's great grief, Samuel had been born in 1816 and Daniel was still to come. At this point five of her children were under ten years old.

Their mother was being praised by William Wilberforce and was in the forefront of the battle against capital punishment for a wide range of minor offences including shoplifting and forgery. She was invited to the Mansion House to meet Queen Charlotte on one of the old Queen's last public appearances in 1818, and reported that, 'There was quite a buzz when I went into the room.' Much more important, she managed to change the barbarous custom by which women prisoners who were to be transported, many of them for nothing worse than petty theft, were chained together and taken to the docks in open wagons, subject to the jeers and pelting of the crowds. She and her committee also looked after the well-being of the unfortunate women as they waited on board for the transport ships to sail, and saw to it that they had the means to make small items on the voyage for sale on landing, to avoid being forced into prostitution.

The more famous she became, both at home and abroad, the more Betsy found herself criticized by fellow Quakers. Her husband sometimes went to concerts, her sons liked to hunt and fish and the girls enjoyed the pleasures of life. All this, according to her Quaker critics, was her fault. Betsy minded, but there was work to be done. She began to journey round England, with her brother Joseph in support, to look at prisons outside London. Joseph was both banker and minister, so they held Quaker Meetings on the way. A Scottish woman described her successful visit, against the odds, to the Glasgow Bridewell. As at Newgate, Betsy got the women to vote on her proposals by a show of hands and carried all before her. She ended by praying with them: 'I felt her musical voice in the peculiar recitative of the Quakers to be like a mother's song to a suffering child.' These women were her children. But her own family took it out of her when she got home. They seemed 'almost jealous of me and ready to mistrust my various callings.' Luckily her husband was 'always willing to make my way and give me up for any religious duties.' Betsy had a miscarriage in 1819. The same year the Empress of Russia took her advice about the treatment of women prisoners and lunatics.

Daniel was born in November 1822, when Betsy was forty-two. They were living at Plashet again by now and when he was six weeks old she took the baby to Newgate where the prisoners and the Ladies' Committee greeted them both with enthusiasm. It did her good but, 'My dearest babe suffered much by the rides to and from town, so that its little cries almost overcame me.' She probably had another miscarriage in 1824 and that was the end of her child-bearing.

Busier than ever, Betsy was a target for every appeal, and she worried about her 'very expensive husband.' Joseph was backsliding as a Quaker and buying pictures by Rembrandt and Canaletto. Their daughter Rachel had married a delightful young man who was not a Quaker so that Betsy could not go to the wedding. Business was bad again, and it was difficult for a public figure like her to economize. Besides, she liked and felt entitled to her comforts. Her Quaker dress was plain but it was the best silk, and her Quaker shawl was lined with ermine. Once again her family rallied to their help and she and her brother Joseph paid a successful visit to Ireland in 1827, warning the Lord Lieutenant against the risk of a potato famine. That same year, Betsy helped nurse her dying sister, preached at her funeral and hurried to be present at the birth of her first grandson, whose life the family believed she saved by her nursing. She also published a book on the treatment of prisoners in which she boldly suggested that there was work for women to do not just in prisons but in hospitals, lunatic asylums and workhouses. She concluded, 'Women's calling . . . has nearly, if not quite, an equal influence on society as men's'.

Disaster struck when their bank failed in November 1828. This time the Gurneys must have thought it beyond saving, but they stepped in to salvage the tea business from the wreckage. From then on Joseph Gurney ran it, with Joseph Fry merely a salaried employee. Everything had to be sold, including beloved Plashet. Inevitably, Quakers had lost money in the collapse of the bank. Joseph was painfully investigated and finally expelled from the Society of Friends. Betsy too was affected by the disaster. When she suggested a mission to Suffolk, she was told that she was not wanted. Too many people there had been hit by the bankruptcy.

It was a bad time. Her husband and sons stopped wearing the sober Quaker costume and her children were leaving the faith. And the authorities adopted her methods of prison reform in ways that contrived to exclude her and her committee of ladies. When she appeared before another Parliamentary Committee on Prisons in 1832 they ignored almost all her recommendations. Betsy must have felt she had outlived her usefulness. But her brother Sam had given them a house near his and in 1833 her husband received a 'powerful visitation of judgement mingled with mercy,' and rejoined the Quakers.

They travelled together a great deal after this, taking a daughter with them as interpreter when they went abroad. Her popularity had grown in Europe as it dwindled at home and they were fêted wherever they went. Royalty listened to Betsy's advice, and prisoners were released from their chains. In Paris they met the King and Queen and were entertained by the Ambassador, Lord Granville, whose wife

Harryo had written to her sister Georgiana Morpeth that, 'The only thing that calms my nerves is sitting at an open window reading Mrs Fry.'

When her companions complained of the pace she set, Betsy was firm: 'Where the will of my God is concerned, then I must have my way.' She also visited Holland, Denmark and Prussia, entertained by royalty everywhere, and herself entertaining the King of Prussia when he visited England. But she was wearing herself out as well as her companions. The doctors recommended more and more opium and port wine and she died of a stroke in 1845, a legend in her lifetime and a very early instance of role reversal in marriage.

* * *

If Mrs Fry was an early example of role-swapping, Sara Coleridge was to find herself in the dubious position of being an early single parent. Her marriage was based on an idea, but it was Coleridge's, not hers. He had met Robert Southey when they were both undergraduates and they had plunged at once into friendship and plans for an utopia that they called Pantisocracy, where everyone would be equal, or almost. For this they needed cooperative wives, and Southey knew just the girls for the job. The Fricker sisters and their mother had been left suddenly penniless by their father's bankruptcy and death in 1786. Mrs Fricker had rallied and opened a school in Bristol. The three daughters at home, Sara, Mary and Edith, helped in the school and supplemented the meagre income from it by doing needlework. Sara, born in 1770, was the oldest and liveliest of the family, and Southey had begun by paying his attentions to her, but then switched to quieter Edith, who was just his age, while Sara was four years older. He now suggested that Sara would be the ideal partner for his friend Coleridge, who had, of course, never met her. A friend of Southey's, Robert Lovell, was already engaged to Mary Fricker, and another friend, George Burnett, proposed to the fourth sister Martha who very sensibly refused him, saying he only wanted 'a wife in a hurry'.

Back in Bristol, Southey was enthusiastically describing the project to the Frickers when Coleridge himself unexpectedly turned up, shaggy from a walking tour. He stayed for a fortnight, spellbound them all with his brilliant talk, proposed to Sara, was accepted, and left, promising to write regularly and return. He did neither. Sara had fallen in love with the amazing young man, she trusted and believed in him. At this stage not even he knew that he was addicted to laudanum as a result of being dosed with it at school. Deceiving himself, it was easy to deceive Sara; and she was to stick to him through all the trials of his increasingly erratic behaviour. Southey, safely engaged to Edith, finally dragged Coleridge back from London, where he had gone to ground in a haze of laudanum and alcohol. At this point he seems to have fallen in love with Sara, who told him that she had refused two offers of marriage for his sake. They were all enthusiastically reading Mary Wollstonecraft's *A Vindication of the Rights of Woman*. Sara and Edith thought nothing of going on long, unchaperoned expeditions with their young men, and Bristol seethed with gossip. The Pantisocratic project was breaking down partly for lack of funds and partly because Southey was discovering just how unreliable Coleridge was, but Sara and Coleridge were by now deep in love and her family urged on their marriage because of the gossip.

It was crazy; it was doomed; they would have to live by Coleridge's brilliant, unreliable pen, but they were ecstatically happy at first, on honeymoon in a tiny isolated cottage with not much beyond a bed and an aeolian harp. They were married in October 1795, when government repression of radicals was at its height. Coleridge plunged into political journalism, inevitably neglecting Sara, who was soon suffering from a threatened miscarriage. But she recovered, throve and showed how well she knew how to manage on little or no money. Their first child, David Hartley, was born in September 1796. Coleridge was entranced with his son, but Sara was beginning to recognize that there was something very strange about her husband.

The random, freelance life continued, with financial help and cottages provided by friends, and Coleridge alternately fiercely creative and plunged into narcotic despair. Then he met another rising young poet, William Wordsworth, and his devoted sister Dorothy, and began to neglect Sara, tied by the baby, and join them on long walks of exciting talk. Returning wet, Dorothy would borrow Sara's clothes without permission. As Wordsworth and Coleridge planned their revolutionary volume of *Lyrical Ballads*, Sara increasingly found herself the odd one out, and her temper shortened. By 1798 Coleridge was writing 'Christabel' and Sara was pregnant again. Berkeley Coleridge was born in May and when Coleridge decided to pursue his studies in Germany, in company with the Wordsworths, Sara stayed at home with the children.

Coleridge throve as an admired mature student at Göttingen and he did not much want to go home. When little Berkeley died tragically of smallpox, Sara was sure her husband would hurry to her side, but he took his time about it. Away from her, he had decided he was better without her. She had also had the smallpox, lost all her hair and made a slow recovery, but Southey and Edith, now comfortably married, stood by her. When Coleridge did return after many delays, he found her tongue sharper than he remembered, but they paid a successful visit to his family in Devon and then moved to London where he wrote brilliant leaders for the *Morning Post*.

This was financial security, but poetry was his life. In 1800 they moved to Greta Hall just outside Keswick, to be near the Wordsworths. At first everything went swimmingly. Sara had another son, Derwent, while Coleridge strode over the hills to visit his dear friends at Grasmere. But the Wordsworths were cool about 'Christabel' and 'The Rime of the Ancient Mariner', the damp Lake District air did not suit him and he was taking more laudanum than ever, neglecting his work and getting further and further into debt. There were scenes. Sara screamed at him; he had narcotic nightmares and woke screaming too. When he was well enough, he walked over to complain about Sara to the Wordsworths who, understandably enough, blamed his wretched condition on her. Two friends of theirs, Sara and Mary Hutchinson, also sympathized with the delightful, desperate young poet, and Coleridge fell in love with Sara. He decided that married life confined him too much; he needed his freedom.

Divorce was impossible; the Wordsworths urged a separation, but Coleridge could never quite make up his mind. He spent some time in London, writing contradictory letters to Sara and to the Wordsworths, but finally returned to Greta Hall. A reconciliation with his wife left her pregnant again, to his dismay. It must have been a hideous time. If he left her, he meant to take his beloved sons with him, and there was no way that Sara could oppose this, a father's rights were paramount. And by now she knew very well what an inadequate father he was. She recognized that in many ways he too must be treated like a child, cherished and protected. In the end, she gave in and promised to become the kind of biddable wife he wanted, giving up what he described as her 'habits of puny Thwarting and unintermitting Dyspathy.' She wrote to his sister-in-law that, 'Nothing but tranquillity keeps him tolerable, care and anxiety destroy him.'

He was away when their daughter Sara was born in December 1802, but 'bore her sex with great fortitude.' By this time they were both becoming aware of the threat posed by his opium habit, and he decided to go to Malta in hopes of a cure. Wordsworth had married Mary Hutchinson by now, and they were supportive to Sara while the Southeys moved into Greta Hall with her. She had a rest and hoped for a new start when her husband returned.

Again he was a long time in coming, and when he did reach England in the summer of 1806 he went to stay in London with his friends Charles and Mary Lamb, saying he could no longer face life with Sara. Visiting the Wordsworths, he told them the same thing and they rashly invited him to come and live with them, though they had been appalled by how he had gone to seed. He finally went on to Greta Hall, was welcomed with open arms, and told Sara he was leaving her. He meant to take both boys, leaving little Sara with her mother, to whom he promised an allowance. She fought his plans passionately and in the end he took only Hartley with him, to the Wordsworths at first. Southey, still installed at Greta Hall, was glad to see him go: 'His habits are so murderous of all domestic comfort that I am only surprised Mrs C is not rejoiced at being rid of him.' Luckily for Sara, the Southeys were glad to settle at Greta Hall, which meant that she still had the essential support of a resident male relative, and she was to prove a welcome counterbalance in the household to her increasingly depressive sister Edith.

Meanwhile the Wordsworths were finding Coleridge much less easy as a member of the family, but did their best by him, with intermissions. Hartley and Derwent were sent as weekly boarders to Ambleside, spending weekends at Grasmere and holidays with their mother. Little Sara was taken on visits to the Wordsworths which she did not much enjoy. Sara Hutchinson, now a member of the Wordsworth household, tried to keep Coleridge at work, but gave it up in despair. Coleridge found himself new friends, a family called Morgan, and then a couple called Montagu, who undertook to take him to London for a cure, but briskly abandoned him when they got there, having been warned by the Wordsworths that he was impossible. But Coleridge could always find friends when he needed them. The Morgans took him in and he felt so safe with them that he even suggested that Sara bring the children to London and join him, but Sara had learned by experience; she stayed at Greta Hall with the Southeys.

Drowning in opium now, Coleridge lost interest in his sons, and when it was time for Hartley to go to University he did nothing to help. Southey gradually took over the support of Sara and her children and Sara paid her way by helping to teach the growing swarm of little Southeys. Her other sister Mary Lovell was there too, and the place came to be known as The Aunt Hill. When little Herbert Southey died, Sara did her best to keep up the tone of the household. Surprisingly, her motto was '*Toujours gai!*' Southey was made poet laureate in 1813 and they were thronged with visitors. While his wife slid deeper and deeper into depression, resilient Sara helped to amuse their guests with her puns and jokes and invented language.

By 1816 Coleridge felt he was in danger of death or madness and put himself in the charge of a Highgate apothecary called Gillman and his wife. They undertook to cure him of his addiction and though they did not entirely succeed they managed to help him control it. Once again, he enthusiastically proposed coming home to Greta Hall, but this time Southey said no, and Sara had to accept this. But the children could visit him again at the Gillmans', the boys sharing his room, Sara more rarely because of lack of space. They were all growing up. In 1819 Hartley was elected a fellow of Oriel College but wrecked his chances by drunken behaviour during a year's probation. Rejected by Oriel, he vanished on the first of many drunken fugues, his hopeful career at an end. Derwent, too, went through a rebellious spell, drinking and turning atheist at Cambridge, but changed his mind and plunged into holy orders and school-mastering after meeting a nineteen-year-old girl called Mary Pridman. He invited his mother and sister to come and housekeep for him until he married, but the Southeys made it clear that they could not be spared. The two of them had become invaluable and if they left they would not be welcomed back. It was too big a risk, and they stayed.

Young Sara was a surprise. She was not just beautiful, she was brilliant too. Her portrait as a highland girl by William Collins had caused a sensation when she was sixteen and by the time she was twenty John Murray had published her translation of an abstruse work in Latin by an Austrian Jesuit, Martin Dobrizhöffer. The £125 Murray paid her gave her mother high hopes of an independent future for her daughter as a kind of nineteenth-century Mary Wollstonecraft, and the two of them visited London the autumn the book came out.

Sara had a great success; Coleridge was entranced with her, and so was his nephew, her cousin Henry Nelson Coleridge, a delightful, brilliant young man at the outset of a career as a barrister. In three months the cousins were engaged. Despite her mother's objections, Sara was determined to wait for Henry. They were married in 1829, Southey giving the bride away, and Hartley, like his father, failing to appear. Sara had her first baby, a son, next autumn and her mother came to be with her for the birth and stayed for the rest of her life. There were friendly family visits across London to see Coleridge, still safe with the Gillmans, until his death in 1834. Sara died, suddenly, in 1845. There had been love in her life, but not what she expected.

II

Love & Friendship

T HE BOND BETWEEN women, whether sisters or just friends, was often at least as strong as or maybe stronger than that between man and wife. Sara Coleridge and her sisters supported each other through thick and thin, and so did the Spencer ladies and the Duchess of Devonshire's daughters, Georgiana and Harryo. The Lennox sisters were another case of strong female family bonding, though this was more complicated, with episodes of feuding as well as friendship. The same was true of Harriette Wilson and her sisters; one gets an impression of solidarity among the ladies of the *demi monde*. The bluestocking ladies had their own support system, and another interesting case is that of the Misses Berry, devoted sisters, and beloved protégées of the much older dilettante Horace Walpole. When charming General O'Hara who so took Lady Elgin's fancy asked Miss Berry to marry him, her behaviour was a little like Jane Austen's. She accepted him, and there was a loving correspondence, but then he was ordered to Gibraltar. He asked her to marry him at once and go too, but she could not bring herself to do it and the engagement gradually cooled and broke. Her relationship with Horace Walpole played a part in this, but so did that with her sister.

Romantic friendship between women was also a feature of the late eighteenth century and carried no sexual overtones. Whereas sodomy was punishable by death, lesbian practice was looked on as a lower-class affair; ladies just did not do such things. It made the smearing of Marie Antoinette all the more serious, carrying a double stigma, but it meant that ladies could indulge their passionate friendships without fear of scandal. Lady Melbourne and the Duchess of Devonshire wrote each other letters full of high-flown endearments; it meant nothing. Hester Thrale would simultaneously write letters of loving flattery to Fanny Burney and carp at her in her diary. But a great deal of the feeling was real and supportive.

When Eleanor Butler was asked to befriend a schoolgirl called Sarah Ponsonby in 1768 it was the start of a friendship that was to be closer than many marriages. They were both ladies of immensely good family. Henry II had taken the original Butler to Ireland with him, and from then on there had been Butlers at Kilkenny Castle. They were Dukes of Ormonde by the time George I came to the throne, but were then denounced as Jacobites and stripped of title and estates. Eleanor's junior branch of the family compounded the Jacobite offence by being Roman Catholic, which meant that they could not hold office under the crown. When they surprisingly inherited, all they got was the castle without the title or much money to support it. Eleanor was born in 1739, the disappointing third daughter, but was followed by a son and heir next year. Her older sisters were good friends, excluding her, and she never got on with her brother; like Mary Wollstonecraft and Elizabeth Gurney she was the odd one out in the family. While her sisters were sent to a fashionable convent in Paris and made good marriages, plain Eleanor went to a convent in Cambrai, was happy there and came home well read, strong minded and still plain. Her education had given her much more experience of women than of men; Casanova remarks in his *Memoirs* that homosexual practices were taken for granted in convents. She came home to find the thriving town of Kilkenny a man's world, its civilization consisting mainly of plenty of pubs where men could meet in the evening. In 1764 her brother John renounced the Catholic faith as a first step towards recovering his putative title of Earl of Ormonde and the fortune that went with it. Like his two elder sisters, he made a prosperous marriage. Eleanor sat in the castle and read a great deal.

In 1768, Lady Betty Fownes of Inistioge, twelve miles from Kilkenny, asked Eleanor's mother, always known as Madame Butler, to keep an eye on a thirteen-year-old cousin of hers whom she had sent to a girls' boarding school in the town. Sarah Ponsonby's was a sad story. Her father had been a junior member of the extensive Ponsonby clan, headed by the Earl of Bessborough. After four marriages and three daughters, he had died leaving his latest wife pregnant with what turned out to be a boy. His widow had promptly remarried and nobody wanted Sarah. Penniless and homeless, she had been taken in by Lady Betty, a cousin of her father, and her successful husband Sir William Fownes. A graceful girl, but shy and sensitive after a difficult childhood, Sarah spent what seem to have been five happy years at the Kilkenny school and she and the formidable young lady from the castle that dominated the town became good friends, despite the sixteen-year age gap. When she was eighteen, in 1773, Sarah left school and went to live with her cousin and her husband in their handsome Georgian house, Woodstock, on its hill above Inistioge. She was to take the place of their own daughter, another Sarah, who had recently married a Mr Edward Tighe. All went well at first, except that nobody proposed for dowerless Sarah, but she loved Lady Betty and was happy until Sir William started to pursue her. His wife was ailing, he felt himself in the prime of life, Sarah was there. He talked of marriage – later. Desperate, Sarah wrote asking him if he meant to drive her from his house. 'I would rather die than wound Lady Betty's heart,' she wrote to a family friend in Dublin. She also wrote to her friend Eleanor Butler at Kilkenny.

Eleanor had a problem of her own. Her mother was pressing her to return to Cambrai and become a nun, thus saving her family most of the marriage portion to which she was entitled. In the happy days when Sarah was at school they had dreamed of a civilized life together, two studious women in a cottage somewhere. Now, at thirty-nine and twenty-three, they ran away to achieve it. Sarah kissed Mrs Tighe (there on a visit) in inexplicable floods of tears, climbed out of a window and joined Eleanor who had ridden over from Kilkenny. Both were in men's clothes; Sarah had a pistol and her little dog under her arm. They managed the twenty-three miles to Waterford, hoping to take the ferry for England, but then things went wrong; they had to hide for twenty-four hours in a barn and were finally caught, a mile from Waterford, 'In a Carr in Men's Cloathes'.

Eleanor was immured in her brother-in-law's house at Borris, and Sarah had to try and explain herself to Lady Betty without betraying Sir William. It was too much. She became ill and Lady Betty wrote urging Eleanor, still a prisoner at Borris, not 'to write volumes to her till she was better.' At last, Eleanor apparently yielded and said she would go to the French convent if she was allowed to see Sarah once more. Given half an hour together, they used it to plan their escape. Eleanor walked the twelve rugged miles from Borris to Woodstock, and was smuggled into the house by a maid, Mary Carryll. While her family scoured the countryside for her, and the district seethed with rumour, she hid in Sarah's room for a day and a half. In the end she was discovered and intense negotiations followed. Sir William fell on his knees. Lady Betty told Sarah that Eleanor had 'a debauched mind, no ingredients for friendship.' It was no use. The two friends were immovable. In the end the Butlers gave way, promised unspecified funding and sent their coach to take the two women on the first stage of their journey to England and freedom. They got into the coach, Mary Carryll in attendance, laughing happily. But they left disaster behind. The stress of it all had been too much for the Fownes. Sir William died of a strangulation, in agony, six weeks later, and his wife only outlived him by another few weeks.

The two fugitives knew nothing of this. Happily planning love in a cottage they landed in Wales and started on a light-hearted sight-seeing tour. There had been four tense days of waiting for the ferry at Waterford; if there had been second thoughts, nothing had come of them. From now on they presented an immensely united front to the world. Sarah started an *Account of a Journey in Wales by Two Fugitive Ladies* and dedicated it to her *Most Tenderly Beloved Companion*. It describes an active life of drives and walks round Pembrokeshire, then into Shropshire and back into Wales to Llangollen, where they climbed the local hill and admired the view of 'the Beautifullest Country in the World.' About that time the news of Sir William's death must have reached them. For a few weeks before they heard of Lady Betty's, Sarah must have known that she could safely go back to Ireland if she wished.

Instead, as summer turned towards autumn, they started looking seriously for somewhere to settle. Money was tight. They had spent more of their savings than they intended on the tour; two ladies travelling alone probably did find things very expensive indeed and neither of them had much practice in managing money. After a dramatic episode when Eleanor nearly drowned in the Dee, they spent an uncomfortable winter deep in the country before moving back to Llangollen and taking lodgings with the postman there in 1779. By now they must have had a fairly good idea of what their financial position was to be and it was not cheering. Lady Betty's daughter Mrs Tighe was giving Sarah £80 a year, but a legacy of £1,000 from her stepmother was being withheld through what Sarah called 'mistaken kindness'. And Eleanor's father had made only 'scanty provision' for her, perhaps £200 a year, or less. Living was cheap in Wales, but they were two ladies used to their comforts. They were going to have to be extremely careful, something for which neither of them was trained.

They found a five-room cottage on a hill behind the village and rented it for twenty-two pounds fifteen shillings a year. They called it Plas Newydd, spent more than they could afford on furniture, bookshelves and carpets, and moved in early in 1780. That remarkable woman Mary Carryll, who had been Lady Betty's housemaid and presumably found herself acting as maid/companion on the tour, now settled comfortably into the kitchen and was soon entertaining village worthies there. She probably made a great deal more difference to their position than they realized. She made them respectable in Llangollen. She must have loved Sarah.

The two women were happily working out their conventual regime, which never changed. They rose at eight, breakfasted at nine, dined at three and retired to their dressing room at nine, so that 'our Domesticks also may go to rest.' If Eleanor woke with one of her frequent migraines, they stayed in their big double bed till it was better, Sarah ministering to her friend. Otherwise, not a moment was wasted. They had projects for themselves, as well as for their house and the four acres of field which were to be their garden. It all cost money. The bookshelves filled with books for their studies. They planned to have flowers, a kitchen garden, stable, dairy, henyard, even vines . . . By 1781, Sarah was writing to demand financial help, as of right, from the head of her family, the Earl of Bessborough, father-in-law of Henrietta Duncannon. He sent her a snubbing letter but enclosed £50, begging her not to send him the purse she was working for him: 'I have, I believe twenty by me which are not of any use.'

While Mary Carryll made friends in the village, her ladies were being gradually taken up by the county. Old Lady Dungannon lived not far off, a friend of both their families, Sir Arthur Wellesley's grandmother. People called on her on their way to Milford Haven for the Irish ferry and soon they were calling at Plas Newydd too, to visit the odd couple who were becoming known as the Ladies of Llangollen. The very extravagance of their lifestyle probably helped in their gradual achievement of status. Aristocrats were expected to live lavishly, and they were bringing work and custom to the village. When they got into debt, people bore with them. Someone would pay in the end, and in fact someone always did.

But it was a serious blow when Eleanor's father died in 1782 and she was not even mentioned in his will. Would the brother she had never liked continue her allowance, or would they be reduced to Sarah's £80 a year? Eleanor's migraines got worse and they were outraged by a letter from a widowed Mrs Paulet suggesting that she come and join her fortunes with theirs. It got her a resounding snub: 'Miss Ponsonby and I can only attribute the proposal . . . to your being Totally Ignorant Who we Are.' Their rank was something they never forgot and nor, presumably, did Mary Carryll. It was unfortunate that they had not the means commensurate with it. In the end, John Butler, who had married a rich wife, reluctantly promised to continue the £200 a year and gave them a lump sum of £500 to clear their debts. It was neither enough nor what Eleanor thought herself entitled to, but it was something, and work on house and garden continued.

The two friends were making their lives and their establishment into a Gothic fantasy like Horace Walpole's Strawberry Hill, and, like Strawberry Hill, Plas Newydd and its ladies caught the public fancy. Hostile rumours might circulate in Ireland about quarrels, illnesses and hypothetical marriages for Sarah, but London's sympathy was stirred. Did the spectacle of two women successfully setting up house together touch some unrecognized contemporary nerve? Tweak some unconscious guilt about the treatment of wives and daughters? Travellers brought back glowing reports of the little house and garden, the good talk, with well-informed Eleanor in the lead, the delicious country food. Queen Charlotte wrote asking for a plan of the garden. The Ladies of Llangollen were in vogue.

The house had a spare room now and they could put up guests, offering: 'Asparagus out of our own garden. Ham of our own Saving and Mutton from our own Village.' They supported three booksellers and had a staff of gardener, footman and two maids, costing a total of £39 a year. Mary Carryll took no wages, but accepted lavish vails, or tips, from guests. They were in fashion, but they were also dreadfully in debt. Why not a state pension? They felt they were proving something, and entitled to support. Sarah approached the Ponsonbys for help, without success, and they turned to Lady Frances Douglas who proved a good friend, working tirelessly on their behalf. At last, in 1787, George III actually granted them £100 a year, but it took some time for it to come through. A surviving account book for 1788 shows outgoings of £444.13.2 against an income of £289.3.1.

Gifts and loans kept them just afloat and the happy life continued. Eleanor read aloud while Sarah drew maps, and listened, and at three they dined off 'Roast Breast of Mutton boil'd Veal Bacon and Greens Toasted Cheese.' No wonder elegant Sarah was beginning to look a little more like her stouter friend. But when the weather was good they made the most of it, going for immense walks and planting out 'our hundred Carnations in different part of the borders.' They might be extravagant but they were never idle. And they were happy. Eleanor called Sarah 'My Sweet Love', recording her kindness when she was ill, but mostly they just called each other 'My Beloved' shortened to 'My B' or, later in life, my 'Better Half'. They meant it. They were literally inseparable.

By 1788 visitors were becoming almost too frequent and they themselves sometimes broke their conventual rule to hire the chaise of the friendly landlord of the Hand Inn and pay visits to their friends the Miss Barretts in Oswestry or as far afield as the Shropshire border and sometimes to Shrewsbury for more books. But the King's madness that winter was a great anxiety, doubtless exacerbated by the fact that the pension still had not started to come through. When he recovered in the spring of 1789 the *World* newspaper reported that 'Miss Ponsonby and Miss Butler . . . Who have settled in so romantic a manner in Denbighshire,' had been 'conspicuous in their rejoicings for the King and Queen.' The one pound sixteen shillings they had spent on bonfires and bell ringing for the King's recovery had proved a sound investment in public relations.

In June that year Eleanor listed the twenty-nine books they had been reading since April. It is a formidable list including the nine-volume works of Racine and sixteen volumes of Metastasio. It is hardly surprising that they were in debt. The owner of the Hand suddenly sent in a bill for over fifty pounds that summer. They left him in high dudgeon, transferring their custom to a rival establishment, and when their friends the Miss Barretts next came to see them and made the mistake of leaving their carriage at the Hand as usual, they cut the connection for a year, despite the embarrassment of owing their friends money. It is a sad story. They could be ferocious if affronted. Later, their friend the poetess Anna Seward was to write to apologize for them to a mutual friend, the Reverend Dr Thomas Walley: 'Lady E., who, when pleased is one of the most gracious of God's creatures, under a contrary impression is extremely haughty and imperious. Her sweet amiable friend who, when she has time, can bend and soften the imperious temper, knows she cannot, and therefore does not attempt to assuage its *extempore* sallies.'

In July 1789 the *General Evening Post* ran a gossipy, inaccurate story about them. It described them: 'Miss Butler is tall and masculine, she wears always a riding habit, hangs her hat with the air of a sportsman in the hall, and appears in all respects as a young man, if we except the petticoats which she still retains. Miss Ponsonby, on the contrary, is polite and effeminate, fair and beautiful.' Outraged, and anxious about their pension, which was referred to, Eleanor wrote appealing for help to their friend Edmund Burke, but he disappointingly advised them to do nothing. They reluctantly followed his good advice; the talk simmered down and the pension was not affected.

There was something else for the world to talk about in 1791, when the Ormonde estates and titles were finally restored to John Butler, and his sister found herself Lady Eleanor. She hoped her brother, now an earl and richer than ever, might increase her allowance but he did not do so. Their garden grew more picturesque, however, and they were extending the house and learning Spanish. In 1793, the new Lord Bessborough wrote to his wife Henrietta: 'At a place called Llangollen ... I ... walked across a field to look at a cottage in a beautiful situation where a Miss Ponsonby and Lady Elinor [*sic*] Butler live . . . a servant came out and asked if I was Lord B, as Miss Ponsonby wished to see me.' He was surprised she knew him as they had not met for twenty years, but of course they would have heard all about him through Mary Carryll's village network. He told his wife, 'They had everything very comfortable about them.' They seem not to have asked him for money.

In 1794 Eleanor's mother died and left her a mere £100. It was a last, bitter blow. One of Eleanor's peremptory letters to her sister-in-law got her a swift, firm answer; expectation was over. It would probably have made no difference if she had been conciliatory. And in 1796 John Butler died, leaving a new cause for anxiety. Would his son continue, or better still increase the allowance? He continued it. But those were bad years. The war-time price rises of the nineties affected them as it did the Austens and everyone else on fixed incomes. They kept anxiously in touch with world affairs and worried about the possibility of civil war, particularly in Ireland, where the French actually landed in 1798, with what might have been appalling consequences. Like other people in the closing years of the century they began to wonder if the end of the world might not be at hand.

The civil list was suspended and their pension was late. But the garden was flourishing and hard times meant that they were actually beginning to sell their produce. It must have been infinitely satisfying. Anna Seward visited them in 1795 and found them thriving. Eleanor was almost too plump, with a round fair face and 'the glow of luxuriant health.' Sarah, she said, had 'a face rather long than round, a complexion clear but without bloom, with a countenance which from its soft melancholy has a peculiar interest.' Sarah was always the quiet one, Eleanor the leader.

A child who was taken to see them in the early years of the nineteenth century described the visit, many years later, for her own grandchildren. She remembered the visit because she herself had behaved so well that when she and her 'Dearest Mamma' left, the old ladies said: 'Come, dear little Mary, and give us a kiss for you have been so good and not meddled with any of our pretty things, so we shall be glad to see you here again and here's a nice peach for you.' Mary Elizabeth Lucy, widowed and living at Charlecote, remembered that: 'They looked just like two old men. They always dressed in dark cloth habits with short skirts, high shirt collars, white cravats and men's hats, with their hair cut short. When they walked out (they never rode on horseback) they carried a stick to look like a whip . . . They were so devoted to each other that they made a vow, and kept it, that they would never marry or be separated, but would always live together in their cottage and never leave it or sleep out for even one night.'

At about the same time, Lady Dungannon's grandson Sir Arthur Wellesley called on them and Lady Eleanor gave him a Spanish prayer book, which he found useful for learning the language as he sailed to Spain to take on the French. Another caller was the Duke of Gloucester, who came to dinner. They actually changed out of the riding habits they always wore in his honour and he wrote them a charming letter of thanks, sorry that they had done so: 'I hope they considered me as a Friend and therefore would not have thought it necessary to make any Alteration in their Dress on my Account.' But strangers who tried to take advantage of them were ruthlessly repelled, which only added to the myth that was building up around them. They were becoming, in their lifetime, a kind of public monument. How did they do it? What was their magic? In 1808 Lady Caroline Lamb wrote to her mother in Ireland: 'I hope if you return through Wales, you will not fail to call on the Lady Elenor [*sic*] Butler and Miss Ponsonby, who, I hear are quite delightful . . . Lady Elenor all sprightliness, brilliancy and carelessness; Miss Ponsonby clever, accomplish'd, gentle and agreeable. Their cottage is beautiful and their only maid a wonder of fidelity and ability – she having given them all her little savings when they were distress'd and done everything for them since.'

When Mary Carryll died in 1809 they had letters of condolence from Princess Amelia and the Duke of Gloucester as well as from a host of closer friends. And when their pension fell into arrears again during the bad years after Waterloo they wrote direct to their friend Lord Castlereagh, and the Foreign Secretary took the trouble to answer them personally, explaining about the bad times. They went right on ordering white wine and Windsor soap and the best candles. They replaced Mary Carryll with two devoted sisters called Elizabeth and Jane Hughes, who looked after them just as faithfully as they got older and more frail. Eleanor's sight failed and Sarah became her loving secretary, but they were still thronged with guests and celebrated George IV's accession to the throne in 1820 with illuminations at Plas Newydd that delighted 'the Mob-ility of Llangollen.' Byron sent them a copy of *The Corsair*, Wordsworth wrote them a sonnet: 'Sisters in love, a love allowed to climb Even on this earth, above the reach of Time!' Sarah read aloud the novels of Sir Walter Scott, another of their visitors.

When Eleanor died in 1829 their old friend the Duke of Wellington saw to it that the pension was continued to Sarah. Both families and all their friends supported her through two solitary, desolate years. When she died, the fortune-hunting tourist Prince Pückler-Muskau wrote what could be their epitaph: 'A well furnished library, a charming neighbourhood, an even tempered life without material cares, a most intimate friendship and community among themselves – these are their treasures.' Theirs was a kind of sublime and sublimely successful mutual selfishness. They left behind some account books, some journals, a collection of letters and the cottage and garden which sold for over two thousand pounds, enough to pay their debts and provide annuities for their servants.

I2

Looking for Love

WHILE ELEANOR BUTLER AND SARAH PONSONBY lived the live of their choice at Llangollen, a child was growing up in London who had few options, and not much love in her life. Princess Charlotte Augusta, daughter of the Prince of Wales and his detested wife Caroline of Brunswick, was born to almost manifest destiny. Unless her father should contrive to divorce his impossible wife, remarry and sire a son, Charlotte was heir to the throne of Great Britain, though not of Hanover, where only men could rule. She was born in January 1796. 'An *immense girl*,' her relieved father wrote to his mother, Queen Charlotte. He had stayed up for two nights, 'Much agitated . . . Notwithstanding we might have wished for a boy, I receive her with all the affection possible.' It may well have been the last time he used 'we' to describe himself and his wife. They were to separate that summer after an acrimonious correspondence which he ended by promising never to come near her even if disaster were to strike the little Princess. The King was appalled. The public had long ago tired of the Prince and his women and his debts. They sympathized vociferously with the Princess, and, adequate provision made, she moved out to a villa on Blackheath, and freedom. The baby, of course, must be left behind at Carlton House with her retinue of nurses, though she was allowed to visit her mother. Savage caricatures satirized the Prince's relationship with Lady Jersey, but no one questioned his right to custody of his child.

The Carlton House nursery was soon under the direction of the dowager Countess of Elgin, widowed mother of a young diplomat who had not yet met his future wife. Lady Elgin ran the little Princess's life for the important first eight years and the fact that the child grew up calling her 'Eggy', as her son's wife would her husband, suggests a loving relationship. The Princess's Aunt, Augusta Sophia, the Princess Royal took an interest in her namesake and after she married and went to live in Württemberg she corresponded with Lady Elgin about her. We get a picture of a bright, outgoing, lovable little creature with a hot temper. A sub-governess, Miss Hayman, described her charge as 'the merriest little thing I ever saw – pepper-hot too.' But when Miss Hayman showed signs of liking Princess Caroline, the friendly mother who dropped in and out of the nursery, she lost her job and went to work for Caroline in her random household on Blackheath.

The Prince did, once, in 1798, invite his wife back to Carlton House, for the look of the thing, but liberty had gone to the Princess's head and she refused. After that, she was on her own. The King was fond of her, she was his sister's child, but Queen Charlotte, who had been against the marriage, was unfriendly and her daughters the Princesses followed her example, though they were all fond of little Charlotte and sang her praises when she came to Windsor. Charlotte was in the classic position of the only child of a broken marriage, but she was well looked after, and throve, though her temper went on giving cause for concern. Her father was fond of her, when he saw her, but visibly fonder of another little girl, Minny Seymour, who was born two years after Charlotte, in 1798, and adopted by Mrs Fitzherbert to whom the Prince publicly returned in 1800.

Caroline, who would have been much happier with ten children of her own, was adopting babies too and ran a kind of orphanage on Blackheath for some of London's abandoned infants. One of them, William Austin, became such a pet after she adopted him in 1802 that the gossip became dangerous. He slept in her room, she called him Willikin and indulged his every whim, but she told Lady Charlotte Campbell (later Lady Charlotte Bury) that he was not her own, though she hinted at royal parentage. Her one friend in the royal family, the King, was mad again off and on between 1801 and 1804 and without his protection the rumours about Caroline got louder. Inevitably the Prince of Wales's enemies became her friends. She enjoyed entertaining and did it well, but thought nothing of carrying off some preferred gentleman, maybe the young politician George Canning or the painter Thomas Lawrence, for long private sessions after dinner. And when the King recovered in the spring of 1804 and sent for her and the little Princess to meet him at Kew, Lady Elgin, accompanying Princess Charlotte, was appalled to find that he was there unattended. She was probably more shocked still when he told her to take the child for a walk in the garden while he saw Princess

Caroline alone. Caroline herself had remarked on the freedoms the old King took with her. The Prince of Wales was furious. It all added to the tension between him and his father.

Princess Charlotte was eight that year and there was a general reshuffle of her household. The King, who was paying for it, took a keen interest in her education and from now on she spent more time at the Lower Lodge at Windsor, near her grandmother and aunts, while in London the little ménage moved from Carlton House to Warwick House next door. Perhaps even the Prince recognized that his extravagant bachelor household, presided over by the sinister Colonel McMahon, was hardly suitable for the bringing up of a girl who was heir to the throne. She had an expensive group of servants, and a formidable timetable of study and organized pleasure, and she wrote her father dutiful letters: 'I shall ever feel the sincerest love, regard, respect and attachment to you, my dearest papa.' But it was little Minny Seymour who sat on his knee and christened him Prinny.

And Charlotte's mother was going too far. Scandalous rumours about Princess Caroline abounded, though she was still infinitely more popular than her husband. In 1804 the Government set up what it called a 'Delicate Investigation' into her conduct. Rumours about William Austin must not be allowed to affect the succession. Naturally there was nothing delicate about the details of servant contradicting servant, unmade or rumpled beds, locked doors and midnight assignations. The papers took sides and loved it, and the public sympathized as always with the Princess. In the end, the commission fudged the issue, finding evidence of imprudence but nothing worse. From now on Charlotte would see less of her mother, but the investigation had produced no grounds for divorce and possible remarriage for her father, so her position as ultimate heir remained unchallenged.

As she got older, her father grew more anxious about her. Lady de Clifford, who took over from Lady Elgin in 1804, reported on her fits of passion. She had even snatched the wig from a prosy Bishop's head and thrown it into the fire. The Prince of Wales had always been his sisters' confidant about their passionate affairs, and he knew about his own sexual habits and those of his brothers. He insisted that his daughter never be left alone with her male tutors. As she became a teenager, Charlotte was increasingly frustrated. Irritated by her tutors, she was bored by her dull, loving maiden aunts. She was musical, but had no outstanding gift except for people, and she began to feel, with justification, that her father neglected her. It was not just that she reminded him of her mother; she shared her mother's popularity. It was hard to hear her clapped while he was booed. He kept her as much as he could out of the public eye. She resented it, but there was not much she could do. She was later to write to him: 'I am ashamed to say . . . that . . . I was ungrateful to a father who tho' he had a great deal of business, I am sure never had me out of his mind but I was sufficiently punished, for you could not bear your daughter ungrateful and therefore you would not see her.' His mother and sisters noticed what was happening and urged him to see more of her. She was growing up into a bouncy, handsome girl, but the older she got, the more she reminded them all of her mother, with all that implied.

When the old King was finally declared mad in 1811 and immured at Windsor, both Charlotte and her mother lost a good friend. Regent at last, but with his powers limited for the first year, the Prince surprised everyone by keeping the Tories in power. The furiously disappointed Whigs blamed this on the influence of the Tory Lady Hertford, little Minny's technical grandmother. Inevitably, they now began to cultivate the rival court of Princess Caroline. Princess Charlotte wrote to her friend Margaret Mercer Elphinstone that the print shops were full of 'scurrilous caricatures' of her father. She had made friends with Mercer, another only child, when she visited her mother on Blackheath, and loved her. It was probably the most stable relationship she had known and was to prove a badly needed emotional safety valve. Mercer was eight years older, daughter of Nelson's superior, the successful Admiral Keith. She was also such an heiress already, thanks to her dead mother, that the Duke of Clarence proposed to her after abandoning Dora Jordan. But Mercer was in a strong position, with a devoted father, and in no hurry to marry. As Charlotte grew up, Mercer provided a safe ear for her grumbles about what were becoming disagreeable duty visits to her mother, carefully confidential ones with her indiscreet Aunt Mary and rows with her unpredictable father. He actually forbade the correspondence after 1811, because Mercer was a Whig and they were now backing his wife, but it went on secretly, and in the end he was grateful to her as an intermediary when his daughter began to defy him.

All the old rumours that had given rise to the Delicate Investigation bubbled back to the surface in 1813, the frustrated Whigs using Princess Caroline as a weapon against her husband, while he began to hope again for a divorce. Once more nothing came of it but misery for Princess Charlotte, now old enough to understand, and shamelessly used by both sides. She visited her mother; she heard her grandmother and aunts talk; she read the papers. There was nothing she did not know. She told her father later that she had always believed Willikin to be her mother's child. It may have been a relief to have her visits to Princess Caroline curtailed, but she was too proud to admit it.

And it was infuriating still to be treated as a child. When her father celebrated his Regency with a lavish party at Carlton House in June 1811, he sent fifteen-year-old Charlotte off to Windsor to be out of the way. It cannot have been much comfort that her mother was not invited either, or that Mrs Fitzherbert stayed away, refusing to take second place to Lady Hertford. Charlotte entertained herself at Windsor by a flirtation with a handsome young Hussar called Charles Hesse, who may have been the Duke of York's illegitimate son. Complaisant Lady de Clifford let him ride beside their carriage in Windsor Great Park, and Princess Caroline actually allowed assignations in her Kensington apartments. Later, in a rare moment of reconciliation with her father, Charlotte told him that her mother had locked the two of them into her own bedroom, telling them to 'amuse themselves'. Charlotte concluded her alarming revelation, 'God knows what would have become of me if he had not behaved with so much respect to me.' She added that her uncle the Duke of Brunswick, her mother's own brother, had warned her that Caroline was capable of disgracing her in a vain hope of getting William Austin acknowledged as heir to the throne. It was a wildly improbable story, but it gives an idea of the atmosphere in which Charlotte grew up.

Another young man she enjoyed riding with at Windsor was her cousin Captain George FitzClarence, Dora Jordan's eldest son, when he was on leave from Spain, but he soon moved with his regiment to Brighton, where he fell in love with Minny Seymour. It is good to think that Charlotte did meet at least one of her great brood of illegitimate cousins. Since the old King had annulled the marriage of the Duke of Sussex, leaving his two children in limbo, Charlotte was the only legitimate member of her generation. It is no wonder that she clung to Mercer Elphinstone. At around this time she wrote to her friend about a book she had been reading: '*Sense and Sensibility* . . . certainly is interesting and you feel quite one of the company. I think Marianne and me are very like in *disposition* . . . I am not so good, the

same imprudence etc. however remain very like. I must say it interested me much!'

Princess Caroline had conceived a passion for an Italian singer now
and was gradually alienating her more respectable friends by her outrageous behaviour. Charlotte's visits were limited to one a fortnight,
and the Whig politician Henry Brougham, who had an axe of his own
to grind, advised Caroline to make an issue of this. The result was a
ferocious exchange of letters between her parents, which ended up, of
course, in the papers. There was more trouble when Lady de Clifford
resigned early in 1813 and Charlotte, now seventeen, hoped for her
own establishment with her beloved Mercer at her side. She boldly
wrote to her father proposing this and he came storming out to
Windsor with his Lord Chancellor, Lord Eldon, to read her a furious
lecture on his absolute power over her. 'If she were my daughter,'
Lord Eldon told them both, 'I would have her locked up.'

It made Charlotte ill, as crises did. She probably suffered, like her
aunts, from the family complaint. In the end, she had to give in and
accept the Duchess of Leeds as her new Governess. The situation
improved a little when Miss Cornelia Knight was added to the household as Lady Companion, but this made Queen Charlotte furious, as
Miss Knight, a literary lady recommended by Fanny Burney, had been
a valued member of her own household. And Princess Charlotte felt,
quite rightly, that her father was keeping her a child far too long. At
seventeen, she had been neither presented nor confirmed, and her
father had made it brutally clear that she would not have her own
establishment until she married. The atmosphere at Windsor must
have been hideous, with the old King locked up there, the Princesses
nursing their various frustrations, and Queen Charlotte in a rage.
Princess Charlotte was relieved to move back to Warwick House that
summer, and was allowed to see her mother for an hour or so at a time
in the house of her other grandmother, the old Duchess of
Brunswick, exiled from her home by the misfortunes of war.

England's fortunes were improving. The Regent gave a garden fête
at Carlton House in the summer of 1813 to celebrate Wellington's
victory over the Spanish at Vitoria, and in his *Reminiscences*, Captain
Gronow reports Charlotte's first public appearance there, describing
her as, 'Fair, with the rich bloom of youthful beauty; her eyes were
blue and very expressive, and her hair was abundant, and of that peculiar light brown which merges into the golden . . . Her manners were
remarkable for . . . simplicity and good-nature.' She danced a good

deal with the young Duke of Devonshire, who had got over the loss of his Cousin Caroline and now thought it might be pleasant to be a royal consort. They became good enough friends to cause gossip, but the Prince Regent told the young Duke it would not do. They were to correspond for the rest of her short life, and after she died the Duke wrote that she was 'full of warm and generous and spirited feelings, yet tractable as a child.' Charlotte was also seeing and liking her cousin the Duke of Gloucester, who was later to make her Aunt Mary so unhappy. But her father made it ruthlessly clear that he would only allow a suitable marriage to a foreign prince. He had learned nothing from his own father's mistakes, or the unhappiness of his sisters.

His daughter's increasing popularity made the Prince Regent more eager than ever to be rid of her. He began to talk about young Prince William of Orange. It was a suitable match in many ways. William was his father's heir to Britain's old ally the Netherlands though father and son had been in exile since the French over-ran the country in 1794. By the autumn of 1813 the European picture was changing rapidly. Napoleon was on the retreat at last, both in Spain and in central Europe, after a crucial defeat at Leipzig early in October. Falling back on Paris, he ordered the evacuation of the Netherlands and young William's father was summoned back, whereupon the Regent invited his son to England to make a dynastic match with Charlotte. In exile, Prince William had spent two years at Oxford before serving on the Duke of Wellington's staff in Spain, where he seems to have been liked by his fellow officers. He was ugly enough to be called Young Frog, and was an unappealing young man who drank too much, but then so did most men, including Charlotte's father and uncles.

From what she had heard of William, Charlotte did not take to the idea: 'Marry I will, and that directly, in order to enjoy my liberty: but not the Prince of Orange.' When she actually met William at dinner at Carlton House in December, he was not so bad as she had expected: she let her father push her into an informal engagement there and then, telling Cornelia Knight next day that he was 'by no means so disagreeable' as she had imagined. But two days later Prince William let slip that he would naturally expect her to spend most of her time in the Netherlands with him. Her father had kept quiet about this; she burst into tears and began to have second thoughts. Meanwhile the old Queen, who had a nephew of her own in mind for Charlotte, was not pleased. The engagement was not made public at once, Charlotte brooded about it through the winter and finally consulted the prominent Whig politician Lord Grey, who had once been the Duchess of Devonshire's lover, about her position as heir to the throne. He gave her good, cautious advice, while Prince William, now back in liberated Holland, wrote about the dullness of the court there and how much he preferred England.

In the spring of 1814, everything changed. The Allies defeated Napoleon. The long war was over at last, or so it seemed. The Prince Regent did not go to Paris for the festivities there, but invited the triumphant Allied sovereigns to a great celebration in England, feeling, with some justification, that the victory would not have been won without the steadfast stance, and money, of the British government, and the genius of Wellington. The sovereigns all came, and so did a hopeful group of young princes, but once again Charlotte found herself kept in the background, along with her mother. The Prince Regent ordered that Princess Caroline be excluded from everything, and even asked the visiting monarchs not to call on her. It was the last straw for Caroline, who began to plan to go abroad, encouraged by her husband, who hoped it would end in scandal and divorce. But as always the crowds took the Princess's side, cheering her and booing him, while they greeted Charlotte with cries of, 'Don't desert your mother'. It made entertaining the Allied sovereigns very awkward for the Prince, greeted everywhere with shouts of, 'Where's your wife, Georgie?'

And he could not keep his eighteen-year-old daughter out of everything, though he tried. The Tsar's difficult sister the Grand Duchess Catherine of Oldenbourg arrived ahead of her brother and took an instant dislike to the Prince Regent and a fancy to his daughter. She probably had her own ends in view. Later, Prince William was to marry her sister Anna. Now she wrote to the Tsar that Charlotte reminded her of a boy, or rather 'a ragamuffin', but had wit and a strong will. Charlotte was at loggerheads with her father again, this time about the terms of the marriage contract. A personal visit from Prince William did nothing to mend matters: she was outraged when he went cheerfully off to all the parties to which she was not invited. And then he went to Ascot, got hopelessly drunk and came rioting back on top of a stage coach.

There were other possible suitors about. Calling to say goodbye to the Tsar and his sister at Pulteney's Hotel, she met a young man on the stairs and recognized a friend of Mercer Elphinstone's. Prince

Leopold of Saxe-Coburg was a handsome younger son with charm and his own way to make in the world. He had served in the Russian army and was now in the Tsar's household. He civilly escorted Charlotte and her companion Miss Knight to their carriage and Charlotte teased him a little for not having called on her like the other visiting princes. He promptly did so and then wrote a careful note of explanation to the Prince Regent, hoping that his visit had been correct. He was a careful young man.

Charlotte did not find him so interesting as thirty-five year old Prince Augustus of Prussia, whom she probably met through her aunt the Duchess of York, a Prussian princess. No one told her about his reputation. He had loved and lost Madame Récamier, among other women, now he put his spell on Charlotte and gullible Miss Knight, who did have a tendency to back what she thought was the winning horse. She had ruthlessly abandoned Emma Hamilton (who had been good to her and let her travel back to England in her curious party) after she got to London and heard the gossip about her and Nelson. Now she connived at private meetings with Augustus. Mercer Elphinstone, calling one day, was shocked to find Charlotte closeted with him and insisted on breaking up what she looked on as a risky *tête à tête*.

The young men, the cheering crowds, the Tsar's friendly sister, all combined to give Charlotte the courage, or the desperation, to break off her engagement, citing as her reason the fact that she would have to spend more time in Holland than she should, as heir to the British throne. Besides, to go abroad would be to let down her mother who, she felt, needed her support more than ever after the snubs of the summer. Charlotte would probably have agreed with Jane Austen's view of her mother, could she have known it. She would support her as long as she could because she was her mother, and also, perhaps, because she did not much like her father. But she was soon to find that the support was not mutual.

The bombshell of Charlotte's broken engagement caused the worst scene yet with her father, which is saying a good deal. He had endured a hard summer with the crowds booing him, the Tsar being difficult and his sister rude, and he had heard the rumours about Prince Augustus by now. He summoned Charlotte to Carlton House and when she said she was too ill to go he stormed across to Warwick House to see her alone and issue his ultimatum. All her ladies were dismissed on the spot. She was to move immediately to Carlton House and then to virtual imprisonment in Cranbourne Lodge, deep in Windsor Forest. It was too much. Charlotte had had a hard summer too. She ran away.

Out in the street, alone for the first time in her life, she was befriended by a kind young man who called a cab for her. She went to her mother's London house in Connaught Place, found she was away at Blackheath, and sent urgent notes summoning her and her uncle the Duke of Sussex and Mr Brougham. Cornelia Knight and Mercer Elphinstone also soon joined the party. At first Charlotte's high spirits and sense of escape carried all before them, but as the evening wore on, the real facts of her case became painfully clear. Her mother was set on going abroad now and made it clear that she was not prepared to support her. And her other advisers pointed out that she was her father's subject as well as his daughter; she had no redress against him. The Duke of York arrived at last with a warrant in his pocket. Brougham took her to the window, to show her the dawn breaking on empty streets. If he took her cause to the people, he told her, they would riot in those streets and probably sack Carlton House. The soldiers would be called out: 'Blood will flow.' If she lived a hundred years, it would never be forgotten or forgiven. She gave in, but first she got everyone present to sign a paper saying she would never marry William of Orange. Then she went back to Carlton House and captivity.

It was bad, though perhaps not quite so bad as she had expected. And Cranbourne Lodge turned out to be a pleasant house, a great relief after the few days of real imprisonment at Carlton House with neither pen nor paper to write to Mercer. Cranbourne Lodge had the advantage of being further from the Castle than Windsor Lodge where she normally stayed. 'If my family are to be at sixes and sevens,' she wrote philosophically, 'perhaps it *is as well* I am *quite* out of the way.' But it was intolerable never to be alone; she was not even allowed to shut her bedroom door at night.

Her father put a man in charge of her household now. It was General Garth, which is a reason to believe that he cannot have been the father of her Aunt Sophia's son Tom, whatever the gossips said. Charlotte found him good humoured, if 'very vulgar in his conversation', but she was allowed to ride in the park with him, which she enjoyed. Her boisterous spirits needed plenty of exercise. The old Queen and the Princesses came to call and she thought they were disappointed not to find her more uncomfortable. She had made a sensible point of getting on with her new group of ladies. Then her father came with news that shocked her. Her mother really was going abroad. He had smoothed Caroline's way by promising her an allowance and organizing a boat to take her; he was delighted she was going. He allowed his daughter into London for a brief farewell visit and Charlotte wrote sadly of her mother's 'indifferent manner of taking leave of me.' Mother and daughter never met again, but the Prince Regent never got his divorce.

Charlotte was not well that summer. Like her aunts, she suffered from a pain in her side and the doctors recommended sea bathing. Her father was so busy with a new family row about his brother the Duke of Cumberland's unsuitable marriage that he did nothing about this. It took public protests to get him to send Charlotte off to Weymouth, the old King's favourite resort. She would much have preferred Brighton, and was shocked, on the way there, when she stayed at General Garth's house and he made a point of introducing young Tom Garth to her. A spoiled boy, she said, who ought to be back at Harrow. She knew all about Tom. She enjoyed being welcomed with open arms at Weymouth, but she was suffering because Prince Augustus had not written since he went back to Europe. Gradually, probably through the intervention of Mercer Elphinstone, she began to think more about that other young man, Leopold of Saxe-Coburg. And he was thinking about her, also doubtless encouraged by their mutual friend Mercer. Everyone who counted was at Vienna now for the great post-war conference that was to reshape the world. News came through from various sources, including her mother, who was enjoying herself enormously abroad and falling under the spell of her courier, handsome Bartolommeo Pergami.

Charlotte went on swimming into October and it did her good. Back at Cranbourne Lodge, she found a letter from Mercer confirming that Augustus was marrying, and the assiduous Cornelia Knight smuggled her a cool farewell letter from him. 'Have I not *échappé belle*?' she wrote to Mercer and went on to talk about Leopold. Her father came to see her, very friendly, and in a rash moment she told him about Captain Hesse, who had refused to return her letters despite the efforts of Mercer and Admiral Keith to retrieve them. The Regent was soon using the letters and the threat of blackmail they carried to try and force her into marriage with William of Orange. But Charlotte was on better terms with her grandmother now and the old Queen actually supported her: 'She was very affectionate to me, implored me on her knees not to marry *ever* a man I did not like.' It is hard to imagine Queen Charlotte on her knees.

There were riots that winter and in the spring Napoleon shook the world by escaping from Elba, and war broke out again. Charlotte suffered over rumours that Leopold was engaged, and was infinitely relieved to learn that in fact it was his brother Ferdinand. The scandal about her mother was much worse. She had promised her father not to write to her, but got his permission to do so when Caroline's brother the Duke of Brunswick was killed at Quatre Bras in the run-up to Waterloo. Charlotte was back at Warwick House by then and could get direct news of Leopold from Mercer, who kept in touch with him. He seemed unsure of his welcome if he should come to England; anyway, like everyone else he had to go to war. Anxiously enquiring, Charlotte was relieved to learn that his regiment had missed Waterloo. But then he went off to Paris for the new round of celebrations there, and Charlotte, sent off to Weymouth again, had to hear of him dancing at balls and supping with Lady Castlereagh. 'Why should he not come over . . . It is so near . . . I quite languish for his arrival.' She was falling in love at a distance.

Weymouth seemed duller this year, with so much going on else-where, but at least William of Orange was now safely engaged to the Tsar's sister Anna. Other princes came to London, but autumn came and there was still no sign of cautious Leopold. Charlotte actually approached Lord Liverpool, the Prime Minister, about the match, but her father would do nothing. He did invite her to Brighton to celebrate her twentieth birthday in January 1816, but when the town planned general illuminations in her honour he discouraged them and they were cancelled. Back at Cranbourne Lodge she sat down and wrote him a firm letter: 'I no longer hesitate in declaring my partiality in favour of the Prince of Coburg.' By then the Prince had had enquiries made and decided the young man would do. He wrote kindly to Charlotte, giving his consent, and also to Leopold summoning him to England, while Castlereagh, who had met and liked the young man in Vienna, wrote to him to explain what was going on. The old Queen was delighted but said that Leopold must be sure to be master in his own house. London seethed with rumours and Charlotte, impatiently consulting maps of Europe at Windsor, wrote to Mercer about the 'Silence and mystery . . . but . . . so *much mystery* is *always* made in this house about every trifle.'

He came. She drove to Brighton to meet him at the Pavilion and found him charming. Everyone was pleased. Parliament was generous; they were to have a town house and Claremont Park, a delightful country place near Esher. The young couple were soon happily planning their household with 'no extravagance, waste, or debts.' It was to be a whole new scene. And Charlotte was giving up riding, which she loved, because Leopold did not approve of such violent exercise for a lady. They were never left alone together, but they corresponded, and there was some trouble when Charlotte, on her fiancé's advice, warned Mercer about a new friend of hers, the Count de Flahaut. It was a reasonable enough warning, granted that everyone knew Flahaut was carrying on a long affair with Napoleon's sister-in-law (and step-daughter) Hortense, who had been Queen of Holland. Things were never quite the same between the two young women after this but they would have changed anyway as Charlotte plunged into the new relationship that was making her so happy: 'A Princess never, I believe, set out in life (or married) with such prospects of happiness, real domestic ones like other people.'

It was what she had always wanted, and never had, a family life like other people. She married him in a splendid ceremony at Carlton House in May 1816. Leopold was almost crushed by the crowds beforehand. Mercer was not there, ill they said, and when the young couple finally got into their carriage to drive away the old Queen told Charlotte's maid to get in between them. Mrs Campbell boldly refused and they escaped to the Yorks' country house, Oatlands, lent them for the honeymoon. It smelled of the Duchess's dogs, but Leopold was 'the perfection of a lover' and they were getting to know and like each other, as well as loving. She called him *'doucement'* because he kept saying, *'doucement, doucement, cherie,'* but they could talk to each other. She had a miscarriage that summer and could not go to her Aunt Mary's marriage to the Duke of Gloucester, and they were glad to get away at last from their unsatisfactory London house to Claremont which was ready for them in August.

They lived a quiet, domestic country life there, as much like ordinary people as they could manage, attending the village church until the enthusiastic crowds made it impossible and they had to retreat to their own chapel. They walked and drove, always together except when Leopold was out shooting. And he was having a calming effect on her. His *'doucement'* was working. Even sharp-tongued Princess Lieven reported that Charlotte was 'greatly attached to him, and very submissive.' Like her aunts, Charlotte had the gift of making the best of a husband, and she was infinitely luckier in her man. Leopold's faithful attendant Christian Frederick Stockmar, who found her too ebullient at first, said she soon calmed down so that one could see 'how good and noble she really is.' Cornelia Knight, coming to call, found them surrounded by papers. 'Come in, come in,' said Charlotte. 'Tis only Mr and Mrs Coburg settling their accounts.' They meant to live within their income, unlike the rest of her family. She had another miscarriage some time that winter, perhaps in January when she did not go to the Grand Ball her father gave at Brighton to celebrate her twenty-first birthday. But they may simply have preferred the humbler local celebrations at Claremont, where they were loved as bringers of employment in that bad winter after the war.

The stories about Princess Caroline grew worse. An intrepid traveller, she visited the Greek islands like Byron, Constantinople like Lady Elgin, and rode into Jerusalem, visiting Lady Hester Stanhope on the way. Pergami was always ostentatiously at her side, and the English travellers who were now flocking abroad brought back all kinds of stories of her outrageous behaviour and dress. Charlotte went on writing to her, encouraged by family-minded Leopold, but her mother did not bother to answer, though she boasted to her entourage in the summer of 1817 when Charlotte wrote to tell her that she was pregnant.

Leopold had given the Prince Regent this news at the end of April and was able to report that his wife was in splendid health. Mercer Elphinstone married Flahaut quietly in Edinburgh that June and settled down to a happy life with him, bearing him five daughters and ignoring his flirtations. Before the wedding, Charlotte had asked Mercer for her letters back, but luckily for us she did not send them. Charlotte's baby was expected in October and they spent a quiet summer at Claremont, entertaining the Prince Regent with Mozart for his birthday in August. She went on feeling very well, walking and driving in the grounds with Leopold, but towards the end experienced Queen Charlotte thought her very large and carrying awkwardly. The old Queen offered to come and be with her for the birth, and Charlotte, politely refusing this, felt she must also refuse the offer of a married friend, Lady Ashbrook.

Queen Charlotte went off to Bath for her health; the Regent was visiting in Suffolk, also unwell. There were three doctors on call and an experienced midwife in the house, but no woman friend. Richard

Croft was in charge. He was Sir Richard now, the fashionable *accoucheur*. It was a long time since he had had trouble getting the Duke of Devonshire to pay his bill. He put Charlotte on a severe reducing diet, purged and bled her. An active girl with a hearty appetite, Charlotte had given up riding to please her husband. Now she gave up eating to please her doctor. Thomas Lawrence, who had once painted her with her mother, was painting her alone now, and liked her, finding 'nothing of that boisterous hilarity which has been ascribed to her.' They had tamed her among them. October dragged on. Labour did not start until November 3rd, and then it was slow. Two nights and a day passed. Charlotte behaved with extreme stoicism, refusing to cry out as the pains grew worse. She was hungry, but Croft would not let her eat. Nor did he send for Dr Sims, the member of the team who wielded the forceps, until it was too late. A large, beautiful dead boy was born at last. Charlotte took even this with great calm, seemed better, grew worse some hours later, when Leopold had finally gone to bed, and died with only Stockmar beside her.

The Prince Regent, hurrying up from the country at news of the prolonged labour was so shocked at the loss of his daughter and grandson that the doctors were afraid for him and he was ill for some time. Leopold maintained a surface calm, but he was never quite the same again, though he found himself a German mistress who looked like Charlotte, installed her at the bottom of the garden and used to read aloud to her in the evenings. Later he was offered the throne of Belgium, married a French princess and founded a dynasty.

Epilogue
End of an Era

CHARLOTTE HAD BEEN the hope of the future, of a new age no longer dominated by the extravagance of raffish royal males. She and her domesticated consort would have been much more in tune with the increasingly moral tone of the nation. Only the Duke of Wellington and Lord Holland had their doubts. Tory Wellington thought Charlotte had been dangerously like her mother; Whig Holland on the other hand thought her too like her father. She might well have struck the happy mean, and anyway there was Leopold's influence to be taken into account. He was still to play his part in the dynastic drama, writing volumes of good advice to his niece Queen Victoria and finally producing his nephew Albert for her.

When Charlotte's death left the succession wide open, the Royal Dukes rushed hopefully into matrimony. The Duke of York was married but childless; the Duke of Clarence's happy marriage to Princess Adelaide of Saxe-Meiningen produced no surviving children. The next brother, Edward, Duke of Kent abandoned his long-time mistress Madame St Laurent and married Leopold's widowed sister Victoria, who had the recommendation of already having two children. Their only child, another Victoria, was born in May 1819, and the public had a new hope. George III died at last the next year and the new King made one more attempt at divorcing his wife, but the Bill of Pains and Penalties reluctantly introduced by the government had to be abandoned because of its lukewarm reception in the Lords. At the time, the public sympathized vociferously with the new Queen, but next year, when George IV was crowned and she was turned away from the doors of Westminster Abbey, the mood had changed and she was booed. She died next year, but her fifty-nine-year-old husband was beyond remarriage. When he died in 1830, his brother succeeded him as William IV to be followed by their niece Victoria in 1837.

It may well be that the best thing the Duke of Kent did for his daughter was to die soon after she was born, so that she was brought up by her mother, with Uncle Leopold in the background. It was a breath of new air in the Hanover family, even if it did mean haemophilia instead of porphyria. The public that had loved Charlotte took little Victoria to its heart too, but it was a different public. Charlotte had grown up during the Napoleonic Wars, Victoria was born in the year of the Peterloo Massacre, and grew up in the 1820s when public opinion was slowly shifting in a direction that would eventually make the great 1832 Parliamentary Reform Bill possible. Elizabeth Fry was ahead of the times in her emphasis on the democratic process, and Jane Austen was right about the rise of the Evangelicals. It was in the 1820s that Harriette Wilson published her notorious *Memoirs* and found it easy to blackmail most of her now respectable clients. Queen Caroline, who had been the public's darling for so long, was taunted at her husband's coronation. Lady Hester Stanhope lost her pension. Mary Shelley had to suppress her husband's works to appease his father's prejudice. Women were being put back into the straitjacket, relegated from the salon to the parlour. The spark of equality that had made it possible for the Duchess of Devonshire and her sister to have illegitimate children, like their men, and yet survive socially, was being snuffed out.

Victoria came to the throne twenty years after the death of her Cousin Charlotte, and she and her husband Albert, Leopold's nephew, were to connive at this relegation of the female, becoming the symbol of a new age of prudery when even piano legs, they say, wore petticoats. More than ever, the choice for women was to be between pedestal and brothel. The careers of Emma Hamilton or Elizabeth Inchbald might have been possible under Charlotte and Leopold, but not under Victoria and Albert. From now on, women were to be seen and not heard. When her dear friend Angela Burdett-Coutts married a much younger man, Queen Victoria cut the connection. Florence Nightingale had to get ill to get free. Charlotte Brontë and George Eliot used male pseudonyms. Mary Wollstonecraft would have been appalled.

Bibliography

The place of publication is London, unless otherwise stated.

Acton, Harold, *The Bourbons of Naples*, 1956

Airlie, Mabell Countess of, *In Whig Society*, 1921

Armstrong, Martin, *Lady Hester Stanhope*, 1927

Askwith, Betty, *Piety and Wit, A Biography of Harriet, Countess Granville*, 1982

Berry, Mary, *Extracts of the Journal and Correspondence*, ed. Lady T. Lewis, 1865

Bessborough, Earl of, *Lady Bessborough and her Family Circle*, 1940

——*Georgiana, Duchess of Devonshire*, 1955

Blanch, Lesley, *The Game of Hearts*, 1957

Blyth, Henry, *Caro, the Fatal Passion*, 1973

Boaden, James, *The Life of Mrs Jordan*, 1831

——*Memoir of Mrs Inchbald*, 1833

Brooke, John, *King George III*, 1972

Burford, E. J., *Wits, Wenchers and Wantons*, 1986

Burney, Fanny (Madame d'Arblay), *Diary and Letters*, 1854

Butler, Marilyn, *Maria Edgeworth*, 1972

Buxton, John, *Byron and Shelley*, 1968

Cavendish, Lady Harriet, *Correspondence*, ed. Leveson Gower and Palmer, 1940

——*Harry-O: The Letters of Lady Harriet Cavendish*, ed. Leveson Gower and Palmer, 1940

Chapman, R. W., *Jane Austen's Letters*, 1932

Childs, Virginia, *Lady Hester Stanhope*, 1990

Clifford, James L., *Hester Lynch Piozzi*, 1952

Creevey, Thomas, *The Creevey Papers*, ed. Sir Herbert Maxwell, 1904

Davies, I. M., *The Harlot and the Statesman*, 1986

Dirleton, Countess of Elgin, Mary Nisbet of, *Letters*, ed. Hamilton Grant, 1926

Edgeworth, Maria, *Letters from England*, 1971

Fry, Elizabeth, *Memoir by her Two Daughters*, 1848

Fothergill, Brian, *Mrs Jordan*, 1965

Fulford, Roger, *Royal Dukes*, 1973

Gérin, Winifred, *Horatia Nelson*, 1981

Glenbervie, Lord, *Journals*, ed. Bickley, 1928

Gower, Lord Granville Leveson, *Private Correspondence*, ed. Granville, 1916

Gower, Iris Leveson, *The Face Without a Frown*, 1944

Granville, Harriet, Countess of, *A Second Self, Letters*, ed. Surtees, 1990

Greville, Charles, *Memoirs*, ed. Strachey and Fulford, 1938

Gronow, Captain, *Reminiscences and Recollections, 1810–1860*, 1892

Guttmacher, Manfred S., *America's Last King*, New York, 1941

Hahn, Emily, *A Degree of Prudery*, 1951

Hare, Augustus J. C., *Life and Letters of Maria Edgeworth*, 1894

——*The Gurneys of Earlham*, 1895

Haslip, Joan, *Lady Hester Stanhope*, 1934

Healey, Edna, *Lady Unknown*, 1978

——*Coutts & Co. 1692–1992*, 1992

Hibbert, Christopher, *George IV Prince of Wales*, 1972

——*George IV Regent and King*, 1973

——*The English, A Social History 1066–1945*, 1987

——*Nelson*, 1994

Hodge, Jane Aiken, *Only a Novel, The Double Life of Jane Austen*, 1972

Holme, Thea, *Prinny's Daughter*, 1976

Holmes, Richard, *Coleridge*, 1989

Howell-Thomas, Dorothy, *Lord Melbourne's Susan*, 1978

——*Duncannon*, 1992

Hunter, Richard and Macalpine, Ida, *George III and the Mad Business*, 1969

Iremonger, Lucille, *Love and the Princess*, 1948

Jenkins, Elizabeth, *Ten Fascinating Women*, 1955

Knight, Cornelia, *Autobiography*, 1861

Lees-Milne, James, *The Bachelor Duke*, 1991

Lefebure, Molly, *The Bondage of Love*, 1986

Lennox, Lady Sarah, *Life and Letters*, ed. Ilchester and Stavordale, 1901

Leslie, Shane, *Mrs Fitzherbert*, 1939

Littlewood, S. R., *Elizabeth Inchbald and her Circle*, 1921

Lloyd, Christopher, *Fanny Burney*, 1936

Longford, Elizabeth, *Wellington: The Years of the Sword*, 1969

Lucy, Mary Elizabeth, *Mistress of Charlecote*, ed. Lucy, 1983

Manvell, Roger, *Elizabeth Inchbald*, 1987

Marshall, Dorothy, *Eighteenth-Century England*, 1962

Masson, Madeline, *Lady Anne Barnard*, 1948

Masters, Brian, *Georgiana, Duchess of Devonshire*, 1981

Mavor, Elizabeth, *The Ladies of Llangollen*, 1972

Melville, Lewis, *Regency Ladies*, 1926

Napier, Priscilla, *The Sword Dance*, 1971

Oman, Carola, *Nelson*, 1947

Palmer, Alan, *Life and Times of George IV*, 1972

——*Encyclopaedia of Napoleon's Europe*, 1984

Papendiek, Mrs, *Journals of Court and Private Life in the Time of Queen Charlotte*, ed. Broughton, 1887

Pocock, Tom, *Sailor King*, 1991

Plumb, J. H., *The First Four Georges*, 1956

Reese, M. M., *Goodwood's Oak, The Life and Times of the Third Duke of Richmond*, 1987

Roger, N. A. M., *The Insatiable Earl*, 1993

Rose, June, *Elizabeth Fry*, 1980

St. Clair, William, *Lord Elgin and the Marbles*, 1967

Scott, Walter S., *The Bluestocking Ladies*, 1947

Sheridan, Betsy, *Journal*, ed. William LeFanu, 1960

Sichel, Walter, *Emma, Lady Hamilton*, 1927

Soames, Mary, *The Profligate Duke*, 1987

Spark, Muriel, *Mary Shelley*, 1987

Stone, Lawrence, *The Family, Sex and Marriage in England, 1500–1800*, 1977

——*Broken Lives: Separation and Divorce in England, 1601–1857*, 1993

Stuart, Dorothy Margaret, *The Daughters of George III*, 1939

——*Dearest Bess*, 1955

Thackeray, William Makepeace, *The Four Georges*, 1855

Tillyard, Stella, *Aristocrats*, 1994

Tolstoy, Nikolai, *The Half Mad Lord*, 1978

Tomalin, Claire, *Mary Wollstonecraft*, 1974
——*Shelley and his World*, 1980
——*Mrs Jordan's Profession*, 1994
Trench, Charles Chenevix, *The Royal Malady*, 1964
Wilkinson, Tate, *The Wandering Patentee*, 1795
Ziegler, Philip, *Melbourne*, 1976

Index

Index

Index